WEST AFRICAN
RELIGIOUS TRADITIONS

FAITH MEETS FAITH

An Orbis Series in Interreligious Dialogue
Paul F. Knitter, General Editor
Editorial Advisors
John Berthrong
Julia Ching
Diana Eck
Karl-Josef Kuschel
Lamin Sanneh
George E. Tinker
Felix Wilfred

In the contemporary world, the many religions and spiritualities stand in need of greater communication and cooperation. More than ever before, they must speak to, learn from, and work with each other in order both to maintain their vital identities and to contribute to fashioning a better world.

FAITH MEETS FAITH seeks to promote interreligious dialogue by providing an open forum for exchanges among followers of different religious paths. While the Series wants to encourage creative and bold responses to questions arising from contemporary appreciations of religious plurality, it also recognizes the multiplicity of basic perspectives concerning the methods and content of interreligious dialogue.

Although rooted in a Christian theological perspective, the Series does not endorse any single school of thought or approach. By making available to both the scholarly community and the general public works that represent a variety of religious and methodological viewpoints, FAITH MEETS FAITH seeks to foster an encounter among followers of the religions of the world on matters of common concern.

FAITH MEETS FAITH SERIES

WEST AFRICAN RELIGIOUS TRADITIONS

Focus on the Akan of Ghana

Robert B. Fisher

ORBIS BOOKS

Maryknoll, New York 10545

The Catholic Foreign Mission Society of America (Maryknoll) recruits and trains people for overseas missionary service. Through Orbis Books, Maryknoll aims to foster the international dialogue that is essential to mission. The books published, however, reflect the opinions of their authors and are not meant to represent the official position of the society.

Copyright © 1998 by Robert B. Fisher.
Published by Orbis Books, Maryknoll, New York, U.S.A.

Manuscript editing and typesetting by Joan Weber Laflamme.
Manufactured in the United States of America.

Library of Congress Cataloging in Publication Data

Fisher, Robert B., 1937-
    West African religious traditions : focus on the Akan of Ghana /
Robert B. Fisher.
        p. cm. — (Faith meets faith series)
    Includes bibliographical references and index.
    ISBN 1-57075-165-X (pbk.)
    1. Akan (African people)—Religion. I. Title. II. Series: Faith
meets faith.
BL2480.A4F57   1998
299'.683385—dc21
                                                                97-48998
                                                                        CIP

In loving memory of
Father Peter Kwaku Owusu
Missionary from Kumasi, Ghana, to the people of Liberia,
who advised on many aspects of this book.
He was exiled during civil strife to the Ivory Coast,
where he was killed in a car accident
26 April 1997

Contents

Acknowledgments

Ye da mo ase. We thank you all. First of all, we always give God thanks for allowing me to live in Ghana among such wonderful people. I learned more than what is contained within these covers. May the great God surround the people, living and dead, with his great love and protection.

> *Okokroko Nyame,*
> *Obaatan pa Nyame*
> *Omfa ne Sunsum mmo mo ho ban.*

Great God, God, mother most wonderful. May God surround you with his spirit.

There were many others right from the beginning who made a sharp cut into my own *sunsum.* Kwame Gyamfi Boateng, who first taught me the Twi numbers. Catechists Thomas Gyamfi at Akim Ofoase and Thomas Frempong at Kwahu Tafo. The Twi teachers, Sam and Douglas, and many others who helped me gather material, including Joseph Antwi-Boahen, teacher, catechist, and oral historian at Akim Ofoase, and Charles Kwame Appiasi of Akim Oda.

But there were others, old friends, students, and cultural youth, Thomas Anokye-Danso, Joseph K. Baidoo, John Asare Dankwa, and many of my students at Pedu in the Central Region. There were those many friends at Kwahu Tafo, the parishioners, and other advisors, like John Kwabena Ansiri and Rev. George Adusei Bonsu. There is my artist friend Edwin K. Nkrumah, who contributed much to improve the images of this book, and Kofi Biney-Afful, close friend and advisor.

Here in the United States, foremost among those who pushed me, pulled me, and really got me to write and to create a course at Xavier University of Louisiana in New Orleans, was Dr. Argiro Morgan. Through her efforts with the Bush mini-grant in summers I wrote much of the text while revising it with teaching aids for a course on the same matter during many semesters. Our other artist friend, Clare Evangelista, also helped me to create new images of West Africa. There were those who lent me summer houses in which to write, Ted and Maria George, Ralph and Marie Anderson (who also had lived in Ghana while Ralph worked for the aluminum plant at Valco). Last of all, I lived in a parish at Slidell, Louisiana, where Msgr. Richard Carroll, his associates, and the parishioners of St. Margaret Mary Church put up with me for a good five months, letting me finish writing the text.

Others have read the text and advised me on it. I wish to thank finally Dr. William Burrows and the staff at Orbis for showing an interest in this text from its earliest stages, along with their readers, including my confrere, Dr. Jon Kirby, from the Tamale Institute of Cross-Cultural Studies in northern Ghana.

I would gather you all, departed and living, in a great *durbar* with Jesus in the middle. The *kete, mpintin,* and *fontomfrom* drums are behind you. The *menson*, or seven great horns, are sounding as Christ is seated in state on an *asipim,* a king's ceremonial chair. The ceremony begins with a pledge of loyalty to Christ by the *afonakurafo,* the sword bearers dressed in kente tied around their waists, and raising their *afona,* the gilded ceremonial swords. The drumming and dancing commences, while everyone sings words of praise:

> *Yeyi waye yekamfo wo*
> *Yehye wo anuonyam,*
> *Nana bre bre,*
> *Ewiase Agyenkwa bre, bre o!, bre o!*

> We praise you and we glorify you!
> We give you great honor.
> Great Ancestor, walk gently.
> The World's Savior,
> Do walk gently, please walk gently.

I join them humbly, realizing that Nyame is great indeed. *Onyame nti, ebeye yie.*

The Nations of Africa

Location of Peoples and Places

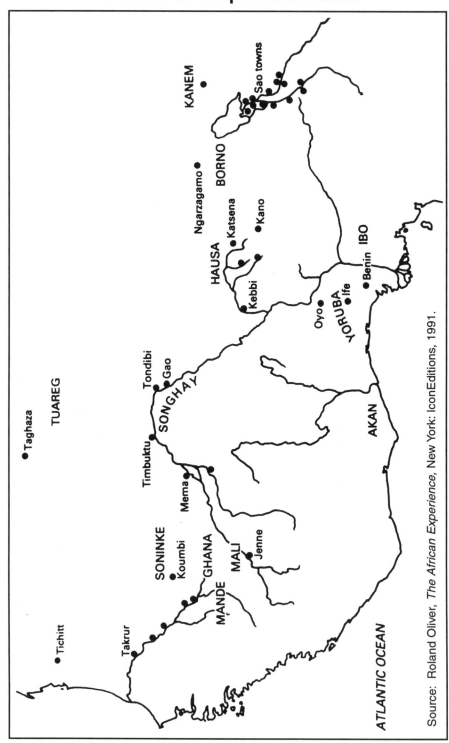

KANEM

Sao towns

BORNO

Ngarzagamo

HAUSA

Katsena

Kano

IBO

Kebbi

Benin

Ife

Oyo

YORUBA

TUAREG

Taghaza

Tondibi

Gao

Timbuktu

SONGHAY

AKAN

Mema

SONINKE

GHANA

MALI

Jenne

Koumbi

Tichitt

Takrur

MANDE

ATLANTIC OCEAN

Source: Roland Oliver, *The African Experience*, New York: IconEditions, 1991.

Ghananian Ethnic Groups
and Administrative Subdivisions

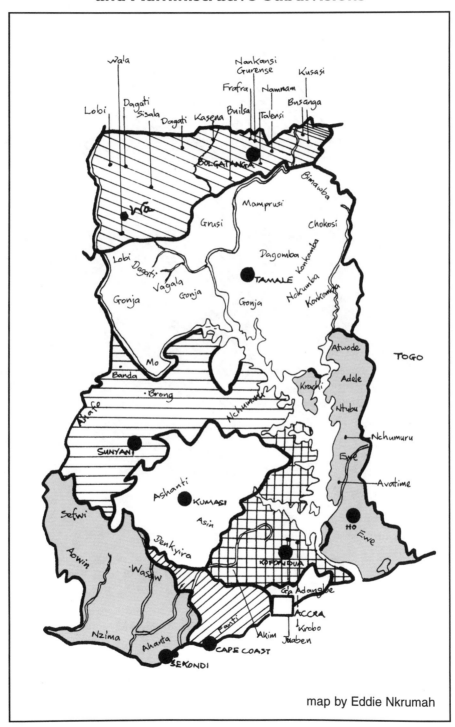

map by Eddie Nkrumah

A Geographic Giant

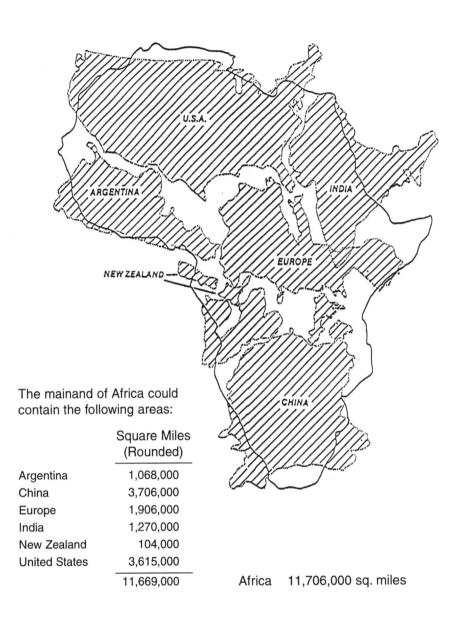

The mainand of Africa could contain the following areas:

	Square Miles (Rounded)
Argentina	1,068,000
China	3,706,000
Europe	1,906,000
India	1,270,000
New Zealand	104,000
United States	3,615,000
	11,669,000

Africa   11,706,000 sq. miles

Introduction

SOURCES FOR RELIGIOUS AND CULTURAL TRADITION IN AFRICA

The Malian (Malinke or Mandinka) novelist Amadou Hampate Ba recalls the significant role of the ancestral figure among the Fulani and the Bambara in the West African Sahel. The Sudanese people of the vast African savanna and desert regard such a person as a *waly,* "a saint of God," whose knowledge of oral texts they measure by how many of them he possessed and transmitted during his lifetime. *En Afrique, un veillard qui meurt, c'est une bibliothèque qui brûle.* "In Africa, every time an elder dies, a whole library burns down" (Asfar 1991, 143).

The waly, like the *griot* among the Mandinka of the Gambia or the *marabout* of northern Africa, was and still is the bearer of something like divine revelation, except that in the area of the Sahel and to the south these "saints" hand down the tradition from the ancestors. In the past the elders were privileged people in the royal courts. Such were the griots or bards (Conrad and Frank 1995) of the people of the western Sudan. Such is the court poet (the *kwadwumfo*) of the Akan in Ghana. Still today, an elder is the interpreter of the clan's traditions. While the community owns its traditions, each elder gives his or her own "twist" to the text according to each one's talents.

Much of our contemporary knowledge of West African Religious Traditions we derive from those oral—now for us the receptors, those aural and visual—traditions expressed in the myths, the folktales, the sagas, the danced-out stories and poems, the proverbs, the rituals and prayers, and even in the tonal rhythms of the talking drums. Moreover, details spring out of those texts that refer to the spiritual world of West Africans, like different names for God, the Creator, God's attributes, references to the exploits of the larger-than-life ancestors of old now revered for their spiritual powers, myths about deities lesser than the Almighty, the presence of evil and death, and the rituals of the annual or monthly festival days. Some of those texts are written in architectonic designs at the shrines and in mysterious symbols and patterns on textiles, gold weights, and carvings. The very institution of royalty with all its archaic ritual even in the humble village is the bearer of ancestral traditions of the clan and lineage where the people find their pride of place in life and in the afterlife. All this we find alive and

well, though increasingly obscured by modern technology and Western un-
belief, long before the advent of Islam or of Christianity up and down the
area of our concern: West Africa. The traditions are many. They are oral,
because the elders spoke or sung them, and in a wide sense they are oral
because the elders danced them and sounded them with drums and other
instruments.

We cannot ignore secondary sources, not only in the case of contemporary African novelists and ethnographers, and recorders of those oral traditions, like Amadou Hampate Ba or Chinua Achebe, for example, but in the
various chronicles recorded by early Arab and North African Muslim emissaries, geographers, and traders, some favorable and some not so partial to
the religious and cultural customs of the inhabitants of sub-Saharan Africa.
Lastly, we are in possession of the written observations of early European
explorers, colonialists, slave traders, tourists, and Christian missionaries.
With the encouragement of such noted scholars as James George Frazer,
government officials and church workers learned the local languages and
recorded customs so they could study how to govern and control the "natives" or translate the Bible in order to convert them from their "savage
heathenism." We recall the work of Robert Rattray among the Asante in the
Gold Coast (Ghana). While valuable in their own right, his studies of the
Akan and Hausa were influenced by an evolutionist notion that the cultures
were "primitive." Geoffrey Parrinder, himself a British scholar of African
religions, notes that it was due to the biased opinions of Europeans that
they described Africans as worshipers of fetishes, juju, and grisgris, or stated
that they were pagans, or heathen, or idolaters (Parrinder 1976, 15-17).[1]

A word of caution is due here when dealing with secondary sources of
the chronicles and letters of early visitors to sub-Saharan Africa. History in
the current sense, and anthropology, sociology, and the various schools of
the study of religion, did not exist as "scientific" methods of inquiry until
the nineteenth century. Even then many observers were influenced by their
so-called scientific biases, such as evolutionist or diffusionist approaches,
as much as the Muslim chroniclers or Christian missionaries were influenced by their cultural and religious opinions about what it meant to be
civilized and religious.

First of all, we refer to the early "outsiders," the medieval Muslim re-
corders. There was the eleventh-century geographer of Muslim Spain, al-
Bakri, who was a witness of "pagan" Ghana (in present-day Mauritania and
Mali). The twelfth-century Arab geographer al-Zuhri attests, probably er-

---

[1] Parrinder notes that the word *fetish* comes from a Portuguese term, *fetiço,* which means "a
manmade object." The word now means a charm or amulet or other magical object, which the
Europeans believed the west-coast Africans worshiped. Later on, the term acquired other meanings about anything one becomes obsessed with. *Juju* comes from a French word meaning
"doll." It refers to African gods or the magic rituals. The French also used the word *grisgris,*
which likewise refers to charms, amulets, and talismans. We will discuss these later.

roneously, that the warrior nomads of northwest Africa, the Almoravids, forcefully converted most of the population of ancient Ghana to Islam. The fourteenth-century historian Ibn Khaldun and, even more captivatingly, that indefatigable world traveler Sheik Abu Abdallah Muhammad ibn Abdallah ibn Muhammad ibn Ibrahim al-Lawati, known to us as Ibn Battuta, were not always capable of understanding the things they observed and wrote about. They borrowed from one another uncritically and very often mistakenly. If they could not grasp un-Islamic elements of Sudanic religious practices, they interjected the phrase, "Allah knows." Yet scholars today regard very highly the chronicles of Ibn Battuta for their rather reliable depiction of the religious and cultural practices along the Niger River Bend in the Sahel, even when he disagreed with either the conspicuous elements of traditional Malian religion or the African appropriation of Islam at the architectural monument, the mud mosque at Djenne (Clarke 1982).

It is worthwhile to examine the Muslim sources a little more thoroughly to comprehend better how an outsider's view influences other outsiders to continue and to build further notions of religion and culture that last even until today in many people's minds. Ibn Battuta was a Moroccan from Fez who had traveled some eighty thousand miles in Africa, Asia, and eastern Europe nearly 650 years ago. He became familiar with India and China, more than Marco Polo had. His last trip was to cross the sand sea, the Sahara, to Mali, where salt was so plentiful the people built houses out of salt blocks. When he arrived at last in Mali, he was bewildered by the beauty of the women. He was surprised by the staunch adherence of the Malians to many Islamic rituals, such as the Friday worship and the education of their children in Arabic and the Holy Qu'ran. Yet, he was somewhat scandalized by the rather liberal social rules concerning women, the regulations of matrilinear succession to the throne and inheritance. He described the Malians as black, not in a racial sense but in contrast to himself, and as devout Muslims, as good as any Muslims anywhere. He noted how affluent the ruling class was. He said the men were handsome and their behavior was different than any other he had encountered in his world travels (Makward 1991).

Ibn Battuta was equally baffled by the submission shown by the Malians to their sovereigns when they bowed before them to the ground, a ritual a Muslim performed uniquely for Allah. He was not pleased by the hyperbole recited by the griots, the court poets, in praise of their king. In the fifteenth century Muhammad al-Lamtuni, writing to al-Suhuti, the Supreme Judge over the Muslim world, complained similarly concerning the matrilinear system among the Tuareg, a nomadic people of the Sahara and the Sahel, and about their laxity in the performance of Islamic rituals and usages. Even peoples closer in distance and culture to the Berbers of northern Africa still adhered to old traditional customs (Clarke 1982). In other words, these negative reports of Ibn Battuta and other chroniclers serve us as positive sources for the culture and traditional religion of the Malians of that time.

The Christian outsiders were not much in disagreement with their Muslim antecedents, except that the former applied their thinking to the whole continent of Africa. It was the "dark continent." It would seem that on that continent everything remained savage and primitive. Culture, if there was one, remained static. Outsiders, whether Arab or European, gave the continent and its interior new names. The area of the western Sudan that Ibn Battuta visited in the fourteenth century was known by the Arabic name of *Sahel,* which means "shore." The area includes the modern nations of Mali, Senegal, Niger, Burkina Faso, and parts of other countries distant from the Gulf of Guinea. It is the savanna belt of grasses and a few trees below the Sahara, itself an Arabic word for the African north desert, the "sea of sand." The northern African Arabs and the Berbers called the area south of the desert *Bilad as-Sudan,* "the land of the blacks." There al-Bakri and Ibn Battuta and others like them tended to lump all the peoples they observed into one whole culture. As far as they could tell, the traditional customs, whether in ancient Ghana or ancient Mali, even when coupled with Islam, seemed remarkably similar.

The Muslims therefore initiated a way of regarding Africa that was to be continued by the European visitors and writers about African religions and cultures even to the present day. Not surprisingly, Geoffrey Parrinder claimed to discover "a great comparative homogeneity of African society in the religious sphere" (Parrinder 1976, 11). Indeed, many others said similar things about other aspects of culture, as they understood it.

Culture is not static. It is in constant flux as a given people, knit together with a common destiny, formulate over time and within a given area a language, a social pattern, and a way to cope with the real world they find around them, whether it is the land, the climate, the forces of nature, or other neighboring peoples different however so slightly from themselves. The whole complex social reality comprised of a system of symbols known to a people as "insiders" is what constitutes culture. One can learn a culture just as one can learn a language. But as far as possible one should learn the culture and language from the insider's view. Total experiential immersion is possible in a here-and-now (synchronic) situation. But it may never be possible in a historical (diachronic) sense, except through knowledge. Sources, therefore, that are secondary are reliable if they evince at least an appreciation of the uniqueness of a given culture as it exists now and in its historical origins. At the same time, one must recognize that over a larger area cultures may be different from one another, even if there are analogous areas of cultural patterns and linguistic similarities, as we shall note in coming chapters. For the moment, we should study the map of the continent of Africa (see p. xiii above). Note the modern nations and their boundaries. Look at another map of the ancient kingdoms (see Kwamena-Poh et al. 1982, 11), such as ancient Ghana, Mali, Songhay, or Kano. Then, if you can, study a map with the various linguistic families and sub-families (see Comrie et al. 1976, 77). Finally, see a map with the multitudes of ethnic groups in Africa (see Demko and Boe 1992, 39) and note how they cross the borders of the modern states. Realize that to study the sources of all of Africa would be an almost impossible task. Even when we narrow them down, as we shall presently indicate, it is not altogether possible. But for the moment, whether geographically or culturally, we must state this: Africa is not a country but a continent; Africa is not one culture, but a rich diversity of cultures; Africa is not one language, but is a polyglot containing many stories; Africa is not one religion, but a shrine of many rituals. If you want to learn the culture and therefore the religious traditions of a people, go to the village and listen to the elders. The Akan of Ghana have proverbs, as we shall later on note. One of them says, One should not go to another's village to insult him. And another says, The mouth of the elder is more powerful than the amulet. In other words, let your sources be genuine, even if they come out of Africa.

THE STUDY OF AFRICAN RELIGIOUS TRADITIONS

A generous number of contemporary authors of comparative religion have paid more attention to secondary sources of the earlier type and quite literally dismiss African Religion globally, since they have filed all of the traditions under one category. African Religion is not, in their opinion, a religion of the book such as Judaism, Christianity, or Islam. It is not as philosophical as Hinduism, or as spiritual as Buddhism. Continuing in the spirit of the negative views of the Muslim geographers and travelers, they have been dismayed by animal sacrifice, for example, forgetting perhaps that such sacrifices are described and practiced in great detail in the Hebrew scriptures (the Old Testament). In some texts of comparative religions African Religion is treated as "primitive," or perhaps more generously as "primal." It is savage, they say, or at least underdeveloped, not in any manner participating in divine revelation. Theologically, Christianity is assumed as the paradigm scholars regard as far superior to any other.

Ethnographers sometimes have attached an evolutionary significance to religions and cultures, and they have relegated African Religion to the lowest level on their scale, thus the category "primitive." They have forgotten that Africans in general are a very religious people and that their traditional religiosity still exists today, even when many have converted to Islam or to Christianity. Educated Africans see no problem when they return to their traditional customs and religious values. Much of sub-Saharan Africa has no Islamic tradition, or even a Christian tradition. The religious dimension of African cultures is not static, nor is it inferior to any other. It is dynamic and contemporary. Perhaps Islam, Christianity, and modern secularist humanism influence African contemporary religiosity, but African Religion is nonetheless a "world religion" and deserves its own place in academia.

The bad press given to African Traditional Religion originated with the medieval Muslim scholars and merchants, but European explorers, slave traders, colonialists, missionaries, and environmental exploiters have enhanced the misconceptions about it. Not understanding the western Sudanese (to use the Arab term unhappily) cultures, outsiders regarded them as static cultures and "pagan" or savage, to say the least. While recognizing that Africans are an "incurably religious people," as Parrinder recorded the impressions of British colonial administrators (Parrinder 1976, 9), they tended to harp on the bizarre and the unusual and play those things down as superstitious. The textbooks for religious studies departments in our universities have continued to treat African Religion in a similar disparaging manner. Take, for example, the last chapter in Leonard J. Biallas's work *World Religions: A Story Approach,* in which the author combines Mayan (Central American) and Ugandan (East African) religions under one theme dealing with sacrifice and death (Biallas 1991).

TERMS, METHOD, AND FOCUS

So, aren't we begging the question here by speaking about African Religion and at the same time of African Religious Traditions, more specifically, those of West Africa? When we say that African Traditional Religion should be ranked and treated together with world religions, the presupposition is with regard to what one considers *religion* to be. Authors provide various definitions, so much so that theologians and scholars of comparative religion place emphasis on a series of possible componential binary opposites, such as the sacred and the profane, the supernatural and the natural, personal and impersonal, spiritual and material, function and structure, and so on. But in West Africa and in most of the continent where Africans adhere to their traditions and are not that influenced by Islam or Christianity, or by Hinduism and Buddhism in eastern Africa, religion and the remainder of the principal cultural complexes, such as systems of kinship, inheritance, governance, economics, education, art, and so on, are for the most part not compartmentalized. In this sense we can speak of *religion* in the singular, because we tend to separate the various symbolic domains in a culture. And only in this sense is there an analogy between religion in Africa and other world religions and even among the various traditions within Africa. Beliefs in a sky-god, the gods of the spirit world, the deity of earth, the ancestors, and the terrible function of evil are present, but each one does not always enjoy equal or similar emphasis. Hence, only in an analogous sense do we refer to Religion in Africa in the singular, and to World

Religions in another sense, just as Islam is a religion, Buddhism is a religion, but each only analogously (Wendland 1990).

We refer, moreover, to African Religions as traditional. There is no one single Tradition, but there are many traditions. We have noted that there are oral and living traditions. The griots, the elders, the storytellers, and the drummers keep alive the corpus of material that serves as a moral guide and as a foundation to the thought and the behavior of a given people within its cultural environment. A tradition is what is handed down from one generation to the next, including the thoughts, the words, and the deeds of previous generations, not as stark history, but as the myths, the exploits, the wisdom of the ancient ones, in the genre of the dramatized stories, the songs, the proverbs, the drumming, and the designs that make up the heritage of the people while also recognizing the uniqueness of each performer. There are many traditions, and they are never static. They normally are modified to meet the situation due to shifts caused by nature, by war, or by contact with neighboring ethnic groups, who may speak the same language or may not. The traditions have been changed by trade, by travel of groups or individuals bringing news, and later on by Islamic jihad, by the slave trade, by colonial domination, education, technology, and so on. Note the changes in dress suggested by Islam. Also note that certain customs, such as succession to kingship by nephews on the king's sister's side of the family, confirmed by the complaints of the Muslim travelers, remained in place. Certain segments of the population adapted to change more easily than others, particularly the more educated and the nobility. Lower classes of society and the rural folk tended to be more rigid than the urban elite. West Africans, whose cultures are quite complex and heterogeneous, have generally remained rather conservative in outlook. Each ethnic group has not been so eager to surrender its traditions to other groups, even if they are similar. At times, however, partial cultural surrender has occurred; for example, when the Ga, along the coastal area near the modern capital of Ghana, Accra, adapted certain Akan funeral rituals and music from the neighboring Akwamu after their defeat in 1681. But over all, the traditions are so disparate that we really can claim we are dealing with West African Religious Traditions.

We intend to examine those traditions as much as possible from the "inside," with what is occasionally termed the *emic* approach. Following the method of Clifford Geertz, I propose that we examine the symbols of West African societies, whether the symbols are known consciously or not by the people, in order to arrive at a "thick description" of their cultures and religiosity (Geertz 1973, 6). We are simply offering an interpretation of the symbols found in the West African Religious Traditions. We are going to seek out the meaning of things, of the actions and the words. We are concerned with the actants, the persons who are the bearers of the deep, hence Geertz's word, the "thick" meaning of the symbols we perceive. We are taking the cultures as they are (a sort of "you get what you see" method) here and now (the synchronic approach, sometimes called the ethnographic present). We do this without denying that the cultures are subject to historical change and therefore that the phenomena we observe may be somewhat different in form and substance today from those of the past (the diachronic approach). While we attempt to do an "insider's" description, we, I for certain, and perhaps you, are mostly "outsiders," not African born and not indigenous to the cultures, who can provide a narrative only at most by way of exemplification. We have to use language we are familiar with. We translate by using models to which we can relate.

One last biographical point deserves attention. The author is a Divine Word Missionary who spent almost thirteen years in Ghana, teaching and serving in the ministry. As a Roman Catholic theologian, I have my own priorities. I am a liturgist, a specialist in Catholic worship and ritual. But I have made it my personal concern over the years to observe rituals of other religions and even secular rituals and body language (ritual studies). My missionary congregation is steeped in the study of anthropology and the history of religious traditions all over the world. I have made use of phenomenological principles to study the language and the culture of the Akan of Ghana, a large linguistic group comprising a number of ethnic groups speaking various dialects, sometimes called Twi. I am also a Euro-American. The Ghanaians say that I am *oburoni koko,* "a pink-skinned person from behind the corn field." While my origin and background may tend to shade my view somewhat, I have tried not to westernize or to christianize either the discussion or my interpretation of West African societies. I focus on the Akan most of all because that is the area of West Africa I know the best firsthand. I am quite familiar with the relatively nearby cultures of the Ga, Krobo, and Ewe, and to some extent those of the Yoruba and the Igbo, from personal interviews as well as research. A number of friends and advisors, mentioned in the Acknowledgments, have over the years taught me Twi and the Ghanaian cultures, written down information for me as a personal favor or in classroom assignments, or let me video-tape them.

So, the title of our study is *West African Religious Traditions: Focus on the Akan of Ghana.* The reader should note that I commence with the phenomena rather than the ideas or beliefs. It is in the performance of the religions that the traditions are actualized and therefore known in an oral milieu. Even recitation is fleshed out with gestures, mimes and sounds, as we shall soon realize in the coming chapters. We begin with dance and rhythm, with song and recitation in a tonal language. An Ifa diviner in Yoruba societies first learns to cast the cowrie chain before he slowly memorizes the 250 poems connected with each throw. To repeat, performance is the locus for the primary sources in oral traditions.

Moreover, in the West African societies we are interpreting, human beings are the central figures of the cosmos, not God, not the deities, not even the forces of evil, but men and women and children among the living and the ancestors among the dead. Hence, I do not start by adhering to the pyramid or triangular illustration of the order of spiritual forces, first proposed by Edwin Smith, followed by Parrinder (Parrinder 1976), followed by E. Bolaji Idowu (Idowu 1975), and to some extent by Kofi Asare Opoku (Opoku 1978). The pyramid or triangle model proposes that God stands at the apex of the African cosmos and is the primary object of value, followed down the theocracy by the divinities, the ancestors, other spirits, totems and charms, with human beings fitting in there somewhere. Actually, human beings rather than God are the center of a rather circular form of cosmos, which we will discuss later. My approach involves the experiential element of religion, which implies that not every West African society and even not every area in a single ethnic group experiences its religion in the same form of ritual or story. Every individual experiences the spiritual world in the context of his or her own community, not only within the larger ethnic group, but also down on the clan and village levels. As John Mbiti says, "To be human is to belong to the whole community." This means to hold all the beliefs, festivals, ceremonies, and rituals of the entire community as sacred. To detach oneself from that religious tradition is to be severed from one's roots, kinship and value system. "African people do not know how to exist without religion" (Mbiti 1990, 2). The same applies to West African Religious Traditions.

While I limit this discussion to the Akan experience and relate it to the experience of a few other West African Traditions, it is my hope that the reader's curiosity will be fired up enough to search out those other cultures of West and Central Africa that formed the roots of so much of the cultural wealth brought to North, Central, and South America and the Caribbean by Africans during those horrendous years of the slave trade.

There are seven chapters dealing with traditional and cultural values. I have tried to describe them as they are without romanticizing about them. There are some rough edges, too, that we must honestly discuss. The last two chapters deal with Islam and Christianity in the West African context. In the end, we shall once more have to admit, West African Traditions have permeated change itself.

BIBLIOGRAPHY

Asfar, Gabriel. "Amadou Hambate Ba and the Islamic Dimension of West African Oral Tradition." In *Faces of Islam in African Literature*, edited by Kenneth W. Harrow, 141-50. Portsmouth, N.H.: Heinemann Educational Books, 1991.

Biallas, Leonard J. *World Religions: A Story Approach.* Mystic, Conn.: Twenty-Third Publications, 1991.

Clarke, Peter B. *West Africa and Islam: A Study of Religious Development from the 8th to the 20th Century.* London: Edward Arnold, 1982.

Comrie, Bernard, Stephen Matthews, and Maria Polinsky, eds. *The Atlas of Languages: The Origin and Development of Languages throughout the World*. New York: Facts on File, Inc., 1976.

Conrad, David C., and Barbara E. Frank. *Status and Identity in West Africa: Nyamakalaw of Mande*. Bloomington, Ind.: Indiana University Press, 1995.

Demko, George, and Eugene Boe. *Why in the World: Adventures in Geography*. New York: Doubleday Anchor Books, 1992.

Geertz, Clifford. *The Interpretation of Cultures: Selected Essays*. New York: Basic Books, 1973.

Holloway, Joseph E., ed. *Africanisms in American Culture*. Bloomington, Ind.: Indiana University Press, 1990.

Idowu, E. Bolaji. *African Traditional Religion: A Definition*. London: SCM Press, 1973; Maryknoll, N.Y.: Orbis Books, 1975.

Kwamena-Poh, M., J. Tosh, R. Waller, and M. Tidy. *African History in Maps*. Essex, England: Longman Group UK Limited, 1982.

Makward, Edris. "Women, Tradition, and Religion in Sembene Ousmane's Work." In *Faces of Islam in African Literature*, edited by Kenneth W. Harrow, 187-99. Portsmouth, N.H.: Heinemann Educational Books, 1991.

Mbiti, John S. *African Religions and Philosophy*. 2d ed., revised and enlarged. Portsmouth, N.H.: Heinemann Educational Books, 1990.

Opoku, Kofi Asare. *West African Traditional Religion*. Accra, Ghana: FEP International Private Limited, 1978.

Parrinder, Geoffrey. *African Traditional Religion*. New York: Harper & Row, 1976.

Wendland, Ernest R. "Part 1: Traditional Central African Religion." In *Bridging the Gap: African Traditional Religion and Bible Translation*, edited by Philip C. Stine and Ernest R. Wendland, 1-129. UBS Monograph series, no. 4. New York: United Bible Societies, 1990.

STUDY GUIDE

1. Beside the word *waly,* as described in the text, familiarize yourself with the terms *griot* and *marabout*. Concerning the ancient notion of the griot, a bard or poet, the king's counselor and historian in an oral culture, see D. T. Niane, *Sundiata: An Epic of Old Mali* (Burnt Hill, Essex: Longman, 1992), vii. For the French word *marabout,* which means a Muslim cleric in West Africa, or at least a person (a man) who is holy, see ibid, 91 n.44.

2. What is the role of the elder in the typical African community? Read John S. Mbiti, *Introduction to African Religion,* (Portsmouth, N.H.: Heinemann, 1991), 68-69, about intermediaries, and 160, about ritual elders. See Oliver A. Onwubiko, *African Thought, Religion and Culture* (Enugu, Nigeria: SNAAP Press, 1991), 28-29.

3. What is meant by oral traditions? Read Isidore Okpewho, *African Oral Literature* (Bloomington, Ind.: Indiana University Press, 1992), 3-19. Note what the author says about the various approaches modern scholars have taken concerning the oral traditions in Africa and why, according to the author, they should be regarded as literature.

4. Which are the secondary sources utilized for the study of certain West African cultures and religious traditions? Why are the Muslim chronicles so interesting and informative?

5. Who was Ibn Battuta? Why are his chronicles so valuable? Read Thomas J. Abercrombie, "Ibn Battuta, Prince of Travelers," in *National Geographic* (December 1991), 2-49.

6. Which geographic terms applied to the continent of Africa by the Arabs and North Africans do we use today? What do they mean, and to which areas do they apply?

7. Define *culture*. What is meant by the synchronic approach to culture? What is meant by the diachronic approach?

8. Map Study:

a. Take the contemporary political map of Africa (see p. xiii above) and become familiar with the names and boundaries of the nations of West and Central Africa.

b. Examine a map of West Africa (Holloway 1990, 2) with the names of the major ethnic groups (we do not use the term *tribe*. Why?). Note the names for the coastal areas as defined by the early European explorers. We will say more about these later.

c. Study the map with the ancient West African empires and peoples (see p. xiv above). Note their names. Where is the Niger River Bend? Where are their capitals?

Ancient Ghana: Koumbi-Saleh, whose people were known as the Soninke in southern modern Mauritania.

Mali (called Mallel by the Arab geographers): Niani, whose original people were Mandinka. The Sundiata (Sunjata) legend is about its founder Sundiata (Sunjata had a griot by the name of Balla Fasseke).

Songhay: Kukiya, then Gao. Its other towns included the university town of Timbuktu and Djenne (Jenne), the latter with its magnificent mud mosque; its peoples are said originally to have been Sorko fishermen and farmers from the Lake Chad area who had moved to live along the Niger River to hunt crocodiles and tortoises.

Kano is the name of a town in Hausa country that gave its name to the Hausa Empire; Katsina was another important town in the area.

d. Identify the areas of the Akan and the subgroups, such as the Asante, the Akim, the Akwapim, the Fante, and the Kwahu (see p. xv above and Opoku 1978, facing p. 1); then also locate the Ga, the Ewe, in Ghana and Togo, and the Yoruba and the Igbo in Nigeria (see p. xiv above).

9. Why should the study of African Religion be on a par with the study of other World Religions?

10. What is meant by *religion* in this context? What is traditional about Traditional Religions?

11. What is the "inside" or the *emic* approach to the study of culture? (see Geertz 1973, 5-10, 14, 27-28). Why is an understanding of culture so important for our study of religion? Do you suppose that the fault of many secondary sources, such as those written by the Muslim travelers and the European traders and missionaries, is that they were composed mainly to entertain and that they did not consider the cultural context of the religions they purportedly described?

12. What is *ethnography?* (see Geertz 1973, 5-6). Who is an *anthropologist?* (see ibid., 14). Note that the social anthropologist is in the business not of studying villages, as Geertz warns us, but the people and their culture in the villages. And, looking ahead to the next chapter, it is the business of paleoanthropologists to study the fossils of ancient peoples.

13. Why is the community so important to African life and religion?

14. What advantage do you suppose the focus on the Akan Religious Traditions has as a model for our study of West African Religious Traditions?

Recommended for viewing at this point:

• "Proud Heritage from Western Africa," a filmstrip in two parts (Mount Kisco, N.Y.: Guidance Associates, 1970). Here the reader can find geographical and historical information about the savanna and forest regions of Western Africa, including a brief look at the medieval kingdoms.

• Similar information is found in the first part of the 57-minute video version of the television series *Africa,* Program 3: "Caravans of Gold," written and presented by Basil Davidson, Home Vision, 1984. For information, call 1-800-262-8600.

I

In the Beginning Was the Dance

HUMAN SOURCES: DANCE AND RITUAL INCARNATE

If the elder is the primary source of African Religious Traditions, then the elder who lived before him or her, the ancestor, is the elder's source. We need to reach back to the origins of the clans and nations for the root sources of their traditions and even beyond to the traditions of other clans and nations that lived before them. Since oral traditions have no written texts to dig up somewhere, we must investigate elsewhere. And where else than the very human beings we are discussing?

The scientists, whose job is to look for fossil remains and to dig for archeological evidence of human origins, have probably demonstrated quite well for us that the earliest human life forms appeared in East Africa over a million years ago. These paleoanthropologists maintain that the first humans evolved in Africa and migrated to Europe and Asia. An older hypothesis called the multiregional hypothesis, which is maintained by most of these scientists, claims that from earlier forms, which they named from the sites where the fossils were found, like Arago man, Java man, Broken Hill man, and so on, evolved the earliest type of human. The earlier form they glorified with the name *Homo erectus* (Leakey and Lewin 1992). So, according to the multiregional model, which later scientists dubbed "the candelabra model," the evolutionary movements consisted in identifiable species changes from the *Homo erectus* to the *Homo sapiens,* with intermediate stages throughout Africa, Asia, and Europe (Leakey and Lewin 1992). There were, therefore, three branches of human beings based on the three general regions—thus the "candelabra" effect of the models. Some scientists have entertained doubts about this for a while. Another hypothesis, proposed by those whose job is to study human genetics, called the "Noah's Ark" hypothesis at first, because it posits a complete extinction over a wide geographical area of the original species after a new form arrived out of Africa, the modern human. The biblical allusion is to Noah's ark and the flood, when, according to the book of Genesis, most of the human race was destroyed (Gn 6–9). Scientists at Berkeley, California, and at Emory, in Atlanta, by looking at patterns of genetic variation of mitochondrial DNA among human populations, determined that Africans, of all existing populations, have the deepest genetic roots (Leakey and Lewin 1992; Fagan 1990). Since only women are the bearers of a type of "genetic time-clock," the African woman stands out as the model of a kind of "Mitochondrial Eve," once again alluding to the biblical Eve, the first human mother. At any rate, the point is that the transformation of an archaic human form to a modern form of *Homo sapiens* occurred first in Africa only about 100,000 to 150,000 years ago (Leakey and Lewin 1992). From Africa this most recent ancestor, probably in small groups, migrated to spread over the face of the earth. We must therefore not imagine this "Eve" to be a lonely woman. There were other human forms around, but the descendants of their mitochondria have long died out. "Eve" is the most recent common ancestor on the purely female line, and she was probably African. There are, of course, other ways to have ancestors, and these can occur along the purely male line (see Dawkins 1995, chap. 2). All human beings are therefore within a very recent time frame and descended from Africans, at least along the female line. Whatever happened to the earlier human forms is anybody's guess. We don't know. But one thing is certain; the human species that developed did so in large part due to adaptation, language, and culture.

This is where neurobiologists enter to speculate concerning the derivation of culture: communication through body language and spoken language, hence, the development of community. Some anthropologists, like Victor Turner, through studies of existing populations in central Africa, had fixed their focus on ritualization in terms of cultural processes. Ritual, as a stylized performance of symbolic activity, in one way conserves a tradition of sociocultural values. Turner has demonstrated that ritual actually goes further by providing ways for a given society to cope with transitions in life and environment and even to effect necessary adjustments to new situations during a period of liminality that results in *communitas,* a Latin word for "community" (Turner 1977). While it is true that in the animal kingdom various species engage in courtship and mating rituals, such activity is not related to survival, coping, and problem solving in a social or religious context, as in the case of human beings. Turner discovered in central Africa that rituals are performed at various stages in life—in rites of passage, for example—in order to create a sense of *communitas,* a temporary statusless bonding that holds a society together after the ritual is over (Turner 1977).

Turner and his wife, Edith, also an anthropologist, have been intrigued by suggestions of neurobiologists because they bear upon the origin of ritual and language. Most authors in the past have believed that myth and speech were primary and that ancient rhythmic behavior followed. The primacy of the word was even speculated by Aristotle. But Eugene d'Aquili, a neurobiologist, paraphrased this postulate by playing on the biblical expression from John's gospel: "[In] the beginning was the word, which danced its incarnation" (D'Aquili 1986, 142). But then he explains that the development of the human brain postulates the structuring of myth and story through ritual enhanced by drumming and dance. Earlier species of *Homo* engaged in ritualistic dance, but as the brain developed, a greater feeling of well-being filled the human heart by means of the physical activity and the variegated drumming and dance, now embellished with reflective song, reiterative call and response, and shouts of various emotions. D'Aquili now takes his former metaphor to give it a new twist: ["In the beginning was] the dance, which gave birth to the word, which then danced its incarnation" (D'Aquili 1986, 142). Later in his monograph d'Aquili concludes that the evidence seems to underscore this metaphor: "[The] dance has formed the word and the word the myth which has guided the dance to an awareness of itself" (D'Aquili 1986, 160; Turner 1986, 144).

The point we make here is that since the cradle of humanity was probably Africa—or, at least, one important segment of the species *Homo sapiens* evolved out of an early genetic pool in Africa—one could claim that dance, ritual, and ceremony are the dramatic elements of the religious traditions that are still extant today all over sub-Saharan Africa and have spread from there over the face of the earth. The African is a person of dance. Africans were the first human beings to dance and reflect on their humanity in terms of a world beyond the physical, the spiritual order of gods and ancestors. Religion and culture are therefore inseparable from the beginning. The Africans were the messengers of art and of the good news about a world beyond the mere mundane earth. But those who stayed behind, especially after the increasing desiccation of the Sahara region from about 4000 B.C.E. onward, migrated in the area of the Sudan or sub-Sahara and eventually set up their cultural centers, such as the Nok of present northern Nigeria and the Ile Ife center of the Yoruba, their linguistic dispersion into the present four basic language families, and their establishment of traditions (Onwubiko 1991). With the independent introduction of agriculture and the use of iron in the Niger River Bend, the pastoral societies organized into urban communities and small town states. Migration into the forest belt in West Africa continued from about 500 B.C.E. until about 1600 C.E. During this time history records for us those ancient empires of the Sahel and the organization of the peoples we will now consider.

DANCE IN WEST AFRICA: DRAMA AND THE STUFF OF CULTURE

In oral traditions words cannot be left to speak for themselves alone (Okpewho 1992). There are many nonverbal and paralinguistic elements that make for dramatic effect in a performance. Many subtle variations to

an oral text include mime and dance for effective delivery to an audience
that understands them with both serious as well as humorous consequences.
The cultural language is as important as the spoken tongue. It creates community; it enhances life; it establishes a religious sense of the presence of
the spiritual order and moral values. It creates the environment for connect-
ing the past with the future and change. Commenting on the relationship
between the dramatic substance of rituals and ceremonies and the religious
power of humans and gods together at those celebrations, Ogbaa quotes
from the narrator of Chinua Achebe's novel, *Arrow of God:*

> The festivals thus brought gods and men together in one crowd. It was
> the only assembly in Umuaro in which a man might look to his right
> and find his neighbor and look to his left and see a god standing there.
> (Ogbaa 1992, 88; Achebe 1974, 203)

To the African, therefore, as Mbiti has remarked, religion is life and life
is religion. Moreover, life is communal. Kinship forms the foundation of
society, which is the mirror of the cosmos. Particularly family and clan are
the society to which a person must essentially adhere for survival. The Akan
have an expression for clan solidarity: If a child commits nine crimes, he
bears the punishment for five. This means that in the *abusuaban* (clan) system of the Akan, the result of a person's misdeeds is not borne by the person alone, but by both person and family. So, in the context of the social
structure, dance, rhythm, drumming, song, and mime all express a way of
thinking, of feeling, and of communicating with one another. While African
dance is not similar in any way to Hindu cosmogonic art performances,
African dance is unique in its celebration of events in life from the significant to the ordinary. The African dances when a baby is born and named
and at puberty rites; the African dances in rejoicing at marriages and in
mourning at funerals. The African dances at festivals, when the yams are
harvested, to thank the spiritual powers for food and life. The African also
dances at festivals just for entertainment and for intersexual excitement.
Africans sing and imitate dance at work. To get a job done, they sing while
they work in the fields, calling and shouting to one another, while moving
in rhythm to the beating of drums or tools. The result is to create solidarity
and harmony (Onwubiko 1991). One of the contributions African slaves
made to American culture was the work or field song.

Africans teach children to dance as they teach them to walk and talk.
When the children see the adults and youth dancing according to their divisions, they run around and jump into the circle without any shyness or hesi-
tation. Olaudah Equiano, one of the earliest Igbo expatriates in England,
wrote about the day of festival, when villagers lined up according to age
sets, the married men and married women, the young men and the maidens,
all did their parts in dancing and rejoicing (Ogbaa 1992). Among the Akan,

the king-elect must learn the royal customs and traditions during an extended period of tutorship. Among these are the significant dances of his clan and community, most important, the royal or court dances. After the enstoolment ceremonies of a king, he dances with grace and with all the majestically deliberate movements expected of a king (Bame 1991).

All over sub-Saharan Africa, singing, drumming, stamping, and clapping in diverse styles and rhythms, coupled with other instruments beside the drum, such as the xylophone and the bamboo flute, come under one heading: *dance*. There are various forms of recreational dancing, but also dances for significant events in the life of the community—for war, for hunting, for harvest, for secret societies, for the royal court, and, through everything, for religion. Many of these overlap, in particular on festivals. On the contemporary scene, even in rural areas where battery-operated radios and imported tape players broadcast contemporary music, recreational dance and song may seem heavily secularized. Villages in Ghana without electricity, for example, invite popular bands to come by truck, loaded down with portable generators, lights, and sound equipment, to set up a stage and play all night while the local villagers dance to the deafening sounds of "High Life." But even many of these songs sing about God and religious values. Thus K. K. Kabobo, in his tape entitled "My Sweet Heart," sings a song called *Nyame ye odo,* "God is love!"

Traditionally, if we focus on West Africa and, in particular, on the Akan of Ghana, there are two general functions of dance: the religious as such and the merely social. We shall briefly consider each of these aspects.

The Religious Function of Dance

The entire complex of African communion with the spirit world, which we shall explain in greater detail in coming chapters, includes dances, but along with them prayers and invocations to the spirits during the pouring of libation or at the beginning of the talking drums activity, trance dances of the priesthood of deities, as well as proverbs sprinkled in speeches, storytelling, and symbols on buildings, carvings, gold weights, and on textiles. Dancing and music often permeate the other forms of religious activities and artifacts. Formerly, dance groups based on age sets of the community among the Igbo and Yoruba created new forms of dance. Religious dances thus have a social function, in the sense that their purpose is to generate systemic control over all forces of good or evil for the harmony between the spirit and material worlds, and as social control over the behavior of the people by means of oracles, shrines, and customs. We now will examine the Akan *Akom* dance.

The *Akom* dance is a series of dances performed to aid the priests at a certain deity's shrine either to work themselves into a trance or to release them from it. During the trance they communicate with the deity and with those who have approached for some personal need. The band for the dances includes several sizes of a variety of drum called *fontomfrom.* The drummers, who are men, and some women gather in front of the shrine some time before the dance commences. Other persons arrive to obtain favors, as well as the curious. Some of the people may know the steps of the dance and begin to dance while the drummers get warmed up. The audience watches, and sometimes individuals jump into the circle of dancers. After some time, the priest *(okomfo)* or priestess arrives in full regalia with a skirt made of raffia *(odoso)* and with talismans all over the body and tinkling bells on the ankles. The face is painted with white clay *(hyirew),* a symbol of victory and joy. The priest is expert in the art of dancing, and so the drums intensify while the singing of the others is heightened. The priest walks around greeting the people while sprinkling them with the white powdered clay carried by an attendant. The priest turns to "the four winds" to acknowledge God, Nyame, and the directions from where his word will come to the priest. The first steps of the dance, called the *adaban,* likewise acknowledge the wholeness and the oneness of God, while the singers invoke the deities. The priest dances with spins and turns for more than a half-hour and is worked into a frenzy as the shrine deity takes possession. At this point the priest performs acts of healing of their ailments for the devotees and delivers messages from the deity to the community of worshipers. At the end the priest dances some more and eventually is released from the trance. He retires or is often carried exhausted to his house (Bame 1991). Sometimes the devotees stay on for the whole day or night. The deity and "his children" enjoy a feast with songs, drumming, drinks, and food.

Other religious dances are performed at festivals, to which we shall return below, to identify witches and sorcerers or other causes for evil. Among the Yoruba, when a female devotee dances in honor of Shango, the spirit of thunder, the deity rides her head. She takes on all the characteristics of the male deity (Drewal 1992).

The above description of religious dance indicates that dance as a part of the whole religious activity serves a social function of a society in its need to solve problems. The priest is the medium between the spiritual world and the "lived" world. The world of human beings is a social as well as an individual world woven into the structure of a people struggling with the problems of life within their own milieu. The dance, according to Victor Turner, developing the theory of the rites of passage of Arnold van Gennep, establishes the boundaries of what he calls "anti-structure" or *communitas.* The in-between period of delivering divine messages to the community of the village and the healing of ailments is called the situation of *liminality.* The dance before the trance was the rite of separation; the dance for dissolving the trance was the rite of aggregation. The aim of the entire ritual was to help people with their problems. Hence, as we have indicated in the Introduction, ritual, of which dance is an early form, is at the heart of the social structure of human beings, particularly in African society. Dance creates a milieu for anti-structure during the period of liminality, which once more re-creates and renews the culture. Ritual is associated, therefore, according to Turner, with social transitions, while other ceremonies are linked with social states (Turner 1986). The spirits are present simply to serve the human society in its origins and in its ends. The rites create a different world of symbols, a world that re-creates and recombines culture in a progressive way. In a manner of speaking, the rites are road maps that point the way to a more profound understanding of the social and cosmic orders, of which the spiritual is a part. The shrine is a space apart and therefore sacred. But the ritual provides even more precise space apart from the rest of life. And that life never remains the same. Once the priest goes to his room and the group goes back to its village, life returns to normal, but with a sense of change. The area of *communitas,* the sacred time and space of communion with the spirit world, re-creates the social order and the culture. The traditions are preserved, and at the same time they are modified to address new problems that have been solved or will be solved in the future.

The Social Function of Dance

Dance is not only the symbolic and therefore real vehicle of communion with the spirit world; it is also a means of communication with members of the clan and community. From earliest times, Africans have expressed through the language of dance the deepest feelings they have about life with one another. Of the many kinds of dances in their repertoire, the Akan have two that illustrate our point quite well, the *fontomfrom* and the *adowa,* both elegant and stylized in their symbolic gestures and intended double meaning. While not religious in the deepest sense, they manifest a sense of values that can also be perversely humorous.

The *fontomfrom* consists in a suite of warrior dances accompanied by one or two groups of drummers with orchestras of large-size and medium-size talking drums and various smaller drums. The dancers may be soloists or several persons in groups. The dance is performed as a warrior's dance of valor in the field, an expression of his pride in service of the king and ethnic group. The dance may moreover express the happiness of the king himself and his pride at being a valiant military leader. The queen mother, the most powerful woman in the royal court, since she is the king maker, sometimes rises to dance of peace, stability, and of motherliness, for which she expects the men to fight and win to preserve those values (Bame 1991).

The symbolic gestures mime combat motifs. They often—and very elegantly among the Akan—express feelings that either enhance the social structure or belittle it. For example, the king wishes to remind his court at a *durbar* (a royal reception) that he is the sole authority present, so in the course of the dance he points his finger at the sky, the ground, and his chest as if to say, "Except God above, and the Earth Goddess below, there is absolutely nobody besides me in authority here." The king may point to the "four winds" and then fold his arms across his chest as if to say, "I own everything in every place I have inspected" (Bame 1991). A commoner doing the dance, instead of pointing to his own chest, points in the direction of the king to assert his authority. If the commoner dances in the manner of the king, he insults the king and must pay a fine in the form of money or by offering a sheep to pacify the stool of the king (Bame 1991). The stool, which we shall explain later, is not only the seat of the king but the symbol of the authority he holds from the ancestors.

The queen mother—who is not the mother of the king but often one of his maternal aunts or a sister—or another woman dances the *fontomfrom* to manifest the grief she or the other women as a group of mothers and wives feel at a death during battle. She points to an eye as if to say, "See what grief has stricken me." She sometimes places the palms of both hands on top of her head to show her sorrow and bereavement. She expresses pain when she places both palms on her stomach with her torso tilted forward. She then runs into the arms of the nearest lineage head or even of the king himself to say that person is her support and she depends upon him for hope of victory (Bame 1991).

Adowa dance is a woman's dance usually performed by an ensemble headed by the queen mother. The coastal Ga people in Ghana acquired this dance from the neighboring Akan group, the Akwamu, who conquered them shortly after they arrived in the area from Benin country in modern Nigeria back in the seventeenth century. The Ga do not have a queen mother, but their *adowa* ensemble resembles the Akan in that it forms an auxiliary women's group opposite the men's *asafo* or military association. At any rate, the Ga still sing the verses in Twi, the language of the Akan. The original purpose of the dance was for funerals, but today it is performed for durbars and for the annual yam harvest festivals in honor of the ancestors (Hampton 1978).

The instruments among the Akan comprise two medium size drums, two small drums, and usually a couple of gongs. The dance is a stylized, symbolic employment of gestures and movements of the body in tune with the rhythm of the gongs. The left hand is extended forward while the right hand brushes over it.

The audience in this dance and in others gets involved when someone sticks money on the forehead of the dancer or others raise their right hands and make a "V" sign with the fingers to indicate pleasure in the performance.

The dance illustrates that sometimes conflict rather than harmony may result. A dancer gives vent to her animosity toward a rival when she clenches her fist and places the thumb over the fingers and points in the direction of her rival to say "she is worse than a beast" (Bame 1991). Similar gestures are indicated, such as brushing the thumb over the buttocks to say that the other person is nothing more than toilet paper (Bame 1991). No doubt even in times of festival brawls sometimes ensue. At any rate, the point is that a dance that has social ramifications may also indicate religious or moral meaning. Certainly to insult the king is worse than insulting a commoner, because a king has "spiritual" status. An offense is a *musuo,* an infringement that requires customary rites of expiation. But the offense against another person is wrong in any case; it is "unfitting" *(eye bone; enfata)* (Wiredu 1991).

The drummers, singers, and dancers refer often to God (Nyame), to the Earth Goddess (Asase Yaa), and to the ancestors. Dance both manifests and teaches a belief that is ongoing and permeates every fabric of society. This leads us to consider how religious traditions are manifest during festivals.

FESTIVALS: RELIGIOUS TRADITIONS AND COMMUNITY TIME

Traditional festivals combine elements of dance and dramatic rituals that require the participation of the entire community. In *Things Fall Apart* Chinua Achebe gives details about the feast of the New Yam among the Igbo of Umuofia (Achebe 1989, chaps 5-6). Achebe takes the occasion to describe for the sake of the reader, whom he presumes to be an "outsider," certain aspects of Igbo culture and cosmology:

> The Feast of the New Yam was held every year before the harvest began, to honor the earth goddess and the ancestral spirits of the clan. New yams could not be eaten until they had first been offered to these powers. Men and women, young and old, looked forward to the New Yam Festival because it began a season of plenty—the new year. On the last night before the festival, yams of the old year were all disposed of by those who still had them. The new year must begin with tasty, fresh yams and not the shriveled and fibrous crop of the previous year. All cooking pots, calabashes and wooden bowls were thoroughly washed, especially the wooden mortar in which yam was pounded. Yam foo-foo and vegetable soup was the chief food in the celebration. (Achebe 1989, 37)

Achebe goes on to explain that part of the preparation includes the cleaning of the huts and painting them in white, yellow, and dark green; the painting of the women with cam wood and drawing patterns on their stomachs and backs; and the decorating of the children's hair, shaving it in beautiful patterns (Achebe 1989). The day of festival consists in sacrifice of new yam and palm oil to the family ancestors and eating much food and having much palm wine with relatives and friends from other villages. The second day consists in other celebrations, especially wrestling among the young men. Drumming, dancing, and singing fill other moments. One can readily observe how the religious and the secular in our terms are not very distinguishable among the Igbo. The yam festival marks the end of the old and the beginning of the new.

Here we must deal with the African sense of time. Religious festivals combine dance with ritual drama, entertainment, and other ceremonies that, like dance, oscillate with the rhythm of time. John Mbiti maintains that African time is two-dimensional, with a long past, a present, and virtually no future (Mbiti 1990). Oliver Onwubiko, a Nigerian, disagrees. Not only the past and the present but the immediate future and the long-distant future are concepts included in African languages, reflecting how people regard their immersion in time. Except under the influence of the West, there is no such thing as "clock time." The African concept is polychronous. An African woman can at the same time be pregnant, balance a load of wood on her head, and carry a baby on her back. Combining responsibilities is an aspect of life which indicates that time is family or social. The African is master or mistress of time and not vice-versa (Onwubiko 1991).

Some personal factors enter into the reckoning of time. For example, a baby sometimes is called a "breast-feeder" during the first two years of life. Physical changes in the body indicate natural growth from childhood to adulthood; a boy grows into manhood and a girl grows into womanhood, each with proper rites of passage. In some societies admission into secret societies marks a defined period of personal time. Historical factors enter in. For example, when asked when a person got married, he or she would say, "In the year when the king was enstooled." There are also environmental indicators for time. A person would say that he got married when there was a great flood. Among the Akan, one determines the hours of the day with the lengthening of the shadows. The morning hours *(anopa)* last from the earliest dark shadows to about 11 A.M., when there are practically no shadows. The Akan have seven days to the week, the names of which are significant for the naming of the children born on those days, as we shall see. The Yoruba and the Igbo, on the other hand, have only four days to their week. The Akan measure time from one Akwasidae festival to the other. Akwasidae is a celebration to honor the royal or stool ancestors in a given traditional area. There are forty-two days from the first Akwasidae to the next one inclusive. In other words, there are six weeks, with a minor celebration, called Wukudae, on the twenty-fifth day, or a Wednesday, to honor ancestors. Each day of the week in this calculation has a name. Finally, the Akan divide the year into twelve months (see below) and four seasons, which are based on the tropical weather. From December to March there is the dry season or *harmattan,* the time when the sky is darkened by the sand from the Sahara blowing southward. This season is called in Twi *opebere.* From April to June there is the rainy season and time for planting *(asusuebere).* July and August are the small dry season *(ofupebere).* And from September to November there is a small rainy season with evening showers *(bamporobere)* (Mensah 1992). For an agriculture-based society the religious festivals are calendar indicators of the farming activities of the people. The ninth Adae is called the Great Adae *(Adaekese).* (The actual Akan year is 378 days if it is divided into nine months of forty-two days.) This major festival in honor of the stool ancestors is called the Odwira (Oh-je-rah) Festival by the Asante, the Brong, the Akwapim, and the Akwamu. It is celebrated in August or September. Among the Efutu of coastal Winneba in Ghana, the annual Aboakyer (Ah-boh-ah-cher), or deer-hunting festival, is reckoned by an old woman keeping knots on a string counted in a box until she gets fifty-two of them in April to announce the new year. The festival itself takes place in modern times on the first Saturday in May.

The above-mentioned festivals represent two of the three kinds of festivities among the Akan, namely, the ancestral and tutelar deities festivals. The Odwira, the first kind, is a harvest festival and represents the dedication of the new year to the royal stool ancestors. At the same time the king, his royal family, and the town lineages gather with much eating of meat and yams and drinking of palm wine and maize beer, while on the streets there is dancing and general fun. The royal family fasts from the first fruits until all the purification rituals (hence the name *Odwira*) are completed, which usually last for about twelve days. In the meantime, thanksgiving is made to God (Onyame), the spirits, and the gods for the good harvest (Bame 1991).

The second type of festival is celebrated in honor of the ancestors. The town king offers up gifts to the gods and the ancestor spirits for the past as well as for the future well-being of the people. This is the time for the dramatization of the myths of origin and legends as well as of actual historical memories of the great deeds of valor of past kings and warriors (Bame 1991).

The third group of festivals is dedicated to the tutelar spirits or deities. The Akan call their divinities *abosom* (the singular is *obosom*). We shall return to a discussion about these deities later on. For the moment, let us keep in mind that these tutelar spirits, called *tete bosom* (teh-teh boh-sohm), have as their main function the protection of villages, towns, and states from all harm, spiritual and physical. They are believed to be the children of Nyame (or Onyame), and are often found dwelling in local rivers, such as the gods Tano and Pra, or in shrines. The tutelar divinities belong to everyone (Opoku 1974), so, on the festival days of these gods, there is much drumming, dancing, eating, drinking, and merrymaking around the rituals. For example, the deer-hunting festival at Winneba, mentioned above, is a feast in honor of Penkye (pen-cheh) Otu, the guardian spirit of the Efutu

State, whose *'kra* (vital force) needs to be renewed by Onyame and return to earth for the common good of the people. Renewal of the god also means the future well-being of all Efutu State. The god is renewed through sacrifice and the flow of blood. Formerly, human sacrifice was required, but when the deity accepted the leopard or the deer instead, the deer hunt became part of the ritual and the enjoyment of all the State, while two competing Asafo Companies (patrilinear or *ntoro* military groupings of father and son in the same company; see below) vied with one another for the prize catch (Akyempo n/d).

Another Akan festival in honor of a divinity is the Apoo Festival at Wenchi in the Brong Ahafo Region of Ghana. The tutelar spirit is Ntoa. As for the Aboakyer Festival, people come from far and wide to witness the rituals and join in the almost decadent revelry, dancing, and eating and drinking. Elaborate rituals and the central Apoo dance with the ritual swords manifest the mythical origins of the Wenchi State, when a founding ancestress and her people emerged from a cave near the river Basuaa (Bame 1991). One of the features of this festival is that a period of liminality is established whereby the competing dance groups of royalty and commoners can sing provocative and insulting songs to taunt the others. It is a time when temporary license is given to all citizens to get off their chest, as it were, any criticism of others even by insults and humiliating remarks against the king and other authorities. It is a traditional annual outlet for any pent-up feelings, animosities, and latent rivalries. Occasionally, since the young men in particular get rather drunk, violent brawls ensue (Bame 1991).

Dance coupled with singing, elaborate rituals, as well as downright horseplay, all join to make the honor bestowed on the spirit world and the institution of the king a genuine event to be remembered or to look forward to. In coming chapters we shall examine certain symbolic elements we have referred to in passing in this chapter. Certainly dance and the extended forms of bodily manifestations of the spirit world have all come together with a reflection on the meaning of human life in the African context. While the liminal stage of worship of a deity *(osom obosom)* or the veneration of the ancestors effects progressive change, we can perhaps understand that among the Akan, as well as other West African ethnic groups, like the Igbo, time is not exactly cyclical, nor is it linear. Even the deities must have their *'kra* renewed in order to embody themselves. The Akan have a term for this mortal embodiment or incarnation; it is *akyeneboa* (ah-chenay-boh-ah) (Akyempo n/d). In this sense, in the consciousness of the West African, time danced out and reflected upon is perhaps best conceived as spiral. Life is a journey that one undertakes and moves on. The Yoruba say it is life's journey *(ajo l'aye)* (Drewal 1992).

If dance incarnates the reflected word, we need to examine all those aspects where, through word and symbol, the West African expresses himself or herself in the cultures and traditions, reaching back to the earliest ancestors.

BIBLIOGRAPHY

Achebe, Chinua. *Arrow of God.* New York: Anchor Books/Doubleday, 1974.
————. *Things Fall Apart.* New York: Fawcett Crest, 1989.

Akyempo, Karikari. *Aboakyer: Deer Hunt Festival of the Effutus.* Accra, Ghana: Anowuo Educational Publications, n/d.

Bame, Kwabena N. *Profiles in African Traditional Popular Culture: Consensus and Conflict.* New York: Clear Type Press, 1991.

D'Aquili, Eugene G. "Myth, Ritual, and Archetypal Hypothesis." *Zygon: Journal of Religion and Science* 21 (1986): 140-60.

Dawkins, Richard. *River out of Eden: A Darwinian View of Life.* New York: Basic Books, 1995.

Drewal, Margaret Thompson. *Yoruba Ritual: Performers, Play, Agency.* Bloomington, Ind.: Indiana University Press, 1992.

Fagan, Brian M. *The Journey from Eden: The Peopling of Our World.* London: Thames and Hudson, 1990.

Hampton, Barbara L., recorder. "Music of the Ga People of Ghana: Adowa." Notes for recording. In *Folkway Releases*, 1-7. Folkway Records, vol. 1. New York: Folkways Records and Service Corp., 1978. 1 audio cassette with liner notes.

Leakey, Richard, and Roger Lewin. *Origins Reconsidered: In Search of What Makes Us Human.* New York: Doubleday, 1992.

Mbiti, John S. *African Religions and Philosophy.* 2d ed., revised and enlarged. Portsmouth, N.H.: Heinemann Educational Books, 1990.

Mensah, J. E. *Asantesem Ne Mmebusem Bi.* Kumasi, Ghana: Kumasi Catholic Press, 1992.

Ogbaa, Kalu. *Gods, Oracles and Divination: Folkways in Chinua Achebe's Novels.* Trenton: Africa World Press, 1992.

Okpewho, Isidore. *African Oral Literature: Backgrounds, Character, and Continuity.* Bloomington, Ind.: Indiana University Press, 1992.

Oliver, Roland. *The African Experience.* New York: IconEditions, 1991.

Onwubiko, Oliver A. *African Thought, Religion, and Culture.* The Christian Mission and Culture in Africa Series, vol. 1. Enugu, Nigeria: SNAAP Press, 1991.

Opoku, Kofi Asare. "Aspects of Akan Worship." In *The Black Experience in Religion: A Book of Readings*, edited by C. Eric Lincoln, 285-299. Garden City, N.Y.: Anchor Press/Doubleday, 1974.

Turner, Victor. *The Ritual Process: Structure and Anti-structure.* Ithaca, N.Y.: Cornell University Press, 1977.
————. "Body, Brain, and Culture." *Cross Currents* 36 (1986): 156-78.

Wiredu, Kwasi. "Morality and Religion in Akan Thought." In *African-American Humanism: An Anthology*, edited by Norm R. Allen Jr., 210-22. Buffalo, N.Y.: Prometheus Books, 1991.

STUDY GUIDE

1. From Leakey and Lewin 1992, 216, or from Fagan 1990, 21, draw the two models of the "Candelabra" and the "Noah's Ark." Read the explanations in the accompanying pages about these hypotheses and about the "Mitochondrial Eve" (Leakey and Lewin 1992, 218ff.). If you are a biology major in the area of molecular genetics, see if you can connect what we are studying here with your field. Also, study maps of the migrations of the various species of humans (Fagan 1990, 72, 118, 130).

2. Explain Turner's ideas on the rites of passage, liminality, *communitas,* and rituals as processes that accompany change. Explain the meaning of the areas of rites of passage as indicated by Van Gennep: (1) separation or the pre-liminal; (2) margin or the liminal; (3) aggregation or the post-liminal. What does Turner mean by *anti-structure?*

3. How does the development of the human brain seem to relate to ritualistic dancing? See Mathieu Deflem, "Ritual, Anti-Structure, and Religion: A Discussion of Victor Turner's Processual Symbolic Analysis," *Journal for the Scientific Study of Religion* 30: 1-25.

4. Read about the history of the early days of Africa in Oliver 1991, especially chaps. 1-4.

5. Show how dance is central to an understanding of ritual. Read Ogbaa 1992, chap. 5, "Rituals and Ceremonies," about how Chinua Achebe makes use of these elements in his novels.

6. Describe the religious function of dance in West Africa. Note the role of women in dances. How is liminality evinced during the *Akom* dance? What is the symbolism of the white clay powder?

7. Describe the social function of dance. Who is the queen mother? What is her role in Akan society? Explain the meaning of the insults in the dances described.

8. Read Achebe's description of the festival in chapters 5 and 6 of *Things Fall Apart.* How do the age sets play a part in Igbo society?

9. Why is an understanding of time so important in the study of West African cultures and religions? Explain the divisions of time among the Akan.

10. Name and describe the three kinds of festivals among the Akan. From what has been said, who are the tutelar deities (sometimes, the tutelar deities are called ancestral gods or deities)? What is their function for humankind? How does the Apoo Festival demonstrate liminality where things are turned upside-down? Is this good for society?

11. How does this analysis of dance in West Africa demonstrate the importance of ritual for the building up of society? How is religion therefore a central feature of West African cultures?

12. If an insult of the king is a serious fault (*musuo*), how do you explain that it is all right to insult him during a festival like the Apoo Festival in Wenchi?

13. Onwubiko describes the importance of culture centers that have strongly influenced African values. Culture centers are like ideological matrices responsible for the cultural life's formation of a people in a given area (Onwubiko 1991, 5). He alludes to the Nok cultural center, which is identified with the Jaba people of northern Nigeria. The history of the Nok is quite interesting (see Onwubiko 1991, 6-7; see also Oliver 1991, 67 and 69). The Ile Ife cultural center is more famous, since it is the center of the Yoruba people. Find other sources about this important religious center. There are also traditions of non-migration and of migration concerning the origin of the Igbo, mentioned by Onwubiko (1991, 8-11). He also refers to a tradition of migration of the Yoruba arriving in Ile Ife from the East. Is this probable? If so, how? If not, what is the clinching argument against such migration, at least in the last six thousand years?

14. Comment on the emerging themes so far:

(1) Ritual precedes word and myth, which is manifest in dance especially during festivals.

(2) The ancestors are the source of the rituals, myths, and festivals.

(3) Elders today, especially the kings and chiefs, represent the ancestors.

(4) Dancing is connectedness to the earth or the land, symbolized by the mythical cave or the religious center, like Ile Ife.

(5) The cycles of festivals have as their purpose to carry the community along with time toward a better future, since each ritual or feast brings along with its liminal period a challenge to renew the gods and humans.

2

Every King Has a "Talking Mouth"

FROM THE DANCE TO THE WORD: THE MEDIATION OF WORD

From prehistoric times, religion has been inextricably woven into the fabric of sub-Saharan African life. The birth of humankind, the birth and the development of culture and knowledge, evokes a hierarchical ordering of a universe that a people sets up for itself to express through symbols the meaning of life. A given people feels at home in the world that it knows. How a group interprets it, copes with it, fears and celebrates it are what we undertake to interpret through the hidden and manifest codes that we discover in a people's religious activity in dance, in ritual, in drumming, in narrative, and in art. If it is true that "dance gave birth to the word, which danced its incarnation," human beings have ascended to the crossroads of the cosmos, the place where the divine and the earthly meet.

In *Things Fall Apart* Chinua Achebe narrates how Okonkwo threw a huge banquet before his departure from his mother's people, who hosted him during his seven years of exile from Umuofia. The elder of his extended maternal family was Okonkwo's uncle, Uchendu. The old man received the kola nut to break and invoked the following prayer to the ancestors:

> "We do not ask for wealth because he that has health and children will also have wealth. We do not pray to have more money but to have more kinsmen. We are better than animals because we have kinsmen. An animal rubs his itching flank against a tree, a man asks his kinsman to scratch him." (Achebe 1989, 154)

The ritual Achebe describes in his novel suggests how people perceive themselves in their world. Family and therefore community are values beyond compare. The realization of that reality, celebrated before in dance and now with a prayer and ritual, for Achebe is a commentary on the Igbo culture. Achebe breaks for us the kola nut of the cultural code and serves it to us to savor. Human beings are more valuable in their family surroundings than animals could ever be.

Similarly, Amadou Hampate Ba, the Malian novelist and interpreter of pre-Islamic Fulani and Bambara oral traditions, underscores the primary function of ritual over word. He adds that "the secret motive of every ritual is the word, which constitutes the foundation, the magic, the active agent, of all ritual" (Asfar 1991, 148). Language is analogous to the waly, the wise man, he says, who is the intermediary between God's word and humankind. Hampate Ba outlines the belief before the arrival of Islam of a supreme and non-definable being named variously Maa Ngala (Master of All), or Masa Dembali (Uncreated and Infinite Master) by the Bambara; and Gueno (the Eternal One), or Dundari (the Supreme One) by the Fulani (Asfar 1991). This God is the creative force of the entire world, material and spiritual. But the Supreme Being is seemingly remote and beyond the reach of ordinary mortals (but see chapter 7, below), therefore there is a need to have a "messenger." The waly is one such messenger, revealing God through his mortal life, and the many gods (which we shall term *deities*) of the traditional religions are the other kind of messengers, active agents of the sacred. Hampate Ba writes that the Fulani and Bambara epic initiation tales express, to the initiate into a secret society, through language within the ritual, how he can reach the terrible and distant Godhead through intermediary prayer. The narrative itself is such an intermediate means of handing on the traditional word. Hampate Ba remarks that the colonials quickly learned that the cook always went to the boss through the houseboy. One had to reach the cook in a similar reverse fashion. This social relationship between the different echelons of society is reflected in the spiritual order. That is why the *interpreter* or *linguist* enjoys such a high position in West African societies. Hampate Ba names the Bambara interpreter with the French term *Répond-bouche,* "talking mouth": "Every king has one; every god has one" (Asfar 1991). Among the Akan, both the drummer and the king's linguist or spokesperson are viewed as such intermediaries. The drummer, called *okyerema* (au-chay-ray-mah), is the symbol of knowledge and therefore one who expounds the stories of the past as well as moral instructions. The linguist (this is not the correct term, since this official is the king's orator and diplomat, but the term is the popular translation in Ghana) is called *okyeame* (au-chay-ah-may), the one who makes everything clear. He is also the bearer of ritual rubrics and serves often as an assistant officiant at festivals, such as the monthly Adae rituals in the royal ancestral stool house (Yankah 1995).

Hampate Ba points out, moreover, that the traditional professions in Africa—the weaver, the potter, the blacksmith, the farmer, and the shepherd, and I might add, the carver—all manifest not only an artistic talent but, through their rituals and forms, the sacredness of reality and the consecration and actualization of divine authority in human society. A human being can invent nothing except with the authority of God (Asfar 1991; concerning the mystical power of the blacksmith among the Mande, see McNaughton 1995). I believe this is where the Akan adinkra symbol summarizes this belief: *Gye Nyame,* "Except for God." Even the professions are intermediaries between their work and God's word. "Only God" inspires African art and culture.

In this chapter the phenomena revealing human reflection on the larger-than-life realities of the cosmos, especially in the context of Akan religious traditions, are the topics of our consideration: the language itself, the talking drum and the drummer, the prayers and the pouring of libation, the folktale and song, and the myth, the proverbs, the adinkra and kente textiles, the stool, the linguist's staff, the gold weights, and the mask.

THE LANGUAGE OF AFRICA

Except for the Indo-European language family introduced from Europe and South Asia through recent colonization in Africa, and except for the Malayo-Polynesian family introduced in Madagascar by earlier colonizers, there are four distinct language families native to Africa: the Afroasiatic, the Nilo-Saharan, the Niger-Congo, and the so-called Khoisan families. Until about 1950 it was assumed that the Afroasiatic language family had intruded into Africa from neighboring Asia, but now it is widely held that it originated in Africa west of the Red Sea (Oliver 1991). It includes the Semitic languages of southwestern Asia, such as Arabic, Hebrew, and ancient Aramaic, and the ancient Egyptian, Berber, Chadic, Cushitic, and Omotic languages of northern and northeastern Africa. One outstanding exception is Hausa, which is spoken by the people of the same name in West Africa. The Nilo-Saharan language family extends to the south of the Afroasiatic and then to the west along the Sahara Desert as far as Mali, where the Songhay branch belongs to this family. Fishermen in the Nubian stretch along the Nile spoke an eastern branch language long before the influx of the Cushitic branch of pastoralist food producers from the Afroasiatic Family (Oliver 1991).

The Niger-Congo family comprises most of the languages spoken in West Africa and in the area southward. The only other family is Khoisan, which formerly was spoken in the entire area south of the equator, but today is located mostly among people living in the southern part of modern South Africa. The language spoken by the !Kung San is one of the most remote languages in the world, remote in the sense of most distance in relationship to all other currently used languages. "Khoisan" is really an umbrella term covering a collection of unrelated languages that are defined by a clicking sound (signified by the !) (Oliver 1991).

Languages are learned, and they influence each other as the speakers interact. The history of the peoples of Africa is interconnected with the history of the spread of the languages. Vocal communication was limited in earlier times, when human beings lived in small communities of twenty to thirty adults while in the food gathering and hunting stages of the Stone Age. As human beings developed agriculture and the domestication of animals, they tended to gather in urban settings of villages and towns and to trade with outsiders. Generally, the pastoralists were nomads and spread over a larger area, but they learned the languages of the sedentary farmers. It was the latter who organized themselves into unions of cities and eventually into larger states. Therefore the spread of the Afroasiatic and Niger-Congo families was due to the development of economies and politics from about 4000 B.C.E. onward.

Our interest lies with the Niger-Congo family, which consists of seven or eight branches. Languages tend to diverge, and linguistic distance often is reflected in geographical distance, although it can also depend on time distance. In Africa the distance is great, attesting to the antiquity of the languages. The language distance also suggests a cultural difference. The Niger-Congo branch reflects this diversity. A small branch, called Kordofanian, is spoken in southern Sudan. For the most part, the Niger-Congo languages developed in West Africa. The most ancient branch is Mande, spoken from Senegal and Mali to Liberia and the Ivory Coast. It already existed some six thousand years ago but developed very much earlier. The only non-tonal section is a branch called West Atlantic. The other branches include Bambara, Malinke, Wolof, and Fula or Fulfulde. The latter is spoken by the Fulani, who are nomadic in character and raise cattle, roaming from northern Guinea to northern Nigeria and Cameroon.

Beside two branches spoken in Liberia, by the Kru and the Grebo, for example, and also in Burkina Faso by the Moré, the two branches of most interest to us are the Kwa and the Benue-Congo branches. We will consider the latter first. Except for a few small groups in northern Nigeria, the largest and most recently spread branch is the Bantu. This is a language group with sub-branches extending from the area north of the forest in the Cameroon area, where it originated around 8000 B.C.E. and migrated eastward (about 300 B.C.E.) to modern Kenya, and southward through the forest area down through the southern savanna in modern South Africa. This is the most "recent" spread of a language and represents a larger group that is more homogeneous in language as well as culture than any other branch except where Islam has imported a uniform religious culture with Arabic.

Bantu languages include Ki-Kongo and Li-Ngala, spoken in the present-day Congo, which were among the languages brought by Africans to America. In his monumental work *Africanisms in the Gullah Dialect,* Lorenzo Dow Turner documents that fact (Turner 1949). Bantu in all its various subgroups is spoken over a wide area of Africa. The most famous subgroup is Ki-Swahili, spoken as a second language over most of the Bantu area. It is, however, not a tonal language and is mixed with elements derived from the various Bantu languages, Arabic, and some Malayo-Polynesian. It was and is a lingua franca in trade in eastern Africa and on the Indian Ocean. Its place of origin is probably the island of Zanzibar in East Africa. The linguistic homogeneity of the Bantu languages also in some ways points to Bantu's more "recent" spread and to the homogeneity of most of the cultures where these languages are spoken (Oliver 1991).

The area of our concern, however, is West Africa, where the Kwa branch of the Niger-Congo family is spoken. This is the south-facing Atlantic coast from the central Ivory Coast to Cameroon and a few hundred miles inland. The major Kwa languages include Baule in the Ivory Coast, Akan in Ghana, Ewe in Ghana, Togo along with Fon in Benin, and Yoruba, Igbo, and Efik in Nigeria.

Akan is the language of a group of people whose languages are also called Twi (Tshi) in the southern two-thirds of Ghana and in parts of Ivory Coast and Togo. All dialects are mutually intelligible, but some expressions may be hard to understand if the dialects are more remote from one another. The dialects include Akwapim Twi, the first grammar for which was published in Copenhagen in 1764; Fante Twi, which is different but has a rather extensive literature; Akim Twi, Kwahu Twi, Akwamu Twi, Denkyira, Nzema, and Asante Twi. Akan is an ethnographic term referring to all the peoples of the area, while sometimes Twi is used to define the language of the Akwapim spoken in the southeast portion of Ghana. For our purposes, we can use *Akan* for both the people and the language, unless we refer specifically to a particular traditional group, such as the Asante or Kwahu. We will use *Twi* for the language only. An interesting feature of the names in Twi is the root form *kwa*, meaning a title of honor and respect, seen in some of the above names as well as Akwasi, Kwafie, Kwabena, and so on.

According to Boahen, the Akan first lived in the open country of modern northwestern Ghana and the northeastern Ivory Coast. They seem to have entered the forest region to the southeast perhaps two thousand years ago to displace or intermarry with the pre-existing peoples, who spoke a related Akan language called Guan, such as that still spoken by the Gonja in Ghana (Boahen 1966). Over a long period the Akan set up various kingdoms with their matrilinear and patrilinear clan systems, their Twi language, and their seven-day calendar. The first powerful kingdom was the Bono-Techiman Kingdom, founded by the Aduana clan around the fifteenth century (Boahen 1966). The Akan developed farms producing yams and palm oil around villages and towns. Because of the discovery of gold at bedrock level, the clans required a consolidation of their towns for protection and trade with the north, especially from the seventeenth century onward. The need for labor to clear the dense forests and to mine the gold required reliance on war and the taking of captives (slaves) (Oliver 1991). The union of several existing states in the eighteenth century by the Oyoko clan under Kumasi formed the basis of the Asante Empire and enabled it to exercise control over trade and politics until British ascendency in the nineteenth century (Boahen 1966).

The Akan language of these interesting people is tonal. It is just as important to pronounce the right tone as the correct consonants and vowels. There are many words distinguished only by their tones. For example, the Twi word *papa*, when it means "palm-leaf fan," is pronounced with two low tones. But *pa'-pa*, meaning "good," comes out with two high tones. An adaptation of the European word for "daddy" is pronounced with a low pitch followed by a high one: *pa-pa'*. In Twi and other tonal languages, there are three contrastive or phonemic tones: high, medium, and low. Moreover, tonal languages require a complicated terraced system where the midtone is always a downstep in absolute pitch from the preceding syllable. The first tone in utterance depends on the natural pitch level of the speaker's voice and somewhat on his or her emotions.

Mention of tonality is significant because of the tonal quality of the talking drums and of the tonality used by oral performers of African call-and-response ritual chants and the telling of riddles. We shall return to the talking drums below. But the tonality of oral performers with its musical appeal to counterpointing of parallel phrases lends itself to a wealth of meaning not intended in the literal context (Okpewho 1992).

Closely related to vocalization of communication and tonality is the employment of ideophones in narrative and song. An ideophone, examples of which will come up soon when we deal with folktales, is simply a sound without any assigned meaning used in oral narratives to achieve a stronger sensual or dramatic impact than words can achieve (Okpewho 1992). Folksongs and folktales, lullabies and nursery songs form much of the tonal participation in the early learning of the tonal languages for children. Linguistically meaningless sounds teach them how to make the right tones (Mphande 1992). The same process is also good for "outsiders" to begin learning an African language as adults. The mistake made by many translators of African folksongs and folktales is to ignore the ideophones and thus lose much of the intended meaning and humor of the story. On the other hand, since they are untranslatable, in a real sense African literature maintains its identity only in African languages (Mphande 1992). Nevertheless, Achebe in *Arrow of God* tried to preserve some of joyous sounds in the old chant of praise at the wedding of Ezeulu's son, Obika:

> *Kwo-kwo-kwo-kwo-kwo*
> Kwo-o-ooh!
> We are going to eat again as we are wont to do!
> *Who provides?*
> Who is it?
> *Who provides?*
> Who is it?

Obika Ezeulu he provides
Ayo-o-o-o-o-oh!
(Achebe 1974, 117)

(Note also the call-and-response verses, as the women call out to each other.)

THE TALKING DRUM AND THE DRUMMER

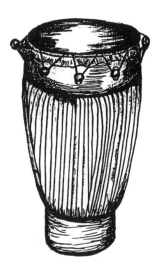

ATUMPAN

There are drums for every occasion and ritual. The sacred royal drums are locked until they are played by specially trained drummers. There are war drums and talking drums. There are other instruments, such as xylophones, castanets, gongs, flutes, zithers, and rattles. They are made of gourds, wood, bamboo, metal, and sticks. Ordinary pots and pans can be instruments. Here we concern ourselves with the talking drum.

The talking drum is not essentially a form of telegraph, although it is used to announce important events. Colonial authorities sought to ban the drums since they announced over distances of twenty-five miles the military campaigns of the Europeans. Missionaries thought of them as something like liberative symbols of satanic forces (Niangoran-Bouah 1991). Primarily, however, the talking drum is an instrument of prayer and of mediation with the sacred order of the gods and the ancestors. There are several sizes with various sounds. Among the Akan, there is the large open-headed drum called *bomaa,* then the medium-sized single-headed drum, called *atumpan,* which comes in twos to sound the low or masculine pitch of the tonal language and the high or feminine pitch. There are other smaller single-headed upright drums. One attractive double-headed drum is the *donno,* or the "armpit" drum, which changes tone when the drummer squeezes it under his left arm.

The drummer, *okyerema,* in the very language of the drum summarizing the myth of creation, along with the court crier and the executioner, represents the stages of creation and life. "*Odomankoma* (the Almighty) created *esen* (crier), then the *okyerema,* and in the end *kwamu kwabrafo* (executioner or death)" (Opoku 1978, 22). The crier stands for order, for it is the duty of the court crier to keep order in the king's court. The drummer stands for knowledge, for he knows the history and lore of the community, and he recites it on his talking drum. The executioner ends all with death. So, in the language of the talking drum itself, there is first order in the world, then knowledge, and finally death (Opoku 1978). The drummer plays from time to time when cases are tried at the king's court. He advises on the drums: "If you are used to doing what is just, you will live long." He advises the prosecutors and witnesses to be fair and just in their statements and decisions, for the pursuit of justice brings the reward of long life and peace (Opoku 1978).

Usually, on festive days, the drummer "warms up" the drums while addressing the drum parts and their spirits, such as the cedar tree, the source of the wood, and the elephant, whose hide forms the membrane over the head and the fibers in the strings and the pegs. He calls upon the dark-blue bird, the *kokokyinaka,* (ko-ko-cheen-akah), the drummers' totem or patron animal. The formal activity commences with prayers offered to God, Nyame; the Earth Goddess, Asase Yaa; and then to various royal ancestors, whose exploits are recalled and celebrated. Finally, the drummer's task is to play the praise of the present stool. Exaggerated language of adulation and praise are drummed out profusely, like the embellished eulogies of the griots.

While the drummer puts his heart and soul into his work, he only carries out the basic traditions of the clan and society. He receives his texts from his fathers, and they from the ancestors. He arouses the collective imagination to the heights of the grandeur and the heroism of the ancestors. He signs when he finishes with the genealogy of drummers and in his own name. The text is therefore sacred. His freedom of embellishment is restricted by the truth. The drum is sacred, too; it is stored away in a safe place afterward.

One may claim, therefore, that African Traditional Religions are religions of a book of a different sort, one not handwritten or printed but recorded in the oral traditions and the memory of the ethnic group. The clanspeople hear, but they move in the rhythm of the story, their own story. The drum instills pride, and fear too, for in its deep rumblings the ancestors speak. The joy of the drum is evident during the Ga rituals of the Homowo Festival. Initially the drums must remain silent, like a form of fasting, or like refraining from saying "alleluia" in Lent. When the drums play again, there is rejoicing, marking the end of a period of liminality.

Perhaps we can end our discussion of the talking drums with this description from *Things Fall Apart:*

> The drums were still beating, persistent and unchanging. Their sound was no longer a separate thing from the living village. It was like the pulsation of its heart. It throbbed in the air, in the sunshine, and even in the trees and filled the village with excitement. (Achebe 1989, 44)

LIBATION AND PRAYERS: *MPAE*

Earlier, we quoted the incident of the breaking of the kola nut and the invocation prayer to the ancestors among the Igbo. Among very many West

African ethnic groups, the ritual of libation—pouring a liquid or dropping some food on the ground accompanied with a prayer—is quite common. The liquid is usually a strong drink, like palm wine, schnapps, or whiskey; the food is something like mashed yam. In West Africa ritual is an act of social communion. Moreover, as Kwame Anthony Appiah remarks, "ritual entails symbolism" (Appiah 1992, 111). We shall come back to the trivial rituals of conversation in communities later, but a similar use of ritual is considered important although not central when dealing with the spiritual world. Appiah claims that "the element of ceremonial is not what is essential; what is essential is the ontology of invisible beings" (Appiah 1992, 112). Even when opening a new bottle of Scotch or gin, the Asante pours a few drops on the floor. It is not that the dead like to drink whiskey—although some will in jest insist that the ancestors have updated their tastes from country palm wine or sugar-cane gin *(akpeteshi)* to imported drinks—it is just that there is a literal belief in the spirits and the ancestors (Appiah 1992).

The ritual of opening a bottle of drink is private, and usually the person doing so does not say a prayer. When an elder utters a prayer while he or she more formally pours libation as invocation, instructions for the dead, or prayers of praise, as Mbiti explains, the words "are a bridge of communion, a people's witness that they recognize the departed to be still alive" (Mbiti 1990, 81). Often, such as on the day of Akwasidae among the Akan, the officiant of the libation memorializes the recently living dead in prayer, and he recites a list of the genealogy from long past. Failure to remember the dead may bring a host of disasters on the community.

We shall return to the veneration of the ancestors, but here we underscore that the pouring of libation is a witness to the existence of the spiritual world. The words are a declaration of the traditions handed down from ancient times, and therefore libation is a human action in line with dance and drumming of the role of traditions.

Among the Akan the structure of the ritual consists in an invocation beginning with God, Mother Earth, and then the ancestors. The petitions and instructions follow, then the concluding remarks, sometimes including curses upon enemies. The officiant must be ritually and morally pure. For example, a menstruating woman may not pour libation or leave gifts at spirit shrines. Among the Akan, when a man pours libation, he partially removes his sandals from his feet and uncovers his left shoulder, if he is wearing the toga-like wrapper cloth *(ntoma),* as a sign of respect and awe in the presence of the elder ancestors. Even the king wears an older cloth *(kuntunkuni)* when he pours libation in the stool house on the Akwasidae festival. He does this as a sign of his mourning for the dead.

The attendants prepare a drink, which is normally alcoholic. The Ga, however, use a nonalcoholic maize beer during the libations at the Homowo Festival. The officiant raises the calabash or glass high to arm's length and calls upon God with grand titles in Twi: *Otweaduampon Onyankopon Kwame nsa oo!* ("Almighty Creator Saturday-Soul God, here is drink!"). The linguist (official spokesperson) standing with uncovered shoulder shouts out *Nsuee!* ("Drink!"). The officiant bends down facing the ground or floor and says to the Earth Goddess: *Asase Yaa nsa oo!* ("Earth Thursday-Soul, here is drink!"). Each time, the linguist responds with the words "Drink!" The officiant pours a few drops on the ground, which he repeats after each following invocation or petition. Although the versions may vary, often the spirits of the eight Akan clans (seven among the Fante) are invoked one by one. If a river or lake is nearby, the officiant addresses the spirits of the waters. Next, he recalls the occasion of the libation, such as the Adae Festival, the Afahye among the Akim, the naming of the baby, a marriage, the outdooring of a new king, times of hardship, or at a burial, for the benefit of the spirits. (If the occasion is special, other rituals may intervene.) In the end he pronounces a prayer for potency for the men, fertility for the women, blessings for long life, for health, for peace, for the honored guests, for the crops and the harvest, for safety during risky undertakings, and finally, he pronounces curses upon the enemies. The concluding remarks include promises to continue to honor the ancestors and threats to other spirits if the requests are not granted. At the end everyone applauds and shouts with one voice a word of approval: *Mo ne kasa!* ("You have spoken well!") (Antwi-Boahen 1988; Yankah 1995).

Depending on the occasion, the people present sit for a round of drinks and conversation or they share in food amid festivity or mourning. Certainly libation pouring is a ritual that is replete with symbol and permeated with belief in a spiritual world.

In conclusion, I want to underscore that this belief in invisible forces is taken quite literally without a need for theory or dogma for belief. Modern and educated women and men with degrees, and often Christian Ghanaians, see no contradiction in this belief. They find no problem, therefore, as Appiah remarks (Appiah 1992), when a Catholic bishop says a Christian prayer at a Methodist ceremony, followed by pouring of libation to family ancestors by one of the Asante king's senior linguists. Similarly, just to add a personal observation, I attended a birthday party of a Ghanaian (a Fante) in Milwaukee, where libation was poured and even the gods of Lake Michigan (if there are any) were honored along with the family's ancestors. Following this ritual I said a Christian meal prayer. No Ghanaian found that to be problematic, since they were all Christians. Only an American objected, thinking perhaps the Christian prayer adulterated the traditionally "pure" African prayer.

FOLKTALES, SONGS, AND MYTHS

While the content of many libations as prayer form is very similar to the content of much of the language of the talking drum, storytelling involves much of the rhythm of the drumming and dancing. The oral performance involves a greater than vocal interaction of the performer and the audience. There is much more play with body language than that called for in the formal rituals of libation pouring. There is more verbal virtuosity shown through tonality, ideophones, plays on words, and the occasional use of proverbs. As the master drummer pulls away from the timing and tones of the other drummers in a form of counterpoint, he lends variations on the same theme. So the storyteller, by means of tonal and nasal qualities of the language and other vocal devices, can evoke a response from the audience, lending to the emergence of song, dance, and acting out of the story in ever creative and novel performances (Abrahams 1983). Throughout West Africa we find this phenomenon vibrant in the living traditions, in the telling of stories, in myths, when sprinkling speech with proverbs, in riddles, and in verses recited during divination. For that reason collections of tales and myths cannot transmit entirely the full significance of the art form. One must be there personally to feel the full impact.

Still, we will try to explain some of what we mean in our discussion here. Paul Radin underlines the Asante humor at the beginning of a story: "We do not really mean, we do not really mean, that what we are going to say is true." Or the traditional ending: "This, my story which I have related, if it be sweet or if it be not sweet, take some elsewhere and let some come back to me" (Radin 1983, 19).

The Folktale

According to Kalu Ogbaa, Achebe reduces all major tales in Igbo folklore, legends, fairy tales, animal tales, myths, and riddles, to *akuko,* stories told by the fireside (Ogbaa 1992). While stories are told on chilly nights by the fireside, I believe there is still a difference, at least for our own understanding of the various forms. Tales are told to the children for entertainment, and so they are useful for handing down the ancestral traditions to younger generations (Ogbaa 1992). Tales sometimes overlap with myths when dealing with the why and the wherefore of things, but myths generally reenact clan or national origin during a ritual liminal period, such as the annual Yam Festival, for the refounding of society.

When the Africans were forced to come to the Americas, their myths often died because their gods had died somewhere in the middle passage. But the rich oral traditions of the folktales remained. They still handed on to their children the lessons to learn from the didactic animal stories, the trickster tales, and the myth-tales, which told the why and the wherefore of things in the world they knew. The Mande speakers from the Sinegambia region, which produced the ancient empires of West Africa—the Bambara, the Fulani, the Mandingo, the Wolof, and the Hausa—brought the Brer Rabbit, Brer Wolf, Brer Fox, and Sis' Nannie Goat stories to America (Holloway and Vass 1993). The Tortoise and Hare stories originated in the Yoruba, Igbo, and Edo-Bini cultures of West Africa. And the *anansesem,* the Spider stories of Kwaku Ananse, arrived intact from Akan groups to the New World (Holloway 1990).

The educational value of West African tales is evident in that, in contrast to Aesop's Fables, for example, normally they do not end with a moral but are open-ended to allow for debate on any possible moral of the story. Such, for example, would be the tale "Killing Virtue," recorded by Abrahams in *African Folktales* (Abrahams 1983). A society considers a tale to be a part of a vast corpus of oral traditions transmitted from olden days from the ancestors. In an oral traditional culture, the determinant factor of moral behavior is whatever the ancestors have enjoined or what has been the custom or the way things have been done since time immemorial.

Modern West African novelists, like Chinua Achebe, Wole Soyinka, Sembene Ousmane, and others, both preserve the tales—mostly in the context of rural, pre-colonial times—and transform them to allude to symbols of the characters in their narratives. When they write about urban affairs, the traditional symbols remain but are more subtle.

Achebe's novels feature several kinds of folk stories. Two of them will illustrate what we are saying here. In *Things Fall Apart* Okonkwo not only literally wrestles with and throws Amalinze the Cat, but he wrestles with the weakness and laziness of his father, Unoka, and with the effeminacy or the incipient weakness of his son, Nwoye, who, he thinks, is just like his father, maybe his incarnation. Throughout the narrative Okonkwo wrestles with himself so that he never appears weak, and that his wives and children, and his village people, perceive him to be a man, to be the "Roaring Flame." In this context the mundaneness of village life appears to us almost without any romanticism. Its stark reality stares out from the pages at us. Achebe has his characters tell their tales in all their opaqueness, their intended meanings explained. Like Geertz, Achebe is describing the traditional Igbo culture "thickly." He cracks the kola nut for us, the symbolic cultural codes. He reveals the hidden semiotic meanings and scatters them before us, challenging us to read the symbols that he, the diviner, is propounding about the passing of the culture, as things fall apart. Then he prophesies about the new British culture and the Christian religion, which Okonkwo's son, Nwoye, will join to become a catechist as Mr. Isaac Okonkwo in another novel, *No Longer at Ease.*

So, among the several folk stories Achebe narrates in his first novel, Okonkwo likes to tell the boys the stories of the land, "masculine stories of violence and bloodshed" (Achebe 1989). But Nwoye prefers the stories that his mother told, about the Tortoise and about the quarrel between Earth and Sky. In the latter tale, Vulture, Earth's emissary, carried rain from Sky in his talons after pleading for mercy on the dry Earth. It had not rained for seven years. When the talons pierced the leaves that contained the water, it rained heavily and Vulture left for another land, where he fed on the entrails left over after a sacrifice of an animal (Achebe 1989).

Ogbaa interprets the tale as folk entertainment, which Nwoye's mother tells the children to explain the universe and natural phenomena. It explains why there are two seasons, a rainy and a dry season in Igbo land, and why birds, like vultures, migrate during seasonal changes. It goes on to explain why the vulture is a scavenger. But, most of all, as a didactic animal tale, the story teaches children to be good emissaries and that people should live in harmony. Otherwise quarrels will result, harming their children, just as the quarrel between Earth and Sky harmed the children of the Earth (Ogbaa 1992).

Ogbaa sees a deeper symbolic meaning behind Achebe's own telling of the story. The tale becomes a symbolic image of Nwoye's own life. He resented everything his father stood for. He hated his own people's religion, the practice of which involved violence. Nwoye was the metaphoric vulture; his talons, while carrying the message of Christianity, got him into other trouble. His conversion alienated him from his father and earned him the admonition of the elder, Oberika. Later Nwoye misused his Christianity. He had lived out the essence of the tale but not its moral, which should end in love, whether in traditional religion or in Christianity (Ogbaa 1992).

Ironically, another mother's fable influences matters in the life of Okonkwo—his mother's story about Mosquito and Ear. Mothers tell this story to children to explain why mosquitos buzz and bite the ear more than they do other parts of the body. In the story, Ear fails to marry an eligible suitor, Mosquito, because he looked skinny. Children are introduced early to the social implications of marriage and how one should not judge the prospective spouse, often proposed by family, because of appearance (Ogbaa 1992). As Achebe reconstructs the story, according to Ogbaa's analysis, Mosquito represents "the lingering and nagging fears of Okonkwo which he fails to marry to his conscience, the metaphoric Ear" (Ogbaa 1992, 153). Okonkwo failed to be reconciled to his own father, and his relationship with his son, Nwoye, and the adopted boy, whom he murdered, Ikemefuma, was always a problem for him. Fathers and sons have not worked out well and, in the end, all that Okonkwo does results in his downfall. His relationship with his daughter, Ezinma, is also ambiguous; he wanted her to be a boy.

Contemporary, urbanized West African authors modify the traditions in plays and in film and television scripts, only changing the characters from animal types to human types, which are often the butt of jokes. Examples, which are most common, are government officials, Christian priests or ministers, Muslim malams, or market women. Ousmane's film *Xala* pokes fun at an influential member of the Chamber of Commerce in Dakar, who is struck with a disease called *xala,* impotence! The interplay between a lifestyle that is pseudo-international and his return to traditional religion is amusing. African films are often modern fables set in an African scene to teach Africans how to cope with new problems, for example, *Wend Kuni* by the Burkinabe, Gaston Kaboré. The director presents a morality play that displays the traditional Mossi values of tolerance, generosity, and cooperation. They are proposed as values that can still shape modern African society against bigotry, infidelity, and cruelty, just as they did in old times before the arrival of Islam in particular. Novelists today sometimes imitate the oral narratives in mocking otherwise reverent religious themes. Certain animals crop up again that are invested with Muslim virtues, for example, on the exterior, while deep down they remain just animals. Among the Wolof in Senegal the cat is said to be Muslim, but in spite of its religion, it remains just a cat—selfish, artfully deceitful, and greedy (Cham 1991). (Note the comparison between a cat and the lazy and sly Mahmoud Fall in Sembene Ousmane's short story, "The False Prophet," in Achebe and Innes 1985.)

Folksong

Like dance, which gives birth to reflection on life in a given context, the folksong forms a part of oral tradition in Africa. It stands between the wealth of history and legend of the talking drum, the praise of the ancestors in the pouring of libation, and the folktale and the proverb in teaching morals and expressing the wisdom of the ages. The griots sang their praises of kings and the important people in their society, often with much hyperbole. Sometimes a story contains a song or is chanted to the accompaniment of a musical instrument or vocal humming. At other times the story reaches poetic heights while the narrator feels the tension in his or her audience, thus giving occasion for a genuine song about the trickster animal, for example. The tonal quality of the African language, together with the narrator's musical ability, may move from normal speech to a form of chant.

Okpewho refers to a study done by J. H. K. Nketia about "spoken poetry" among the Akan, "which is recited and not sung" (Okpewho 1992, 131). At the installation of a king or at other state ceremonies a member of the court praises the king with a high-pitched and fast recitation of the king's abilities. The speaker manipulates the tones of the language a bit more than normal speech to achieve tension in his or her story (Nketia 1960). At funerals a person often half sings and half recites the deeds of the departed.

The song reaches the highest level of vocal manipulation. The singer, now accompanied by instruments, exploits the high and the low tones of speech at different levels to create a melody (Okpewho 1992). In the song the poet reflects on his or her vision of events, whether the return of warriors or a cradle song (Nketia 1960). In the Gambia griots exploit all three styles—the speech mode, the recitation or chant mode, and the song mode— to tell the Sundiata story (Okpewho 1992). One should note that there are solo performers, often accompanied by a choral group and instrumentalists. This is where antiphonal or call-and-response song may result in the form of a question-and-answer performance. We noted this in the song quoted earlier from Achebe's *Arrow of God*. In normal speech, as well as in song, the use of ideophones achieves a form of instrumental effect, as we remarked about the same song, where people are drawn to the wedding festivities by the loud singing of the town's women.

Like the proverb, the song teaches lessons about life, including sexual matters, love for clan and family and even love between persons, and marriage and death. Thus, scholars classify the songs as praise songs, war songs, lullabies, marriage and sex songs, and dirges. There are the play songs of the children, which sometimes teach and sometimes poke fun at something. There are the work songs, which lighten the burden of the work and the heat of the day. Sometimes the proverbs are inserted into the text. Even modern "High Life" songs sing about love in the context of the old maxims.

Particularly in West African traditional rural communities, music, with drumming, dancing and song, matches the pattern of the agricultural year, including the royal festivities, games (like wrestling or soccer), birth rituals, marriage, death, and other key events in the lives of individuals. On almost every occasion traditional religions permeate the activities. However, modern, urban, anglophone West Africa sings and dances to "High Life," a product of traditional rhythms and local language mixed with Western instruments. The sentiments of the songs are largely observations of urban life and changing values. While proverbs are often interwoven, love and life and death are still the major themes. Almost everyone is a "high lifer." In a sense, "High Life" levels all members of society to one democratic whole at West African parties.

To conclude this discussion, we can illustrate how story and song merge into one whole with the children's play song from the Fante in Ghana entitled "The Lazy Hawk."

> The hawk's mother is dead and he catches chickens.
> He says he's not going to work and he catches
>   chickens
>   Chorus: He wonders, wonders, wonders,
>   wonders, wonders, and wonders,
>   and he catches chickens.
> He says he's not going to work and he catches
>   chickens.
>   (Klein and Robbins 1986, 6; translation mine)

The actual story told by the Fante tells about the lazy hawk who spends all his time flying around looking for chickens to steal. All the other animals in the animal kingdom decide to isolate the hawk for its greed and laziness. Later on, the hawk decides to stop killing baby chicks because it no longer wants to be ignored and left out by everyone (Klein and Robbins

1986). Of course, children singing the song together with the recounting of the story learn that they need to fit in to be accepted by other children.

The Myth

The peoples of West Africa express their cosmologies with their myths. A myth is first of all a ritualized story that tells the why and the wherefore of reality as it is perceived without any scientific or philosophical explanations. While the folktale may have suggested a "reason" for things in the animal world, with applications to the human world, in particular for the education of children, the myth delves deep into the cosmos of human beings, reaching into the spiritual world. Sometimes the myth mixes with the folktale to explain, for example, that human beings acquired the use of fire from Kwaku Ananse, the Wise Spider, who got fire from God. A primordial ancestor in another myth brought language, a festival, or a special kind of dance to an ethnic group. A "spirit of the wild" (the dwarfs) revealed a special herbal medicine to heal a disease. At other times genuine historical events and persons are transformed with legends and myths to describe the origin of a nation or cult, for example, the myth of the Golden Stool, which explains the origins of the Asante Nation, or the myth of Shango, the king-god of thunder, who is worshiped among the Yoruba and their descendants in the New World. As we shall see, myth furnishes the particularization of a given ethnic group, distinguishing it from others.

Myth is not only a story that, when ritualized, refounds a society, as on a day of festival; it is time and space. We have already indicated how time can manifest the liminality of a ritual as "time in between." But space can draw the limits of liminality within a given parameter. Mythical space is clearly evident in the place of a shrine or demarcated area within a shrine, such as an altar or the place where the deity resides. Mythical space in West and Central Africa is indicated by circular drawings or circles and by crosses signifying crossroads or intersections.

Robert Farris Thompson in *Flash of the Spirit* describes the "Kongo Cosmogram." It consists of several elements. There is a cross, the *yowu*, representing the point of intersection between the ancestors and the living. At the points of this cross are discs that stand for the four moments of the sun. A horizontal line divides a "mountain" of the living from a mirrored counterpart in the kingdom of the dead. God is said to be at the topmost part and the dead at the bottom. The summit also symbolizes noon, maleness, north, and the peak of a person's strength while on earth. The bottom signifies midnight, femaleness, south, and the highest point of a person's strength in the otherworld (Thompson 1984, 109).

I mention this symbolism because there is a similar notion found in West Africa. When driving through the "bush," I have seen sticks left at crossroads, probably symbolizing an offering to a local spirit. The mythical spatial symbol marks the spot where a person is in communication with the world of the living and that of the dead, or, for that matter, the realm of the spirits.

Similarly, the circle stands for the culture, a circle of life. At the center of each circle the local people reenact their myths; rituals, such as libation, are performed; and the elders deliver their speeches. Simon Gikandi comments on the circle described in *Things Fall Apart.* Whenever Umuofia meets, it forms a circle, which, Gikandi claims, "functions as a synecdoche of Igbo culture and a symbol of its cosmological configuration" (Gikandi 1991, 33-34). The circle is summoned into being, he says, by the beating of the drums; "these drums provide listeners with the surrogate language of the cosmos" (Gikandi 1991, 34). We mentioned above, when discussing the drums, how Achebe described the drums reflecting the pulsating of the village heart. "The drummers were possessed by the spirit of the drums" (Achebe 1989, 46). Gikandi believes that the concentration of the drum voice has transferred its power to the community gathered around the silk-cotton tree. He quotes Soyinka, who says that the village is called by the drumming to its "pristine existence," where language has become "the embryo of thought and music and where myth is a daily companion" (Gikandi 1991, 34).

The circle has a dual purpose. It permits the village "to evoke its identity in an organic world of resemblance, similitude, and order" (Gikandi 1991, 34). It also allows the narrator (Achebe) to expose the alienation and dysfunction that the circular order conceals. Achebe admits that the circle and the ritual were for men. The women were excluded. Achebe points to a certain cultural blindness of the people. Later on in the novel, Achebe tells how the *efulefu*, the "worthless empty men," whose words were not heeded by the assembly of the people, converted to Christianity. In other words, they were not included in the cultural circle. That they had no voice with other men meant that they were deemed less than anyone in society. The centrality of the word in male society coupled with the ritual at the village gathering was not their privilege. The colonial church contradicted this cultural shortcoming when the *efulefu* became its new leaders (Gikandi 1991).

Myth, however, has its good points. The myth is truth in the sense that it describes a metaphysical reality, a cosmology that is deeply symbolic in that it is human. The myth points to a way out of a bad situation or simply to the fact that the world and everyone and everything in it can run down. A return to the creative moment, when chaos ruled, and God established order while creating the earth and its creatures, restores order to society, bolsters the authority of the king and the institution of chieftaincy, and sets the world clock, as it were, forward to face up to any vagaries afflicting society. The zone of liminality, the "betwixt and between," to use Victor Turner's phrase, is what myth is all about. Passages from birth, through puberty and marriage, to old age and death and beyond to the realm of the ancestors are all ritualized and explained in the recital of the myths. The person and the community, immersed in the context of the story through ritual and recital, enter the zone of liminality and therefore the timeless and the spaceless twilight of the spirit world at the heart of a people's culture.

The Akan myth of creation, for example, tells of order and of the goodness of creation. When the Creator, *Onyame odomankoma,* made the world, he started with the sky, then the earth, rivers, and plants. He continued, creating animals and human beings. The animals fed on the plants, and both provided food for human beings. Since the humans are the center of the universe, the Creator furnished them with river spirits, forest and grove deities, and spirits in the rocks for their protection from the presence of evil lurking in those places.

The Akan have a proverb that states frankly that God did a good thing in creation: "The hawk says: 'All that God created is good.'" We have noted how universal order is reflected in human society when God, according to the drum language, created the main characters of the royal court, the drummer, the crier, and the executioner. Creation mirrors the spiritual order.

There are fall myths in most cultures to explain why God is now so distant from creation and the world of human beings. Such myths describe how God designated created spirits to care for the needs of human society.

Myths called charter myths recount the origins of clans and nations. These sometimes tell of a common ancestress, as in the Apoo Festival at Wenchi. The ancestress appeared from "the bosom of the earth . . . from a cave near the source of the river Basuaa, about eight miles south of the present Wenchi town" (Bame 1991, 88). She and her people founded the Wenchi State.

The most famous myth of the Asante relates the origin of the Golden Stool and the foundation of the Asante Confederation. At one time there was no Asante Nation. Kumasi, its capital, was only one of many kingdoms under the hegemony of the king of Denkyira. But in 1701 King Osei Tutu of Kumasi, at the firm suggestion of the high priest, Okomfo Anokye, called all the kings and queen mothers of the neighboring paramountcies together to Kumasi on a Friday. The priest brought down from the sky the Golden Stool (*Asikadwa Kofi:* "Friday's Golden Stool") to settle on Osei Tutu's knees (Sarpong 1971). He collected nail clippings and hair from the royal personages, made a potion of them, and smeared the mixture on the Golden Stool. He had them all drink of the potion. With that, Anokye proclaimed that now the *sunsum* (the soul) of the Asante people resided in the Stool. The destruction of the Stool meant the destruction of the Asante as a unified people. No one ever sits on it; it may not touch the ground; and it is reserved in a secret, sacred place. It is more important than the *asantehene,* the first among equals of all Asante kings. Osei Tutu was a historical person, but the myth, mixed with history, tells of the foundation and the symbolic meaning of the Asante Nation.

The sacredness of the symbol of the Stool as a corporate soul was tested in 1900, when the British governor of the Gold Coast, Hodgson, arrogantly marched on Kumasi to demand the Golden Stool so he could present it to Queen Victoria. He never got the real stool but only a false stool after a year-long battle under the leadership of the queen mother of Ejisu, Nana Yaa Asantewa. The false stool is still on display at the British Museum in London. When the *asantehene*, Prempeh I, refused to surrender the genuine article, he was imprisoned for a while in a cell at Elmina Castle on the coast. The governor in his ignorance and arrogance mistook the Golden Stool for a throne instead of what the myth tells us about its real meaning: It is the soul of the Asante Nation (Sarpong 1974). Moreover, it has become a symbol of Asante resistance to colonialism and of the permanence of the *asantehene*'s rule in spite of the modern state.

Other West African societies tell similar charter or foundational myths. One of the most revered myths is the epic of Sundiata, a narrative celebrating the founder of Old Mali. The ancient Mande culture and cosmology are mapped out to illustrate how the order of the cosmos and that of the empire of Mali were deeply rooted in the primordial order of the universe.

The Yoruba recite the myth of Oduduwa, the founder of Ile Ife and the ancestor of all Yoruba. He seems to have been a historical warrior-king who led a new people into the land to displace an older civilization (Abimbola 1991). Not only does the charter Yoruba myth center at the town of Ile Ife, but the Yoruba creation myth gravitates around the same place. It remained the symbolic world center of Yoruba religion and social life. The Yoruba have a huge number of deities in their pantheon, and very many of them are enshrined at Ile Ife.

Modern West Africa authors, like Wole Soyinka, Chinua Achebe, Ayi Kwei Armah, and others, employ these and similar myths, like twice-told tales, to speak to their Yoruba, Igbo, and urbanized Accra peoples, as well as to other Africans outside their own cultures, and help them to look beyond the banalities of ordinary home life in order to perceive the deeper meanings of their distinct cultures. Although these novelists have created their stories in the colonial languages they inherited, they have attempted to translate their cultures and values into a form that expresses what it means to be Yoruba and Igbo and an Accra city dweller. These authors have had to expand what it means to be a member of an ethnic group into the continental African while writing in English. Their myths keep them linked to their identities in their distinct cultures, which today they may simply call "Nigerian" or "Ghanaian." If myth is a story about the why and the wherefore of reality, the myth when adapted continues to establish a critique of the new world the authors live in. Just as there is no single "African" religion or culture, there are no "African" myths. The storytellers—Akan, Yoruba, Mandinka, or whatever—have always defined themselves according to the mythic origins of their people, with their peculiar cosmologies. Mythical circles and caves may seem analogous, but each symbol is distinct. Only an Umuofia circle is special to that traditional land area. In Umuaro, it defines what it means to be Igbo, yet the villagers at Umuaro despised their fellow Igbo in another village, Okperi, just six miles down the road (Achebe 1974). The circle, then, means something a little different in each traditional area. Identities of peoples are defined in terms of their villages. Achebe comments on this when he says that where he came from the word *Igbo* was a term of abuse. But with the Biafran War, *Igbo* became a symbol for a very powerful consciousness (Appiah 1992). Myths defined a people in the traditions, but new economic and political needs redefine the myths too. Sometimes these lead into false notions or false myths about who a Nigerian is, or even what an African is. We must at least respect the plurality of the myths, the religions, and the cultures.

THE PROVERB AND THE RIDDLE

This short passage from *Things Fall Apart* is quite precise: "Among the Igbo the art of conversation is regarded very highly, and proverbs are the palm oil with which words are eaten" (Achebe 1989, 10). When the wife prepares cooked, sliced yams, she pours some palm oil over them or she makes palm soup to enhance the flavor of the yams. Proverbs embellish normal speech to make it interesting.

First of all, the art of conversation in most African rural societies seems to an outsider to be very formal. Much time is spent on stock greetings, trivial questions about health, the condition of one's home and of the road just traveled. The speakers add emphasis to their words by handshakes, such as the West African palm-snap, holding of both hands, and minute courtesies such as offering a drink of water, called in Akan "tired water." Only after these formal greetings have been exchanged do the host and visitor get down to the purpose of the visit. The speech at this point is heightened with perhaps a proverb or two, and verbal combat may ensue.

Oral traditions require face-to-face interaction of the spoken word. From all that we have said so far in this chapter we can infer that African tradition, while ritualistic, establishes a certain power in sound and word. African oral tradition is both phonocentric and logocentric, symbolized very appropriately by the call of the drum to gather in community around the circle (Gikandi 1991). The proverb, a concise statement made in the third person with the accumulated wisdom of the ancestors and elders, stands at the center of the authoritative power of the word. The drum speaks in proverbs, dances are nonverbal proverbs, libations are proverbial. Among the Akan, Ga, and Ewe in Ghana, the words for proverb, *abe* or *ebe,* mean not only the short, oft-quoted expressions of wit and wisdom, but parables, illustrative anecdotes, and even longer stories, such as the Akan *anansesem* (Spider stories), when used as anecdotes to illustrate a point (Yankah 1989). So the proverb in its concise form overflows into other areas of speech and sound, and into symbol, such as textiles, architectural designs, and carvings.

Nonliterate societies from ancient times have produced proverbs. The book of Proverbs in the Bible is a collection of the wisdom of the Israelite people from their oral traditions. Europeans first encountering African civilizations collected the proverbs. Richard Burton in 1865 collected 2,268 proverbs from several West African ethnic groups, including Efik, Ewe, Ga, Twi, and Yoruba (Yankah 1989). In 1879 J. G. Christaller compiled 3,600 proverbs from the Twi of the Asante and Fante; these were translated into English in 1990 by Kofi Ron Lange (Christaller 1990). John Mbiti has collected some 12,000 proverbs from various parts of Africa (Mbiti 1991). The trouble with these collections is that the proverbs are not situated in a natural context. Their interactional elegance is missing; their double entendre is altogether taken out of context. The advantage of Achebe's novels is that the narrator employs proverbs in the mouths of his speakers. And he creates new variations to build up an extended context. Only in such contexts does the palm oil lubricate the yams of ordinary, banal speech.

Igbo society is acephalous; that is, it has no chief or king. It is ruled by a council of titled elders and by religious leaders, such as the chief priest. In *Arrow of God* Achebe has his male characters deliver some very fiery, harsh, and many times earthy, speeches. Proverbs lace every expression, indicating the rhetorical ability of the speakers. Proverbs in such a context are not necessarily the final word, but they add force to the address. There are many examples in this novel; Ezeulu's (the chief priest) speech in chapter 13, for instance, shows how proverbs in context mean more than what they apparently say. The priest apologizes for not bringing palm wine for the elders to drink. The speech indicates that the priest realizes he is bound by a certain decorum. He hails the assembly of men: "People of Umuaro, respond to my greeting!" To which they reply "Hem!" This is an appeal to unity, for the men to respond as one people. The priest then proceeds to the second stage, which is to cultivate good will. He thanks the elders for gathering in assembly, and he apologizes for the lack of palm wine. He explains why: the white man's summons to appear immediately at court in Okperi. He rounds off his speech with two proverbs, a way of explaining the situation: "Unless the penis dies young it will surely eat bearded meat," and "When hunting day comes we will hunt in the backyard of the grass-cutter" (Achebe 1974, 142-43). The grass-cutter is a rodent often cooked in a soup for its tasty flavor. Both proverbs evidently urge patience. The first one counsels youth to exercise patience and not engage in premarital sex. "Bearded meat" is a metaphor for the genitalia of a mature woman, not the type a boy plays with when young. Men tell jokes about their own genitals, but they do not do so about women's, for every woman is a potential mother (Ogbaa 1992). In *Things Fall Apart* Okonkwo's maternal uncle, Uchendu, says, "Mother is supreme" (Achebe 1989, 151).

So this simple proverb, Ogbaa explains, propounds sex education and morality, but in the situation it exhibits the ability to handle rhetorical persuasion, which is essential to Igbo oratory, and folk humor, which helps the Igbo men to keep their sanity in a time of crisis (Ogbaa 1992). Both proverbs together promote patience as the virtue of the moment.

Among the Akan a sign of good breeding is the ability to control words in *dwamu kasa,* public speaking (Yankah 1989). They observe that a child salivates and utters meaningless chatter. Thus lack of eloquence is likened to the drivel falling from a baby's mouth. But a good speaker, one who is crisp and witty, earns the complimentary remark *n'ano awo,* "his mouth has dried up," meaning that he enjoys the gift of linguistic wit or eloquence with dry lips (Yankah 1989, 333-34).

We have referred to symbolic action when persons dance. Proverbial actions, or parables, like speech, are indirect ways of communicating advice or opinion. Written proverbs are wholly or partially displayed on the sides of tro-tros (locally made buses) to convey to the public the owner's philosophy. Many of them are in English, but they are also in Twi or pidgin or mixed. For example, "God dey" means God is present. "No time to die" is an aphorism for hard work. Some are more profound, like *Onyame bekyere,* "God will provide"; *Nnipa hia mmoa,* "People need help"; *Onyame nnai,* "God never sleeps." Others are maxims that indicate again the male-centeredness of speech, "Men suffer, women don't know," "No Business No Wife," "A beautiful woman never stays with one man," and "Fear woman and play with snake" (Yankah 1989, 330). While some men complain about marital problems on their vehicle, displayed for all the world to see, there are other proverbs—for example, "A good wife is wealth," or "A good wife is more precious than gold"—that indicate appreciation for a good marriage.

Proverbs teach children good behavior, and sometimes proverbs teach parents how to bring up their children to fit into society. Some would be useful in a more permissive society, for example, "If your child is dancing clumsily, tell him: 'You are dancing clumsily'; do not tell him, 'Darling, do as you please.'"

Other proverbs teach about God, or about charms and witchcraft. How to deal with good behavior but also how to deal with bad behavior and the ever-present forces of evil are all the stock of the wisdom of the ages. "One does not teach a child about God" does not mean what it says literally but means that there is an innate sense of the existence of God (see chapter 9 below). Among the Akan there are no shrines to Nyame, so anyone can pray to God: "If you have anything to say to God, say it to the wind." We say, "God helps those who help themselves," but the Akan say, "It is God who pounds the fufu for the one-armed man," and "It is God who drives the flies from the tailless animal."

We have referred to the eloquence expected of the king's linguist or spokesperson (in Akan, the *okyeame*). His ability to express himself clearly is even more important than the eloquence of the king, since he often speaks for the king. He is like the prime minister in the presence of the king. His perception of guests and of other states must be absolutely transparent. Most of all, his knowledge of ritual and proverb must be totally in line with tradition. His staff by itself is silent eloquence.

The use of proverbs in courts of traditional law garnishes the words of both defense and prosecution. The judge and the jury members may rise to speak, lacing their speech with proper maxims. However, the proverbs themselves are not the final authority.

There is a game played in Ghana called *dame;* it is similar to checkers. The game depends, like most, on skillful moves of the pieces. However, the players also must be skillful in their mastering of words, of humor, and of satire. The moves in the game have to be reinforced verbally with satirical remarks, jeers, and invectives from players and audience alike. Praise, abuse, and flourish of gesture all come together, taken in good spirit. Opponents are often peers, but uneven social status does not change the situation. In other words, mastery of language is part of the game, and a period of liminality is established where even a king may be jeered at, if he plays with a commoner. Proverbs are the chief means of verbal exchange. For example, when a trap is discovered by an opponent and he counters it, he says, "The tsetsefly stands in vain on the back of the tortoise" (Yankah 1989, 341).

At this point, we may ask what all this has to do with West African Traditional Religion? While there are many so-called secular occasions mentioned here about the use of language, the wisdom literature of oral tradition reflects the antiquity of the West African societies, reaching back to those ancestors still evoked in libation and remembered in the proverbs. Even when a speaker invents a new twist to an old proverb, he generally prefaces the remark with "As they have said," or "As the elders have said." A good proverb is always at home. However, modern authors have indicated that Africans themselves can be divorced from their own culture in an urban setting. Thus a person bastardizes a proverb to manipulate and wheedle neighbors, digressing from the ancestral tradition for personal gain. Ayi Kwei Armah, in *The Beautyful Ones Are Not Yet Born,* illustrates how the defeated Koomson bribes the boatman to help his escape. "You used to repeat a certain proverb," said Koomson. "'When the bull grazes, the egret also eats.' Do you remember?" The boatman replied with a surly "Yes," as if to indicate that time and change ought to modify the truth of all proverbs (Obiechina 1975, 180). Koomson, while a fugitive, still tries to retain his economic advantage. The boatman realizes times have changed. Perhaps the ancestors have died, too?

Just in passing, I mention the use of riddles in African society. A riddle is usually a verbal puzzle in which one statement challenges another statement to match it. The humor pokes fun even at body parts or at animals. The skill in matching the question depends not only on meaning but also can exhibit ability with the tonal qualities of the language as a form of amusement, greeting, explanation for an action, an indirect way of cursing, or even double-entendre eroticism to joke about sex among men and to insult women. For example, young men among the Ibibio in Nigeria greet one another with riddles rather than the more formal stock greetings required by etiquette (Okpewho 1992). Children and youth engage more often in riddling. They make use of a large amount of sexual and scatological expressions chiefly for tongue-in-cheek humor. As far as I can see, riddles, while similar to proverbs in some cases, like puns and tongue-twisters, offer no religious and very little cultural value.

TEXTILES

Before the invention of wooden looms to weave threads from cotton or wool in West Africa, the most common cloth worn was from hand-woven raffia-palm strands, now mostly worn by religious dancers. There was much more nudity than later on. Okpewho quotes a praise-song of Seydou Camara from Mali, who praised his patron, a hunter, heading off to his hunt barebodied: "Naked Buttock Battler and Naked Chest Battler . . . " (Okpewho 1992, 27).

From Senegal in the west to Cameroon in the east, West African narrow-strip cloth, woven only by males on horizontal looms, at some unknown time in history became quite common. Cotton may have been domesticated well before the Common Era. Archeological evidence indicates the manufacture of threads from cotton in Old Ghana by 1000 C.E. At any rate, myths speak of weaving at the core of creation. Textile production and the trade in fabrics from the Mediterranean world and from the Orient already existed as early 500 B.C.E., when Berbers attempted to cross the Sahara as far south as the Niger River Bend. Egyptian cotton, oriental silks, and Arab brocades were brought to Ancient Ghana and worn by the aristocracy, as witnessed by al-Bakri (Gilfoy 1987).

West African textiles formerly were made of woolen or cotton threads. When royalty imported silk, the material was unraveled and new threads of various colors were made, mixing silk with cotton, both imported and local. Woolen cloth was too impractical in the humid forest regions, but the kings used wool to cover their palanquins and to protect the state drums when not in use. They placed their state swords over wool when the king sat in state at a durbar.

Probably the two most symbolic of West African fabrics are the wrapper cloths worn today in Ghana, the kente and the adinkra. The kente is worn usually by distinguished persons on joyous occasions, while the adinkra is worn when people are sorrowful or mourning. The word *kente* (ken-teh) is associated with the Fante word for basket, *kenten,* since Asante weavers carried the cloth down from Kumasi to the Fante coastland for trade in baskets (Gilfoy 1987). The origin of kente cloth is shrouded within both history and legend. One version claims that a man observed how a spider wove an intricate web and reported it to his people at Bonwire. The town chieftain, Nana Bobie, reported this new technique to the founder *asantehene,* Osei Tutu, who claimed the discovery as part of a royal prerogative (Gilfoy 1987). Most likely, the method of horizontal weaving was brought from trade with an area called Bondoukou, in the modern Ivory Coast. The Asante developed the technique by mixing various threads and developing the designs. Stripes and checkerboard designs, crisscrossed rectangles and triangles, contrasts of dark and light colors, also found on masks and on architecture, are used to symbolize life on earth and in the spiritual realm. Contrasts symbolize, for example, forest and the cleared community area, chaos and control, male and female (Gilfoy 1987).

The *asantehene* commissioned weavers at Bonwire to design a kente so unique that no one could ever repeat it. The weavers gave it a name, *adweneasa,* "my skill is exhausted." In the past only the *asantehene* wore it. Then the king sent some pieces of the material to cover shrine altars. Now the kente is worn by men and women for significant occasions. A man's cloth is wrapped around the back of his body, passed over the left shoulder and wrapped around again with the left arm holding the bulk of the material. The right shoulder is bare. When even a chief shows respect to deceased elders and ancestors, he lowers his cloth on his left shoulder down to his chest level. The readjustment of the cloth is itself a ritual, like a dance. The wrapped body stands in a stately pose.

According to Sarpong the weaving and the colors relate to the wisdom of the proverbs. The square or rectangle symbolizes the sacredness of masculinity of both God and man. It stands for the territory over which a man rules, whether in his family or ancestral land. The square appears on the kente in various combinations with other symbols and colors to depict feelings of warmth, welcome, and security (Sarpong 1974). The chevron stands for growing anew or the vitality of fresh growth (Sarpong 1974). A staircase design calls for a proverb: "Death's ladder is not climbed by one person," which means that we all shall die one day (Yankah 1989). The female cross in the form of an X stands for ill-will or bad intentions (Sarpong 1974). In fact, it is considered ill-manners and regarded as contempt of court to cross one's legs. Yet, the only drum among the Akan a woman may play is the armpit drum *(donno),* which is shaped like a female cross. The design is found also on stools. The spiral is a female symbol of both frailty and growth, and of peace and mercy. The zigzag stands for prudence and the manifestation of political wisdom.

Colors on kente and other textiles express a rich symbolism. Gold or yellow represents royalty, the presence of God, maturity, and prosperity.

White marks victory and joy. White clay, talcum, or chalk on the ground or in circular designs on the body, or a white headband, signifies happiness over success in life's battles, whether in childbirth or at court (Oduyoye 1986). White is the color of semen and is related to the male principle *(ntoro)*, Nyame, the water deities, the mythical python, and the father-child bond throughout life. On the other hand, red is related to blood *(mogya)*, the female principle, the clan system, and also to sadness, defeat, war, witchcraft, and death. It is the color most worn at funerals (Turner 1977). The combination of red with gold on kente indicates a certain power over sickness and defeat. Green symbolizes fertility and the prime of life. Green with white stands for a bountiful harvest. Black symbolizes death, evil, and the force of evil. The kente staircase design in green, gold, and black probably signifies that there is hope of life after death. Blue is the color for love and female or motherly tenderness. The queen mother often wears blue.

The manner in which the kente strips are sewn together with color and geometric designs suggests to their creators or even to the market women who sell them proverbs or names of animals or birds, plants or trees, or significant individuals (Gilfoy 1987).

Perhaps the adinkra cloth, while less known outside Ghana, is more symbolic though less colorful. The adinkra cloth is worn by the Akan and their neighboring ethnic groups as a wrapper, mostly for funerals. Originally the cloth was woven in long white strips, but later larger pieces of white cotton, calico, dyed cloth, and khaki have been adapted. Russet brown, red-orange, and bright red *(kuntunkuni)* are the main colors. The uniqueness of the adinkra, however, is due to the symbolic designs stamped onto the cloths in a black ink made from boiling the bark of a tree, called locally *badie*. Patterns are cut from dry gourds or calabash, dipped into the ink and stamped onto the cloth. There are more than sixty different designs.

The origin of the adinkra, like the kente, lies in both history and legend. It also seems to have originated in the modern Ivory Coast. A certain king, Nana Kofi Adinkra in Gyaman, now in the Ivory Coast, not only possessed the secret for making this cloth, which is named after him, but he dared to proclaim he owned a golden stool. In 1818 the *asantehene*, Nana Osei Bonsu, waged war against Gyaman to avenge the honor of the Asante Golden Stool. Nana Kofi Adinkra was defeated and, for his insolence, his head was chopped off as a trophy. Other spoils included the adinkra stool symbol, the adinkra cloth, and the technique for making it. It is also significant that the word *adinkra* in Akan is derived from *'kra,* the breath of life from God or personal deity, which at death leaves the person and returns to God. So, the cloth is a "farewell to the soul" cloth worn at funerals (Glover 1992).

The adinkra designs are not only stamped on cloth but are painted or carved on walls, into stools, on drums, and on other appointments. One of most famous designs is the *Gye Nyame,* "Except for God," meaning the omnipotence and immortality of God. The female symbols of roundness, such as the crescent moon, also the shape of the stool seat, bear all the beauty and female qualities of the woman, tender kindness, gracefulness, and serenity (Sarpong 1974). The triangle is another female figure, often found on the royal pectoral pendants or on headgear and sandals; it stands for pride of state, charm, and friendship (Sarpong 1974). Many adinkra symbols refer to God, such as the *Nyamedua,* "God's tree," or *Bribi wo soro,* "God, there is something in the heavens," a sign of hope. Others inculcate virtues for the head of state, like *Akoko nan tia ba, na ennkum ba,* "The hen treads on her chicks, but she does not kill them," a sign of firmness tempered with gentleness. One adinkra symbol popular among African-Americans is the *Sankofa,* "Return and bring (it) back," which means learn from the past heritage and build on it for the future. The symbol is twofold: a large bird with its head twisted backward; a heart with swirls on the two top sides of the cusp.

These textiles and modern tie-and-dye, or wax-dyed material, as a whole, are named with suggestive proverbs, for example, "Precious beads are silent," or "It's a sweet pawpaw tree under which lies a plucking stick." When in 1982 Flight Lieutenant John Jerry Rawlings staged a coup, his overzealous soldiers harassed the market women in Accra, Ghana. The women, ever so wise to the vagaries of politics, designed a cloth to make a political comment, which was given the name of an Akan proverb: *Ehuruhuru a ebedwo,* "Boiling water cools," meaning, even this first fervor will pass (Yankah 1989, 332).

THE SACRED STOOLS, *OKYEAME* STAFFS, AND GOLD WEIGHTS OF THE AKAN

Every king has a "talking mouth" or representative of his office. His chair or stool among the Akan and neighboring groups and the staff of his spokesperson, the *okyeame,* are expressive of this symbolism. Before the introduction of chairs, probably by Muslim traders from North Africa, the stool was nothing more than a piece of furniture. A stool is composed of three parts, the base, the middle or waist, and the top or seat. It is rectangular at the base and the seat. It is the middle portion where designs are made. The choice of the wood depends on the kind of spirit or spiritual character the stool should possess. According to Sarpong, there are three trees in Asante forests that have powerful or vindictive spirits; their wood is used by carvers to make drums, stools, and umbrella frames. They are the *Tweneboa, Nyamedua,* and *Sese* trees. The wood is soft, white, and light. The carver has to offer sacrifice of eggs, fowl, or sheep before he fells the tree. It is expected that the spirit returns to inhabit the stool, although another spirit could live in it. For this reason, it is customary to set an empty stool on its side or against a wall to keep any wandering spirit from entering it (Sarpong

Stools Used in Ghanaian Life

Asantehene Gwa

This stool may be used only by the *asantehene*, the paramount chief of the Asante.

Osebo Gwa

The Leopard Stool is used only by the *asantehene*; it signifies his power and influence.

Ahema Gwa

This stool may be used only by the queen mother. Its similarity to the Asantehene Gwa may show how close she is in rank to him.

Krado Gwa

The Padlock Stool. This stool is used by chiefs and linguists.

Drawings and explanations of stools courtesy of
E. Ablade Glover, M.Ed., Ph.D., F.R.S.A.,
University of Science and Technology, Kumasi, Ghana

1971). The stool carver is almost like a minor priest because of the sacredness of his art. He deals with spirits, and his design is an expression of a supernatural word.

The stool, *akonnwa,* is a piece of furniture, even a "two-penny" white stool made of white wood and occasionally white-washed for the ordinary commoner. But there are the silver stools and golden stools—white stools plated with silver or gold leaf. There are stools for children, for grown men, and for women. There is the king's stool and the queen mother's stool. The royal ancestral land is called "stool land," or "stool farm."

Only the *asantehene,* the paramount king of all Asante, has the first Golden Stool, the famous *Asikadwa Kofi,* "Friday's Golden Stool." According to the myth of the foundation of the Asante Nation, you may recall, the high priest, Okomfo Anokye, called down the Gold Stool from the heavens, upon which the royalty present placed the *sunsum* (soul) of the Asante Alliance, of which Nana Osei Tutu was the head (Sarpong 1971). The Golden Stool rests on its side on its own chair in a secret location. Its last public appearance was in August 1995, on the occasion of the silver anniversary of the reign of Asantehene Otumfuo Opoku Ware II.

Only the *asantehene* may own the Elephant Stool and the Leopard Stool. The *Kotokodwa,* Porcupine Stool, is the symbol of the Asante State and is also used exclusively by the *asantehene.* The Asante queen mother and the paramount king of the Mampong State in Asante both use the silver stool. The mamponghene is the vice-regent of the Asante Alliance in the absence or indisposition of the *asantehene.*

There are as many stool designs as there are kings and sub-chiefs. The seat, in the shape of a crescent, symbolizes a mother's embrace and love, suggesting the origin from a common mother. The middle portion is where the soul-name of the stool is derived. The *Esono Gwa,* Elephant Stool, and the *Osebo Gwa,* Leopard Stool, are both symbols of the great powers of the *asantehene.* These two animals are considered the most powerful and most feared animals of the forest. According to Sarpong, the proverb *Wodi esono akyi a hasuo nka wo,* "When you follow the elephant you do not get wet," means that if you follow the owner of the Elephant Stool you will be free of any unlawful attack or provocation (Sarpong 1971, 24). The porcupine, with its sharp quills, is the totem or symbolic animal of the Asante Nation. When the *asantehene* and his paramount kings and priests sit in council, the Porcupine Stool is used. The Asante believe that the porcupine shoots its quills at its attackers and grows new quills to replace them. The porcupine is the perfect specimen of Asante moral, physical, and numerical invincibility at war. The national motto for centuries has been *Asante Kotoko, wokum apem a, apem beba,* "Asante porcupine, if you kill a thousand, a thousand will come" (Sarpong 1971, 24). Asante Kotoko is even the name of the Kumasi soccer team. The Asante are proud of their Alliance.

Linguist Staff and Symbols

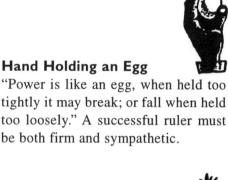

Hand Holding an Egg
"Power is like an egg, when held too tightly it may break; or fall when held too loosely." A successful ruler must be both firm and sympathetic.

Pineapple
"The pineapple is plucked and eaten only when it is ripe; otherwise it is sour." Everything at its own time; or "God's time is best."

Rooster and Hen
"The hen knows it is dawn but leaves the announcement to the rooster." Know your position in society.

Elephant
"If there were no elephant, the buffalo would be the biggest creature." No matter how big you are, there is always someone bigger.

Drawings and explanations courtesy of E. Ablade Glover, M.Ed., Ph.D., F.R.S.A., University of Science and Technology, Kumasi, Ghana.

When treating of the ancestors below, we shall return to the custom of blackening the royal ancestral stool and the celebration of the Akwasidae. The stool that is blackened on a chief's death is usually the one he sat on the most, such as at meals, or the one he sat on when he took his bucket bath. This stool was most intimate to his soul, and therefore the attendants blacken it with soot and egg to keep it in the royal stool house, where other ancestral stools are kept and honored during the Akwasidae and other festivals.

Just a note about the *okyeame*'s staff. Since the so-called linguist's job is to put the chief's or king's mere whispers into poetic and eloquent language and to be his ambassador outside of court, he carries a staff as a symbol of the state he represents. The staff is wooden, wrapped with silver or gold leaf, and its top depicts an animal or human form to symbolize a proverb. One of the more famous symbols is of a hand holding an egg. Power is like an egg, it wants to say. When held too tightly, it might crack open. When held too lightly, it may fall and break. In other words, a successful ruler is both firm and sympathetic. Another rather obvious symbol of three heads means *Odomankoma Nyansaboa se, tikoro nnko agyina,* "The God of Wisdom says, 'One head cannot go into counsel.'" As we say, "Two (three) heads are better than one" (Yankah 1995).

Gold weights—actually brass weights used for weighing gold—serve a similar mnemonic purpose. Cast in brass by the lost-wax method, the weights are often geometric in form, representing proverbs, historic persons and events, as well as animals and legendary characters. A rather common figure is that of two crocodiles with a common stomach. It signifies two competing persons with a common interest. (Of interest also are the state swords, *afona,* and the umbrellas as part of the royal regalia).

MASKS

Masking (masquerading) is not a major feature of Akan religious and cultural experience. I have observed masked figures going about during the Christmas season looking for gifts in Akim Ofoase, but I do not believe they were as significant as similar masked men among the Igbo and the Yoruba.

Chinua Achebe in his novels refers to masked men standing in for the ancestral spirits. In *Things Fall Apart* Achebe refers to the council of elders of the nine villages of Umuofia, called the *egwugwu,* dressed in masquerade to manifest the ancestors to the people. Their purpose was to exercise social control over the local community (Ilogu 1991). They looked awesome as they emerged from their lodge, bodies dressed in raffia, masks painted white, and their leader, Evil Forest, emitting smoke from his head (Achebe 1989). As we shall see when speaking about the ancestral cult, among the Igbo and the Yoruba masks feature prominently. In *Arrow of God*

Achebe makes use of the dancing mask as a symbol of traditional authority and as a force for change.

As a paradigm and as a metaphor, the mask in *Arrow of God* expresses the tension between tradition and transformation (Gikandi 1991). Masks are figures of ambiguity and therefore of symbolism in a deeper sense. Among the Yoruba, the mask is a symbol of masculine unity with the ancestors, especially during ancestral *egungun* rituals. The ancestral rituals express through masquerade the participation in the very presence of the ancestral spirits. While women in Yoruba society nurture the gods, men mask and represent the ancestors. The circle of men excludes women in the veneration of the ancestors in Yoruba society (Drewal 1992).

We shall return to ancestral veneration later. As we conclude here, we wish to say that the human person stands at the center of West African religion and culture. From dance through language and into various aspects of culture, religions manifest themselves as primary, permeating every dimension of society. The ancestor looms large over all.

BIBLIOGRAPHY

Abimbola, Wande. "The Place of African Traditional Religion in Contemporary Africa: The Yoruba Example." In *African Traditional Religions in Contemporary Society*, edited by Jacob K. Olupona, 51-58. New York: Paragon House, 1991.

Abrahams, Roger D. *African Folktales: Traditional Stories of the Black World*. New York: Pantheon Books, 1983.

Achebe, Chinua. *Arrow of God*. New York: Anchor Books/Doubleday, 1974.

————. *Things Fall Apart*. New York: Fawcett Crest, 1989.

————, and C. L. Innes, eds. *African Short Stories: Twenty Short Stories from across the Continent*. Portsmouth, N.H.: Heinemann Educational Books, 1985.

Antwi-Boahen, Joseph. Written interview with Antwi-Boahen. Edited by Robert B. Fisher. Akim Ofoase, Ghana, 1988. Manuscript private collection.

Appiah, Kwame Anthony. *In My Father's House: Africa in the Philosophy of Culture*. New York: Oxford University Press, 1992.

Asfar, Gabriel. "Amadou Hampate Ba and the Islamic Dimension of West African Oral Tradition." In *Faces of Islam in African Literature*, edited by Kenneth W. Harrow, 141-50. Portsmouth, N.H.: Heinemann Educational Books, 1991.

Bame, Kwabena N. *Profiles in African Traditional Popular Culture: Consensus and Conflict*. New York: Clear Type Press, 1991.

Boahen, A.Adu. *Topics in West African History*. Burnt Mill, Essex, U.K.: Longman House, 1966.

Cham, Mbeye B. "Islam in Senegalese Literature and Film." In *Faces of Islam in African Literature*, edited by Kenneth W. Harrow, 163-86. Portsmouth, N.H.: Heinemann Educational Books, 1991.

Christaller, J. G. *Three Thousand Six Hundred Ghanaian Proverbs (from Asante and Fante Language)*. Translated by Kofi Ron Lange. Lewiston, N.Y.: The Edwin Mellen Press, 1990.

Drewal, Margaret Thompson. *Yoruba Ritual: Performers, Play, Agency*. Bloomington, Ind.: Indiana University Press, 1992.

Gikandi, Simon. *Reading Chinua Achebe: Language and Ideology in Fiction*. Portsmouth, N.H.: Heinemann Educational Books, 1991.

Gilfoy, Peggy Stoltz. *Patterns of Life: West African Strip-weaving Traditions*. Washington, D.C.: Smithsonian Institution Press, 1987.

Glover, E. Ablade, compiler. "Adinkra Symbolism." 3d ed. Kumasi, Ghana: University of Science and Technology, 1992.

Holloway, Joseph E. "The Origins of African-American Culture." In *Africanisms in American Culture*, edited by Joseph E. Holloway, 1-18. Bloomington, Ind.: Indiana University Press, 1990.

Holloway, Joseph E., and Winifred K. Vass. *The African Heritage of American English*. Bloomington, Ind.: Indiana University Press, 1993.

Ilogu, Edmund. "African Traditional Religious Systems of Social Control: A Nigerian Example." In *African Creative Expressions of the Divine*, edited by Kortright Davis and Elias Farajaje-Jones, 142-57. Washington, D.C.: Howard University School of Divinity, 1991.

Klein, Rosine, and Stacia Robbins, compilers. "African Folksongs: Children's Songs of Ghana." Teacher's Guide to tape. In *Spoken Arts*. New Rochelle, N.Y.: Spoken Arts, 1986.

Mbiti, John S. *Introduction to African Religion*. 2d ed. Portsmouth, N.H.: Heinemann Educational Books, 1991.

McNaughton, Patrick R. "The Semantics of 'Jugu': Blacksmiths, Lore, and 'Who's Bad' in Mande." In *Status and Identity in West Africa,* edited by David C. Conrad and Barbara A. Frank, 46-57. Bloomington, Ind.: Indiana University Press, 1995.

Mphande, Lupenga. "Ideophones and African Verse." *Research in African Literatures* 23, no. 1 (Spring 1992): 117-29.

Niangoran-Bouah, Georges. "The Talking Drum: A Traditional African Instrument of Liturgy and of Mediation with the Sacred." In *African Traditional Religions in Contemporary Society*, edited by Jacob K. Olupona, 81-92. New York: Paragon House, 1991.

Nketia, J. H. Kwabena. "Akan Poetry." In *An African Treasury,* edited by Langston Hughes. New York: Crown Publishers, 1960.

Obiechina, Emmanuel. *Culture, Tradition and Society in the West African Novel*. Cambridge, England: Cambridge University Press, 1975.

Oduyoye, Mercy Amba. *Hearing and Knowing: Theological Reflections on Christianity in Africa*. Maryknoll, N.Y.: Orbis Books, 1986.

Ogbaa, Kalu. *Gods, Oracles, and Divination: Folkways in Chinua Achebe's Novels*. Trenton: Africa World Press, 1992.

Okpewho, Isidore. *African Oral Literature: Backgrounds, Character, and Continuity*. Bloomington, Ind.: Indiana University Press, 1992.

Oliver, Roland. *The African Experience*. New York: IconEditions, 1991.

Opoku, Kofi Asare. *West African Traditional Religion*. Accra, Ghana: FEP International Private Limited, 1978.

Radin, Paul. *African Folktales*. New York: Schocken Books, 1983.

Sarpong, Peter. *The Sacred Stools of the Akan*. Tema, Ghana: Ghana Publishing Corporation, 1971.

————. *Ghana in Retrospect: Some Aspects of Ghanaian Culture*. Tema, Ghana: Ghana Publishing Corporation, 1974.

Thompson, Robert Farris. *Flash of the Spirit: African and Afro-American Art & Philosophy*. New York: Vintage Books, 1984.

Turner, Lorenzo Dow. *Africanisms in the Gullah Dialect*. Chicago: University of Chicago Press, 1949.

Turner, Victor. *The Ritual Process: Structure and Anti-structure*. Ithaca, N.Y.: Cornell University Press, 1977.

Yankah, Kwesi. "Proverbs: The Aesthetics of Traditional Communication." *Research in African Literatures* 20, no. 3 (Fall 1989): 325-46.

————. *Speaking for the Chief: Okyeame and the Politics of Akan Oratory*. Bloomington, Ind.: Indiana University Press, 1995.

STUDY GUIDE

1. Read one of Achebe's novels, either *Things Fall Apart* or *Arrow of God*. Take notes on the plot and on other questions that come to mind. Be prepared to discuss this with a group or class.

2. Go back over the novel you read and note the Igbo names of persons and the names of the traditional area and the villages. Pay attention to the context of the names and the references the characters make to them in their speech. What is the attitude villagers have toward villagers who do not belong to their union? Save some of this information for discussion after the next chapter.

3. Summarize the folktales, the folksongs, the proverbs, and the myths used by Achebe. Be particular about their contexts in the story and about how the author uses them himself. Note the kind of circle where the proverb, for example, is used. Is it a circle of male elders? A circle in the *ilo* or park where the wrestling occurs? At home in the mother's hut, together with their child or children? How does the literary piece fit in with the context? Are ideophones or onomatopoeia used? How?

4. How do drums express the language of the ancestors? How do the talking drums transform a people? What is the position of the drummer in society?

5. View a film by a West African director, for example, *Wend Kuni* by Gaston Kaboré. On first viewing, try to get the feel of the plot and get used to the subtitles. View it again and pay attention to the common stock greetings, the gestures, the body language of the characters within their context. Keep in mind its Burkinabe context and the time setting. How does the director use this story as a fable of traditional Mossi values before the arrival of Islam or Christianity both as a critique of what is good as well as what is not so good about his own culture? Compare this with the values Achebe brings out, both good and bad.

6. Study strip-cloth weaving in West Africa. Do a study of various kente designs, being careful to be authentic. Study also the adinkra designs and how cloths have names given to them by market women. Relate these to proverbs. How do combinations of symbols sometimes suggest a new name for the whole cloth? How should a kente be worn? What about the colors used by the Akan? If dance groups wish to be authentic, should they be careful about the use of colors?

7. Study the proverbial symbols of the Akan stools, the linguist (spokesperson) staffs, and the gold weights. How do the designs relate to the structuring of Akan social status among the kings and chiefs? What is the role of the linguist in the king's court? What does his staff mean? Show the proverbial meaning of various staff designs (see question 15 below).

8. Do a study of masks. In connection with coming discussions about the ancestors, how do the masks relate to ancestral veneration, festivals, and judicial courts among the Yoruba and the Igbo? What are the dancing masks and the age-set masks mentioned in *Arrow of God*?

9. Do a study of myth and investigate its meaning in connection with a town or clan founding. Does the myth indicate the patrilinear or matrilinear origin of the people? How does the myth relate the people with their own locality. Does the myth connect the people with a deity? How do myths in one place differ from those in other places?

10. Investigate the archeological studies about the Nok culture in Nigeria. Do another investigation about the myth of the origin of the Yoruba. How do the myths tell of the origins of central shrines, such as Ile Ife? What is the story of Sundiata? How does it set up the foundation of the peoples of Old Mali? Do the myths tell of a migration or of a settlement of a people?

11. Study the significance of the circle in a particular society. Be careful not to generalize. Try to particularize the symbol, as Achebe does in the

context of the union of Umuofia and Mbaino; or of Umuaro and Okperi. Or study it in terms of the gender set or age set. Which are the accompanying symbols, for example, the masks? Note the circle of the nine *egwugwu*, the nine ancestral founding fathers, representing the nine villages of Umuofia. How does the power of the drumming and the spoken word give meaning to the circle? Explain the function of the durbar in Akan society as a form of circle.

12. Related to this, but not discussed in chapter 2, is the frequent mention of the market place, the market days, and events of the market area. What is the symbolism of the market even in the traditional society? How did the village of Umuike explain the power of its market to an old woman sweeping it before cockcrow?

13. Do a study of the Asante, the confederation, the Golden Stool, and the role of the *asantehene*. Which are the more powerful symbols? How does the use of kente and adinkra feature in the proverbial symbolism of Asante?

14. If you are an artist, design an adinkra cloth with various symbols and give it an appropriate proverbial name. It can make a political comment, too. What about batik material?

15. While the role of the drummer in Akan society as a medium of the traditions marks him out as divine, somewhat prophetic, like the ancient griots or bards of Mande-speaking peoples, the *okyeame,* or the royal spokesperson, is truly the "talking mouth" of the Akan kings. Ritual specialist and expert in the oratorical value of the proverb and other linguistic devices, the linguist is a buffer against the evil speech and eye cast upon the royal figure of king, chief, or queen mother. Read in detail Yankah 1995.

16. Find out about lost-wax casting, possibly from an art department. How were the gold weights cast? How was the gold trade tied to the development of Asante culture? How did the Asante acquire their weight system?

3

"All People Are God's Children"
Nnipa Nyinaa Ye Onyame Mma

THE HUMAN CENTER OF THE UNIVERSE

John S. Mbiti has stated: "Traditional religions are not primarily for the individual, but for his community of which he is a part. . . . To be human is to belong to the whole community, and to do so involves participating in the beliefs, ceremonies, rituals, and festivals of that community. A person cannot detach himself from the religion of his group, for to do so is to be severed from his roots, his foundation, his context of security, his kinships, and the entire group of those who make him aware of his own existence" (Mbiti 1990, 2). Later, to counter the Cartesian maxim *Cogito ergo sum,* "I think and therefore I am," Mbiti says, "I am because we are; and since we are, therefore I am" (Mbiti 1990, 106).

Without fear of generalization, we can say that the human person in Africa stands at the center of the universe. Although its Creator, God stands outside of it. Further, Africans see themselves belonging to a community, which for them is central, even more important than the individual. Every other creature exists for the community. The content of the dance, the drumming, the myth, the folktale, the proverb, and other rituals and artifacts revolves around the human being in community, whether family, lineage, village, clan or ethnic group, living or living-dead. No one dances alone but with or in the presence of the community. No reflection is born except together with others. In a sense, African thought expressed through these means is humanistic, but not like Western humanism, which is anti-divine and contrary to the spiritual and supernatural. As we shall see presently, the Akan regard human beings in an exalted fashion. Each human being has the "spark of God" in him or her, the *'kra.* God is the Originator and Provider of the human being. The Akan have a maxim that acknowledges this central belief: *Onyame bekyere,* "God will provide."

Each human being in community is valuable from birth until death. Even after death the worth of the human person continues to be respected, because the dead person is living on in the community of the ancestors. Even the deities are subject to the interest of the human community. If they continue to answer prayers and deliver the goods, as it were, they receive human worship and sacrifice. If they fail, however, they fall into oblivion or their devotees will ignore them (Ehusani 1991).

So, the human person in community is where the cosmos lies. Akan and most African cosmologies are therefore anthropocentric, human-centered. The Akan have a proverb: "All people are God's children; no one is a child of the earth." Or again: "The human being is the thing. If I call 'Gold,' gold does not respond. If I call 'Clothes,' clothes do not respond. The human being is the thing." The "divine spark" guarantees that human beings are ends of themselves. The moral conclusion, therefore, is that human beings may not be used as a means to anyone's ends. Everything else God has made, natural or spiritual, is for the use of human society (Mbiti 1991). Mbiti (1991, 40) has suggested a diagram that expresses the mythical and proverbial sense of what we have tried to say:

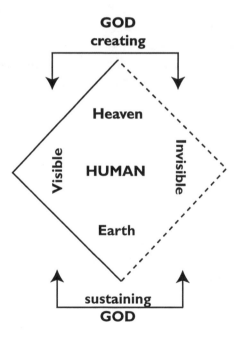

In this chapter we shall consider the human person within society in terms of himself or herself as the mirror of the cosmos, then puberty, marriage, and birth. In the course of our discussion we shall consider briefly the social organization of the group. The next chapter will deal with death and the ancestors and the problem of evil.

THE AKAN AND THE COMPARATIVE CONCEPTS OF THE HUMAN PERSON

At the village, the Asante man or woman meet each other on a path and engage in the rituals of conversation. The reader is asked to excuse the use of Twi, but I merely wish to set the stage, if I may.

Owura, maakye!	Sir, good morning!
Yaa, nua.	The same to you, sister.
Wo ho te sen?	How are you?
Onyame adom, me ho ye.	
Na wo nso, wo ho te sen?	By God's grace, I'm fine. And how are you?
Me ho ye. Ofie te sen?	I'm fine. How's home?
Ofie dee bokoo.	Everything at home is fine.

The two neighbors are actually oiling the wheels of their social relationship. Conversational conventions keep village life running smoothly. Note the reference to "God's grace," the concern about health, and the mention of the word *ho*. While conventional, the stock greeting mentions briefly belief in God, Divine Providence, God's creative goodness, a constant concern about health, therefore the well-being of the "house," meaning the family, and concern about the body. *Eho* means "the whole exterior body," where health or sickness is felt. The word for "strength" in Twi is *ahooden,* literally meaning "body-firm." Another way of greeting asks about "the joints":

Wo mpomuee?	(Literally) How are the inside joints?
Me mpomu dee bokoo.	My joints are soft.

In other words, "My bones are well-greased." Or, as we might say, "Everything is cool."

The point we make here is that the physical, the body, features very centrally when thinking about the health of a person. If the body is fine, the whole person is fine and everyone else is happy and in harmony. This holistic outlook is important, and we shall return to it.

Although the Akan elders do not always agree, as we note from the reports of scholars who give different opinions (Christensen 1954; Ephirim-Donkor 1997), we can probably state the following: The human person consists of a body *(nipadua)* made of an exterior body *(honam),* or "body-flesh." The body comprises a spiritual element from the mother's blood *(mogya);* another spiritual entity from the father's semen *(ntoro),* from which the individual receives his own spirit; the spiritual entity that is bearer of his or her personality *(sunsum);* and the spiritual entity, which we mentioned above as "the spark from God," the *'kra* (Appiah 1992). Each of these spiritual elements, we shall explain, indicates a relational dimension in a person's life to the cosmos or world in which he or she lives. We will discuss the last element first of all, the *'kra.*

'Kra

One should be careful not to equate this terminology to any Greek, Cartesian, or other Western psychology. So, if we say *body, spirit,* or *soul,* we do so only analogously. We may therefore call the *'kra* a soul, but it is sort of a life force, like breath *(honhom),* the bearer of one's destiny *(nkrabea)* from God (Appiah 1992). Before a person is born into the world, he or she stands before Onyame, God, who gives the person a destiny to fulfill. The *'kra* is a person's double linking him or her to God. It acts like a guardian spirit or personal god, sometimes offering good advice to keep one out of trouble, sometimes offering bad advice and failing the person. When a person's *'kra* provides protection, the Akan say, *Ne kra di n'akyi,* "His soul protects him." He will worship his spirit and even "wash" it with offerings (this ritual is called *akraguare,* "soul-washing"). If the *'kra* gives bad advice and fails to guide the person, the Akan say, *Ne kra apa n'akyi,* "His soul failed to guide him" (Opoku 1978, 96). During life the *'kra* is stable and never leaves the body, but at death the *'kra* returns to God to give an account of its earthly life, called *obra* or *abrabo* (Opoku 1978).

This characteristic of the *'kra* is similar to the Igbo *chi.* Achebe has Nwaka tell the assembly at Umuaro, "If a man says yes his *chi* also says yes" (Achebe 1974, 27). In *Things Fall Apart* Achebe writes about Okonkwo's father, Unoka:

> Unoka was an ill-fated man. He had a bad *chi* or personal god, and evil fortune followed him to the grave, or rather to his death, for he had no grave. (Achebe 1989, 10)

The story is about how Okonkwo resisted the father's *chi* by following his own, or at least he thought so, when he was young. The narrator reflects the general opinion of the young men in the village:

> If ever a man deserved success, that man was Okonkwo. At an early age he had achieved fame as the greatest wrestler. That was not luck. At the most one could say that his *chi* or personal god was good. But the Ibo people have a proverb that when a man says yes his *chi* says yes also. Okonkwo said yes very strongly; so his *chi* agreed. And not only his *chi* but his clan too, because it judged a man by the work of his hands. (Achebe 1989, 29)

Achebe says that Okonkwo was ruled by one passion more than by "the fear of evil and capricious gods and magic, the fear of the forest, and of the forces of nature" (Achebe 1989, 16-17), and that was a fear of failure and weakness. In other words, he hated everything his father had been. His life-long fight was really against the choice he tried to make in life against the *chi* he had chosen before birth. Toward the end of his life, after his son had converted to Christianity, Okonkwo realized this, perhaps as he lay think-ing in his hut one night:

> Why, he cried in his heart, should he, Okonkwo, of all people, be cursed with such a son? He saw clearly in it the finger of his personal god or *chi*. For how else could he explain his great misfortune and exile and now his despicable son's behavior? (Achebe 1989, 142)

Okonkwo was beginning to understand that he had rejected his father's gentleness and had refused to honor him as an ancestor. He feared now that because his own sons would soon all leave their gods and ancestors when they joined the Christians, "a lot of effeminate men clucking like old hens" (Achebe 1989, 142), he also would be forgotten. His own *chi* was to blame for making a bad choice (Ogbaa 1992).

Similar to the Akan notion of the *'kra* as the "breath of God," the Yoruba believe they have an *emi* given to them by God, who receives it again at death, because God is "the owner of the spirit," *Elemi* (Opoku 1978). On the other hand, the Yoruba regard the *ori* as the personality, like the Akan *sunsum*, but also as the bearer of destiny and guardian spirit, like the *'kra* (Opoku 1978). Obviously one must always return to the myths for the defi-nitions of beliefs. These are not always consistent with definitions else-where.

Since the *'kra* is unique to human beings, providing them with a worth above all creatures of God, certain rules of etiquette and of grammar apply only to humans. One does not give another person, for example, the left hand, or greet one with the left hand, since it is considered dirty. Greetings are given to all in a circle or line starting from the right to the left, even when the most important person stands in the middle. When you count two chickens, you say, *nkoko abien.* When you count two people, you say, *nnipa baanu.* When you describe an animal, you place your palm prone. When you speak of the height of a child, for example, your palm faces upward.

After a child is born, it is usually kept indoors until the eighth day, when the family performs the "outdooring" ritual, which we will study below. The child is given a name, called the *kradin,* the name of one of the seven spirits for each of the seven days of the week; in English the name is some-times called the soul-name, but erroneously the day-name. The name corre-sponds to the name of the day in Twi, one for the male child, and one for the female child. We give here the names in both Asante and Fante, the latter in parentheses.

Day (English)	Day (Twi)	Male	Female
Sunday	Kwasida	(A)Kwasi (Kwesi)	Akosua (Esi)
Monday	Dwoda	Kwadwo (Kodwo)	Adwowa (Adua)
Tuesday	Beneda	Kwabena (Kobena, Ebo)	Abenaa (Araba)
Wednesday	Wukuda	Kwaku (Kweku)	Akua (Ekua, Ekuwa)
Thursday	Yawda	Yaw (Yao, Kwao)	Yaa (Aba)
Friday	Fida	Kofi (Fifi, Eko)	Afua (Efua, Efuwa)
Saturday	Memenada	Kwame (Kwamena, Ato)	Ama (Amba)

If you know the day of the week on which you were born, you can figure what your name is. You can determine the day, if you don't know, by consulting a perpetual calendar.

Each child receives a characteristic spirit corresponding to the spirit-deity said to preside over a particular day. Thus:

Akwasi—Bodua (whisk = leader),

Kwadwo—Okoto (crab = peaceful),

Kwabena—Ogyam (fire or compassion = *obarima* = manly),

Kwaku—Ntoni (*sika* = gold or rock, thus controlling),

Yao—Preko (boar = courageous),

Kofi—Okyin (adventurer = restless),

Kwame—Atoapoma (spear = target, tenacious).

There may be more than one child with the same soul-name in a family. In that case the elder one will be called Kese, and the younger one is called Kuma or Kakraba. Thus the elder Wednesday's child is called Kwakukese. Sometimes the Fante add another characteristic, such as *good,* to a name. Quite commonly one hears a boy called Paakwesi, "Good Sunday's Child."

Other ways of naming children will come up as we speak of the different spiritual and family attributes. We shall also return to the rituals of outdooring later in this chapter.

Soul-washing, mentioned above, occurs when a person has recovered from a serious illness and wants to give thanks to his or her guardian spirit for aid in the time of crisis. It consists in a traditional meal prepared with African yam, eggs, palm oil, and chicken or mutton. Friends are invited to share the meal. On this occasion no food is dropped to the floor to honor the ancestors or the paternal water deity, since the 'kra is honored by swallowing all of the food (Christensen 1954). Communication with the 'kra is sometimes achieved by consultation with a shrine priest through ritual or by means of divination with a diviner in the marketplace. The purpose is usually to determine the reason for an illness. A puzzled mother may seek to communicate with the *'kra* of an unborn child to ask why it is delaying entrance into the physical world (Christensen 1954).

Sunsum

The second spiritual element of the human person is the *sunsum*, the personality or character (manifest in a person as *suban*). Unlike the *'kra,* the *sunsum* may leave the body momentarily during life—for example, during sleep—and roam about. Witchcraft is an example of how a person's *sunsum* leaves the body at night to seek out the weak *sunsum* of another to "eat." During dreams the *sunsum* is the actor of the person dreaming. So, if you dream you have committed an offense, you have actually done it and this may be used as evidence against you in a traditional court. A man who dreams he has committed adultery with another man's wife is liable for the adultery fees that are paid for daytime offenses (Appiah 1992). The *sunsum* as personality is subject to illness and the machinations of sorcery and witchcraft. Men are expected to have a "heavier" *sunsum* than women, who have a "light" *sunsum.* If, however, a male is retarded, a coward in life or battle, or otherwise is effeminate, the Fante call him a *banyin obaa.* A female, who has aggressive and masculine qualities is said to have a "heavy" *sunsum.* The Fante call her a *obaa banyin* (Christensen 1954). Anyone with a very "light" *sunsum* could be suspected of witchcraft. Usually a woman is the guilty party, but if a man tends to be too talkative, considered a characteristic of woman by men, he too may be suspect. A strong personality is therefore a remedy against witchcraft and illness. Ill health is often the result of turmoil inside one's *sunsum* toward another, which may similarly cause that person to get sick. Hatred, rash judgment, and whatever evil enters one's head causes sickness in mind and body. For this reason, once a year during the major festivals, such as the Odwira among the Asante or Brong, a person has the freedom to speak out about what bothers him or her about someone else, including the king or queen mother. During this period of liminality, *communitas* is created and the rules of etiquette are loosened. Afterward, when the community returns to real life, they say the *sunsum* of people and of the whole society has cooled. Good psychology.

Families, ethnic groups, and whole nations have a *sunsum*. We noted how the Asante Nation has a common *sunsum* enshrined in the *Sikadwa,* the Golden Stool. The symbol of the Asante Nation, the Golden Stool is closely guarded. What happens to it, happens to the nation (Opoku 1978).

Curiously for a matrilineal family system, the father has the prerogative of naming his children. The proverb is clear: *Oba se ose, nanso owo abusua,* "A child resembles the father but belongs to the (mother's) lineage." Through the father's *ntoro,* he endows his children with something of his own *sunsum.*

The spiritual and psychological characteristics come from the father, while the physical qualities, such as height and features, are derived from the mother's *mogya*. Beside the *kradin* and its by-name, noted above, which are bestowed automatically from the day on which the child is born, the father now chooses names for the child based on characteristics he wishes the boy or girl to develop in life from *his* family and even from his friends. A proper name is given based on the father's *ntoro* group (see below, pp. 72, 83, 86), such as Owusu for a boy or Owusuwaa for a girl. He may, moreover, give his child a number name, such as Mensah, which means "third-born." However, Mensah is as common in Akan as Smith is in English and no longer carries the original meaning. It is just a name. In modern times, for legal reasons, the child may combine the name of the father with the *sunsum* name, like Owusuwaa-Osei. Finally, the father may bestow other names mentioned below.

Ntoro

The *sunsum* is an individuation of the patrilineal group, which is the third spiritual entity, the *ntoro*. Each child inherits the *ntoro* from its father. For this reason the child receives another name and is related to the father's river deity, which the Fante call the *egyabosom*. Some Akan do not distinguish the *'kra* from the *sunsum,* claiming that both come from the father's river deity; the first is more stable, while the second can be developed, since it represents the personality. Thus the Fante say, "When you say you worship your father's deity, it is your father's *'kra's* deity" (Christensen 1954, 81, 90). I do not think this contradicts what others say about the *'kra* as the life force created directly by Onyame. God always works through the mediation of God's creatures, even if they are deities. Always, in every Akan tradition, the *'kra* carries the person's destiny or fate, which is determined before the person's birth and about which the *'kra* reports to God after death. However, the *sunsum* is directly related to the father's *ntoro,* which literally means "semen." After a man's death, his *sunsum* returns to the father's river deity with a possible reincarnation in the father's line. This spirit, however, is not the ancestor. A woman's *sunsum* after marriage and her first pregnancy is transferred by her husband to his *ntoro*.

The son reveres the deceased father by invocation of his *sunsum* and his river deity. Christensen describes a libation invoked by a Fante son who is ill:

My *Egyasunsum Tewiah* (Father-personality-spirit born-after-twins), come for a drink. My *Egyabosom Bosompra* (Father-river-deity Spirit-of-the-River-Pra), here is a drink for you. Help me to get well. If I do get well, I will offer for you a sheep. (Christensen 1954, 93)

Among the Akan, except the Fante, there are twelve patrilinear groups based on their *ntoro,* the Bosommuru, Bosompra, Bosomafram, Bosompo, and so on. Each represents a water deity, who is male, and is one of the *tete bosom,* the ancient tutelar deities, whose function is to protect villages, towns, and states from harm (Opoku 1974). Each *ntoro* is identified by a certain characteristic peculiar to its members. For example, those whose deity is the spirit of the River Pra are said to be tough (Mensah 1992; Ephirim-Donkor 1997). There are given names, now associated with family names in modern Ghana, attached to each *ntoro;* for example, for the Bosompra *ntoro* there are the names Agyeman, Asare, Amoako, Boateng, Boakye, Acheampong, and so on. Each has its day of observance, so that those whose deity is the ocean (Bosompo) observe Tuesday and they have a totem or sacred animal, the water buffalo. They have a taboo, an animal whose meat they do not eat, in this case, the tortoise and dog. Even a reply to standard greetings is appropriate. So, if you are greeted, for example, *maakye,* "Good morning," by someone from the Bosomtwe *ntoro,* you reply with *Yaa Ason,* or *Yaa Twedo* (Opoku 1978; Mensah 1992). We shall say more about the deities, the totems, and the taboos later.

Water rituals are associated with the *ntoro* and the tutelar deities. Water is a symbol of cleansing, purification, and is related to white, the color of victory and happiness, the color of semen and of white cloth and clay on the body.

Another feature among the Akan, and preserved quite well by the Fante, is the *asafo,* or the military institution. The *asafo,* from *sa,* "war," and *fo,* "people," is patrilinear, based on the *ntoro,* and only men belong to it. The primary function is defense of the state and support of the paramount king. In a given state, the *asafo,* while democratic, has a general, the *tufohen.* The *asafo* is divided up into companies on the local level, under the command of an officer, called the *supi.* There are company captains, the *asafohen,* a number of lesser officers, flag carriers, drummers, horn blowers, and priests. The *asafo* has much to say in the governance of the Fante state and in the choice of the next king. These institutions are involved also in social and philanthropic activities, including entertainment, traditional dancing, road-works, and sanitation projects. There are two colorful works of art associated with the *asafo:* their shrines, decorated with fantastic monsters; and their flags. Flags today are expressions of the oral imagery but include European coats of arms and flags, naval ensigns, and trademarks of trading companies and other regalia (Adler and Barnard 1992). They express proverbs and the military might of the *asafo.* They combine ancient beliefs in ghosts, bush spirits, and ancestors with modern technology, such as the airplane. Thus a new proverb has been born: "Like the airplane, we can go anywhere." Most images are meant to taunt rivals with challenges and insults (Adler and Barnard 1992). The Elephant *Asafo* taunts the Palm *Asafo* with this flag: "An elephant can uproot the palm tree." The Palm *Asafo* has a reply on a flag with the symbol: "The elephant can't uproot the palm tree but makes friends with it."

Mogya

The fourth spiritual entity is the *mogya*, or blood, which is by no means the least, since it signifies blood kinship on the matrilinear line, the most important for the Akan. Akan traditionally believed that a baby is formed when the semen of the father combines with the blood of the mother. While the father's contribution is stronger, the mother's is more basic. The blood gives the child membership and status in the clan *(abusuaban)* and lineage, the *abusua*.

Matrilineal societies, such as the Akan, determine inheritance, status, and royal succession from the side of a person's mother. In every village or town in Akan territory there are people from different clans. On the local level the section of the clan is called a "lineage," according to Peter Sarpong. Every lineage has a head man, *abusuapanyin*, who, together with other lineage head men, forms a council with the local village head man or chief, from the ruling lineage, who is not the head of his own lineage (Sarpong 1974).

Among all Akan, according to Opoku (1978, 99), there are eight clans with one or two corresponding subdivisions:

1. Oyoko (Anona in Fante)   (Dako)
2. Bretuo   (Tena)
3. Aduana   (Abrade or Aberade)
4. Asakyiri   (Amoakaade)
5. Asenee   (Adonten)
6. Agona   (Toa)
7. Asona   (Dwumina or Dwum)
8. Ekoona   (Asokore)

(But also see Obeng [1996, 17], who says there are seven clans; he groups Bretuo and Agona together.)

The same clans are found among all the Akan, whether the Twifo, the Fante, the Akyem (Achem or Akim), the Akwapim, the Asante, the Kwahu, the Assin, the Wassa, the Nzima, the Ahanta, the Denkyira, the Adansi, or the Akwamu. Wherever the clans are found, members regard themselves as brothers and sisters, no matter where they come from. They cannot intermarry within the same clan, a rule anthropologists term *exogamy* (Sarpong 1974). Clans founded similar small states to gain control of trade with the Mande to the west and the Hausa to the north. Moreover, in the seventeenth century the Atlantic trade was growing and the interior peoples were anxious to trade with the Europeans directly without the middle men among the Fante or the Ga or even other Akan (Boahen 1966).

Through marriage, diplomacy, and war, the Oyoko clan established its supremacy over other founding clans in towns like Tafo and Ejisu. Under the first three Asante kings, Obiri Yeboa, Osei Tutu, and Opoku Ware, the clan system was organized into a political entity that dominated the structure of society from the early eighteenth century onward even when the Asante lost political power at the hands of the British. The Oyoko clan ruled several charter Asante towns; its rulers regarded themselves as brothers from the same lineage. They recognized the king of Dwaben as the head of the clan. They called the king of Nsuta *wofa* or "uncle." The Kumasihene later became the *asantehene* or political and religious head of the Asante Union. Under the advisement of the priest Okomfo Anokye, Osei Tutu organized the basic plan. By means of the Golden Stool, he persuaded the other rulers to recognize Kumasi as the capital of the Union. Kumasi was declared the religious center, where the Owdira Festival was to be celebrated by all together once a year for prayers, for settlement of disagreements among the various states, and to sit in council to make plans for expansion. Second, Osei Tutu devised a constitution whereby he, as head of the Kumasi state, was head of the Asante Union. Below him were the kings, the *amanhene,* of the other component states, who were sovereign and independent in their own territories (Boahen 1966). The *asantehene* was therefore first among equals, but moral head of all on account of the Golden Stool. At the peak of its power in the late eighteenth century under Osei Kodwo, the Asante Empire consisted of three divisions following Osei Tutu's basic plan. There was Kumasi itself, where the *asantehene* was supreme. The second division comprised the surrounding Oyoko *amantoo,* or states, and the first conquered states, each with its own *omanhene.* The third level was the weakest link; it included the later conquered states in the far reaches of the empire, such as the Gonja in the north, and the Akyem, Denkyira, or Ga to the south.

The third element in Osei Tutu's plan was the organization of the military, an idea from the Akwamu that he borrowed and improved upon. This consisted of a military formation or phalanx method of organizing his kings and chiefs. He did this first of all to overthrow the oppressive rule of the Denkyira state and then for expansion. Osei Tutu made the king of Mampong, from just outside and north of Kumasi, the *krontihene*, or commander-in-chief, of the national army. Other Oman kings he elevated to the rank of general of the forward division *(adonten),* the rear *(kyidom),* the right *(nifa),* and the left *(benkum).* Each *omanhene* divided his division into similar formations (Boahen 1966).

Finally, Osei Tutu consolidated trade in Kumasi with the Muslim north when he appointed Muslims from Mali and North Africa to serve as secretaries and bookkeepers. He appointed an Asante to be *gyasehene,* his palace administrator; this person supervised the economy as the Asante Nation improved trade with the north and with the coastal region through tariffs on all imports and exports, by taxation of the provinces, and by the proceeds from stool lands or royal estates.

The many functions of the kings in the modern state of Ghana are assumed by the civil politicians and government. Still, the kings retain their titles and perform their rituals. They continue to enjoy certain judicial functions over stool lands and over traditional practices, but other than that, the institution of chieftaincy has lost much of its prestige today.

So, while the spiritual elements of the human person describe an individual, each element points to a relationship, both spiritual and communal, among humans. The tiny Oyoko family dream grew into the mightiest kingdom of West Africa in the seventeenth and eighteenth centuries. The clan system ensured the rule of a people, in which succession was kept in family, but not by direct inheritance. Each of the Asante *ahenfo* (chiefs) was a nephew of his predecessor. The queen mother *(ohemaa)* was the hidden power in the family who nominated the next ruler.

In conclusion, I wish to recall how the Muslim traveler from Spain to Ancient Ghana, al-Bakri, remarked, about the year 1067, that the King of Ghana, Tunka Manin, inherited his throne from his uncle, King Basi, who himself had ascended to rule Ghana at the ripe age of eighty-five. Al-Bakri noted that the kingdom was inherited by the son of the king's sister (Boahen 1966). In modern Ghana among the Akan we note the same custom. Similarly, the king supervised the government of the capital, Koumbi-Saleh, the immediate metropolitan area, and the outlying provinces in a way that Osei Tutu later devised for the rule of his Asante Empire. He, too, succeeded his uncle, Obiri Yeboa.

THE AKAN MARRIAGE CELEBRATION AND THE ROLE OF WOMEN

The political power of the Akan royalty may have waned, but its moral authority is strong to this day. The clan system of kinship, based on inheritance from the mother's side, is very real. The traditional royal clan of an area determines the rulers of the place. Once more, let me explain the order of Asante society. The *asantehene* is the head of the Asante National Council, composed of the *amanhene* of the divisional states. Each *oman*, or state, is governed by a king or chief *(omanhene)* and a queen mother *(omanhemaa)*, who is constitutionally his "mother" but is usually in fact his sister or aunt. Every town and village in an *oman* has a chief or village head; together these form the divisional council, whose president is the *omanhene*. On all levels of the hierarchy the kings, the queen mothers, and the chiefs are chosen from the ruling matrilineages in their towns. They were usually the first to occupy the piece of land or were the leaders of the first migration to the area and therefore had the right to provide the ruler. As we mentioned before, the Oyoko clan of Kumasi provides the *asantehene*. Likewise, the Asona clan chooses the *omanhene* of Offinso (Sarpong 1977). So, in one place one lineage may be the rulers, while in another place the lineage of the same name and the same totem may be commoners. It happens, when no one locally wants the job of chief, that a lineage seeks out a commoner from another place and asks him if he wants to become chief. He must be a member of the same clan; blood relationship *(mogya)* is the basic condition for becoming a chief. An honorary chieftaincy is therefore only a superficial and empty title.

Blood kinship and marriage are essential ingredients for the continuity of the ethnic group or clan *(abusuaban)*. The role of women in society is therefore at the heart of kinship relationships. While every ruler, king or chief, is a man, beside him sits the queen mother. (There are rare exceptions, see Yankah 1995, 71.) In every clan or lineage there is a man who is the elder, the *abusuapanyin;* he represents the lineage on the chief's council. There is also the senior woman, the *obaapanyin,* who is responsible for the women in a lineage and is concerned with their marriages and divorces. The queen mother advises on marriage questions in the royal lineage, even if she is not the female leader of her lineage. She has her own stool, spokeswoman, and council. Nevertheless, she does not control all the women, since female supervision is done by the lineage female head. The queen mother officially dresses much like a man. Her head remains uncovered, and her hair is short. She supervises nubility rites, when young girls are admitted to adulthood. The most important task of any queen mother, beside advising the king or chief and even freely scolding him in a way not permitted the councilors, is to nominate the next king or chief from among her nephews.

The biological bonding of all Akan with their mothers and sisters is a strong unifying element in society. Perhaps the myths of a common mother are at the heart of this bond. Although there is spiritual bonding with the father through the *ntoro* groupings and the naming by the father, the matriclan system is stronger among the Akan. The mother's brother, the children's uncle, is an authority figure; he probably exercises a stronger influence on the children than the father among the Asante. Among the Fante the maternal bond is a bit weaker, which is why the Fante regard the father's *sunsum* so significantly and why it is venerated after his death.

Sarpong underscores the centrality of fertility and marriage among the Akan, especially the Asante. When pouring libation, two petitions are addressed often to God and the ancestors: one for potency for the men; another for fertility of the women, so they may bless the family with many children. A barren woman is a disgrace to her clan, providing grounds for possible divorce. Constantly agonized that she cannot furnish children to enhance her clan with members, she offers libations and sacrifices at shrines. Divorces also occur when the man is impotent. He is scorned even by children, who refuse to run errands for him, and he has no children of his own to do his chores. The children snicker at him and call him *kote krawa,* "wax penis" (Sarpong 1977).

So, to be blessed with many children, even to have twins or triplets, is considered an achievement of the highest magnitude. Formerly the Igbo killed twins and looked upon them as some form of curse. They mercilessly murdered even their mothers, because of the decree of a divine oracle

(Achebe 1989). The Akan, however, have always believed that to have children of any sort is good. Infertility and impotence are denounced as evils. Traditional doctors claim they have magical herbs that can cure these conditions.

It follows, since the Akan appreciate all children as precious treasures, that having baby girls is even a greater gift from God than having baby boys. Why? Because the girl is a potential mother, one who may provide successors for her lineage. Sarpong reports that when the news of a baby's birth spreads around the village, the women ask, *Oye deen?* "What is it?" On hearing it is a girl, *obaa,* the women say, *Ye da Onyame ase!* "We thank God!" When they hear it is a boy, *barima,* they shrug and say, *A eye,*"Well, it's OK" (Sarpong 1977, 8).

It's not that boys are not appreciated. When a boy becomes a father, he has the prerogative of perpetuating the famous names of his own clan in his children. The women look to their men for protection for themselves and their children. Formerly, a man went to war; he still pays the bills and builds them their house. He pays the school fees. As an uncle, the man provides for his sisters' children, especially when their fathers die or are sick or irresponsible. He helps pay the funeral bills in the lineage. A girl depends strongly on her brother. He knows this. At an early age the boy begins to exercise a small position of authority over at least some of the women among his relations. You will see him strutting around, ordering a girl to wash his clothes or to feed him at any hour. He orders his sister to fetch a chair for a guest. He orders her children to bring drinks. And they obey without a murmur. This spills over into other levels of life. You see a man ordering another woman not related to him to do things for him around the house. And she does them.

Family training is partly the reason for these attitudes. A little girl clings to her mother, who is very affectionate toward her. The mother teaches her daughter feminine manners and duties around the house and on the farm. The Akan girl learns how to be respectful toward her father, uncles, and even to brothers younger than herself. It is not that she is inferior, but until the day when her maturity is guaranteed through marriage and childbearing, she has to exercise patience.

At a very early age the Akan boy gravitates toward his father and often to his uncles. His father treats him sternly. The use of the cane is not out of the ordinary. The boy learns to look after his mother and sisters. His father forbids him to do womanly chores and activities, such as cooking, sweeping the floor, and eating with women. His father shows him how to farm and to plant yams, a man's task, while the women plant cassava. He takes his son to funerals and to meetings to show him how to behave. As the proverb says, "If a child knows how to wash his hands, he eats with the elders." Boys do not have initiation rites into puberty among the Akan probably because of this stern training from their early years by the men, who serve as role models for them. Sometimes in the past, however, when the father chose the boy's future wife, the young man received a cutlass or another trade instrument as a sign that the time for marriage had arrived (Sarpong 1977).

Girls formerly underwent a puberty or nubility ritual. These days the custom is waning due to school education and the influence of Islam and Christianity. Akan girls did not have to experience tests of endurance or physical mutilations or scarifications, often part of rituals elsewhere in Africa (Sarpong 1977). The rituals still performed do not last for more than one week. They are essentially religious in nature, referring to the lineage ancestors and the traditions from of old. They are symbolic of mature womanhood and motherhood.

The queen mother determines the timing of the rituals when enough girls are ready for her inspection of their bodies. She determines if the breasts are developed enough and if the first menstruation has occurred in girls from thirteen to twenty years old. Thus delays do occur, because rituals are not performed until several girls in a village are ready.

A serious problem arises if a girl is discovered to be pregnant. In former times the boy who offended was severely fined and beaten, and, if he had not already bolted, banished (Sarpong 1977). The girl had to undergo rituals of purification and was also banished. The queen mother performed these and other rituals to appease the ancestors (Sarpong 1977).

Since the above crime rarely occurred, nubility rituals have been joyful celebrations among women and girls. Drumming with the armpit talking drums, rigorous dancing that would wear out even the strongest man, songs of explicitly sexual fun-making, folktales, play acting, and rituals of bathing and instructions in womanly skills, virtues, and traditions make up the stuff of a week of liminality that changes a girl into a woman. All rituals are performed by the elders among the women, especially women with spiritual power. The rituals exclude men and boys except at certain points when young boys are invited for food and for playing so-called love games (Sarpong 1977).

In the old days, at the end of the rituals the new women took up residence with the queen mother for forty days to serve in her household. Custom required this to assure the elders that the new women were ready for marriage. If one or the other was already betrothed, the marriage rituals were the next step. If not, then a young man could freely look around to see if one of the young women was his choice. In the present days, where the nubility rites are held, the queen mother inspects the women and then sends them to their parents to await the rituals of marriage (Sarpong 1977).

The nubility rites serve as a notice to young men that the "new" women are available for marriage. (For first marriages, the man may be from twenty-five to thirty years old. The woman may be from fifteen to twenty years old.) It is improper for a young woman to look for or ask for a husband.

After the nubility rites the men know they can express their wishes. Normally a man goes to his father through his mother or another elderly person to indicate his wish to marry a certain girl. If his father and the family approve, they approach the girl's family heads to initiate the procedures for the marriage between their two children. The girl's parents ask for time and both families enter into a form of mutual spying (Sarpong 1974). They try to find out, for example, if there are any hereditary diseases in the family, like madness, epilepsy, and so on; if there is any criminal activity going on; or if there is a huge debt outstanding. Anything that might bring embarrassment or disgrace on either family is investigated. Once both parties are satisfied that there is nothing harmful in the way, they notify each other of their approval.

The young man's father proposes a day for the betrothal or "knocking at the door" ceremony *(aponakyibo)*. The father and a family delegation appear at the girl's family house with gifts, such as drinks, like whiskey or rum, and token cash presents for the girl's mother and other women in the family and the girl's brothers and male cousins. This is all there is to it. After this almost informal ceremony, the young man and his betrothed may appear together in public, but they do not consummate their marriage. If she is still required to undergo the nubility rites, she must do so when it is convenient, and the man must wait until the rites are over before he can complete the marriage rites.

The marriage ceremony *(awadee)* is also a very simple matter. The central ceremony that binds the couple in marriage is the giving of the "bridewealth," called the *tiri aseda* (the appreciation for the head) or the *tiri nsa* (the head rum). On the appointed day the two families come together, the young man's and the young woman's, together with a group of neutral persons, who act as witnesses. The groom's father gives the bridewealth, which among matrilineal clans is rather small. It usually consists of a small amount of cash and the drinks taken during the ceremony, all provided by the groom's father and family. The purpose of the alcoholic drinks is for the bride's *abusua* to pour libation to inform the ancestors of the marriage. The bridewealth is not purchase of a wife but rather a gift to the wife's family and a deposit to ensure the husband of her fidelity and devotion. The amount of the bridewealth varies according to the social status of the groom and his family. It also depends on the social status of the bride, since less may be given for an uneducated girl. The bridewealth may have to be returned in the event of a divorce, which among the Akan is quite common.

Once this important ceremony has been completed with the full payment of the *tiri nsa*, the families decide upon another day when the bride prepares a sumptuous meal *(aduane kese)* for the *ayehyia,* the "wife-meeting" day. The groom's aunts and friends bring the bride to the groom's father's house, where the two families enjoy the meal. The final ceremony is the setting of the bride three times upon the groom's knees and the touching of their foreheads three times. After the banquet of fufu and soup, and dancing and singing, the crowd disperses to let the couple go to bed together for the first time. The next morning, if the groom found his wife to be a virgin, he sends her *abusua* a full bottle of strong drink tied with a white cloth. If she was not a virgin, he sends them a half-bottle of drink wrapped in a black cloth (Christensen 1954).

Sarpong lists the qualities of a good wife. She is obedient to her husband, faithful, hardworking, and not quarrelsome. She knows how to keep matters between herself and her husband confidential, for the proverb declares: "Nobody knows the secrets between a husband and wife." She prepares his food and she washes his clothes. Becoming a mother is her principal motive for marriage. Hence, motherliness is a quality every mature woman should achieve; motherliness includes providing food and shelter for her children, and, when there is need, for the children of other mothers and even for strangers. There are several sayings recited in dirges at funerals of successful mothers, such as, "Grandmother, the big cooking pot that entertains strangers," *Aduane ne naa yensre:* "We do not beg for food or sleeping place." Generosity and hospitality are feminine qualities that a man may have, as illustrated in a verse sung at the funeral of a kind and generous man, *Agya mmofra ni,* "A father who was mother to children" (Sarpong 1977).

Having many children is the boast of both the husband and his wife. When either parent joins the ancestors after death, the children keep his or her memory alive in the stories, the naming of babies, the pouring of libation, and other rituals. Likewise, having more children enhances the prestige of a man in his society. He has enough wealth to support him, he has enough help on his farm not to hire outside workers, he will be supported in his old age. When a marriage is not productive enough, when perhaps only girls are born, then a man resorts to polygamy, or, more precisely, polygyny. A household with more than one wife insures a man against not having children to come after him and guarantees eternal remembrance after death. In former times, when men went to war for the clan and nation, many were killed. Women needed the security of a home and of children. It was not uncommon for women to marry a husband who already had two or more wives just for their own security and pride. Because of taboos against sexual intercourse after pregnancy and well into the period of lactation, there were other wives to satisfy the sexual needs of the husband. If one wife was impeded because of menstruation or sickness, there were other wives to care for the children or to cook for the husband.

This does not mean that polygamous marriages are all sweet, like palm oil on yams. Achebe's novels show jealousy and conflict among the wives and favoritism on the part of the husband. On closer inspection the husband may have provoked the jealousy. An Akan proverb matter of factly states this: "A man with two wives is double-tongued." Yet polygamy survived. If women did not realize that bickering was part of family life, polygamy would have died out long ago. Men also realize that they depend upon women to have their children and to provide them social and economic prestige. For that reason, though they complain that "many wives are many tongues," they also know that the song the girls sing in the Asante nubility rites is true to life: *Etwe yare a, kote ahye akomfo,* "When the vagina is ill, the penis commits suicide" (Sarpong 1977). So, the tro-tro saying—"Fear woman"— is borne out in a positive sense, though the man may boastfully declare: *Obarima nsuro wuo,* "Man does not fear death!"

In the past families arranged infant marriages to cement the social relationships between them. This custom has largely died out. Other arrangements are made to ensure that children are available. For example, when a man dies, his brother becomes the real husband of the man's wife and the children of the deceased now belong to him. If a man or woman is unable to have children, fictional relationships are arranged so that another person's children are said to be the children of that person. It is very important among the Akan and other Africans who venerate their ancestors to generate progeny for the ancestors' sake and to have children to remember them after they die. For example, if a man dies without being betrothed, or was betrothed but not married, another man marries the bride to dedicate a child to remember the deceased. Or if a man has only daughters, his eldest daughter becomes his fictional wife to have a son for him. Although homosexuals are presumed to exist in society, as implied by terms which point to effeminacy in men or masculinity in women, homosexuality as a way of life does not exist because of the desire to have children for the ancestors. So arrangements made between two men or two women do not constitute a homosexual marriage but a fictive although legal relationship that assures the barren partner a child through a relative of the opposite sex.

Divorce among the Akan and other matrilinear clans is quite common and easy since the bridewealth is not expensive. Among the Akan, infertility and impotence are grounds for divorce. Cruelty on the part of the husband, talkativeness, witchcraft, immoral life, laziness, or incompatibility on the part of both can become obstacles to a successful marriage. Among patrilinear nomadic clans, where cattle are an important commodity, the bridewealth significantly increases. Divorce in such a case, at least for a woman, requires second thoughts, because if the wife is at fault, the bridewealth must be returned to the husband's family. If the husband is at fault, he forfeits the bridewealth. A small religious ritual (called *aware gyae*) is performed once the extended families agree to dissolve the marriage. It consists in a form of absolution from obligations to the husband's *abosom* and his *ntoro* grouping. The husband smears some white clay mixed with *adwira* leaves on the ex-wife's shoulder, which she must wear in the market or town for the populace to learn of the divorce. He pours libation informing his river deities of the divorce but keeps his children under their protection. The woman breaks a palm branch and leaves the place. She is free to seek another husband. The husband still has obligations to support the children. The proverb rather crudely states: "We kill the wife, but not the children" (Christensen 1954).

PREGNANCY AND BIRTH

Marriage and having children is a religious duty as well as a social duty. So pregnancy for a woman is a cause of joy. As her abdomen enlarges, she is proud to display to all the world that she is going to have a child. Yet as the time approaches for the baby to be born, her anxiety increases for several reasons. In the past women died more frequently during childbirth; moreover, stillborn children were more common or infants died rather soon after birth. If a woman already has children, but has had too many of the same sex, she worries about that too. Her concern is to have a good labor and a happy outcome. She resorts to several natural and spiritual means to secure this. She makes mixtures from tree bark and roots, seeds and leaves, and special types of food, like palm-nut soup *(abenkwan),* as natural medicines. To prevent the evil forces that roam the world, witches and sorcerers, from harming her or her child, she enlists the aid of a deity or she wears talismans around her waist. She hangs charms at her door, and at night she mixes herbs with steaming water to purify the air. She is obligated to observe several taboos, such as abstaining from certain foods or drinks, avoiding the sight of blood, and not seeing or hearing about something monstrous or ugly lest her child be ugly. Today we would say that such practices are a mixture of common sense based on experience, good medicine, and superstition.

If the mother's labor is hard, some may consider the possibility of her infidelity toward her husband. So some women in difficult labor confess to false infidelities to ease their labor (Sarpong 1974). If a woman dies without confessing her sin, she will not be accorded the normal funeral rites given to a departing ancestor. The midwives try their best through massages, manipulations, threats, and coaxing to bring the baby forth. Other women, usually her own mother and aunts, assist and help to cut the umbilical cord and to bury it ritually. Once the baby is born, the Asante wash the baby as many as nine times with specially prepared water to make sure that the baby does not develop a body odor (Sarpong 1974).

Other methods are used to make sure that the child develops a round or oval head, or a flat back of the head. Elders often circumcise boys privately in early infancy. The Akan, however, do not perform other forms of scarification, tribal marks, and mutilations, as do some other peoples in northern Ghana. Shedding of blood and the disfigurement of the body are regarded as signs of enslavement and inferiority. Mothers sometimes scratch a facial mark for medicinal or magical purposes in early infancy. Until recently, any form of bodily scar, even circumcision, disqualified a person from becoming an Akan king or other official (Sarpong 1977).

Mother and child remain in seclusion for eight days. The mother feeds the child from her breast milk and gives it water mixed with herbs and sometimes the bone of a powerful animal, like the leopard, in the belief that it will help the child develop strong bones. Although the child automatically receives the *kradin* and a by-name with it—as Akwasi, Sunday's child, is also called Bodua—the father must consult with his family about other names for the ceremony called the "outdooring of the baby." Usually the father's sister, as representative of their lineage, suggests some of the names. These other names are bestowed at the outdooring rite by the grandfather or an elder of the father, since this is the privilege of the *ntoro* grouping. Meanwhile, the father gathers gifts for the ceremony, including a cloth, fish and meat, and some gold dust or money for the mother; and a metal spoon, two metal bowls, a new mat, a pillow, a comb, and a small cloth for the child. He also procures a cutlass, if it is a boy, or a basket, if it is a girl. The mother, still at her mother's home, takes care of her "ghost child." If there is danger of its death, she names it a strange name to scare off any evil lurking about, like Sumina, meaning "incinerator." If it dies during the eight days, the people consider it only a visitor from the ancestors, and they dispose of the body quite unceremoniously without mourning. They call it a "pot-child" and throw it on the dung heap. If they decide the child has come to stay among the living, they announce the naming ceremony. This may consist of two separate occasions, with the actual outdooring, or bringing into the light, on the eighth day, and the naming ritual with a solemn meal a few days or even weeks later. At any case, the *ntetea* rite, the naming ceremony, is essential, for naming is humanizing (Sarpong 1974).

Robert Rattray describes how early in the 1920s the maternal grandmother arrived before dawn of the eighth day to pick up the baby and carry it to the edge of the village. There she left the baby's excrement in order to claim the child from the ancestors. She returned to the house to disguise the child with shea butter and to paint the eyebrows heavily. She daubed three spots with white clay on the forehead. She then placed the child on the new mat and pillow just as the sun arose. The mother emerged dressed in white and smeared with white clay, symbols of joy. The mother also spoke ceremoniously over the child, "Thank you for not causing my death." The grandmother then took the metal spoon to feed the child some mother's milk, the first time a utensil was used. If the child's naming was not to follow immediately, the child was brought inside. Otherwise, the naming began (Rattray 1954).

The *abadinto,* the naming itself, is the prerogative of the father's side of the family, by the child's paternal grandfather, or, among the Asante and some other Akan, by the father's eldest sister. On the appointed day, if not at the outdooring, the family and guests arrive early in the morning at the father's house. The rituals vary from place to place, but the one that follows is essentially the same among all the Akan. The child is laid on the elder's lap and then on the new mat on the floor. For the first time the elder names the child. The elder bestows a cutlass, if it is a boy, or, for a few moments, covers a girl with a basket. The cutlass is symbolic of the boy's future role as provider and hard worker. The basket symbolizes the girl's future role as food-maker. She will carry food stuffs from the farm to the kitchen. The family spokesman prepares for the libation and other rituals. Water *(nsu)* is poured into one glass or calabash three times, a few drops at a time, and schnapps or whiskey *(nsa),* which should be clear as water, is poured into a glass another three times. The elder pours libation, saying:

> *Tweaduapon Onyakopon Kwame nsa oo!*
> Dependable God, Kwame, here is drink!

To which the linguist cries out:

> *Nsuee,*
> "Drink!"

(The elder only shows the drink to Nyame.) Then the elder continues:

> Asase Yaa, Earth mother, Yaa, who never refuse any
>   living creature,
> here is drink! (Here the elder pours some on the
>   ground.)
> Ancient stool spirit, here is drink!
> Ancestors of the Aduana clan, here is drink!
> Today, Sunday, is a happy one for me to invoke your
> help in naming this your child. (Here the elder pours
>   libation.)
> Nana Twum-Antwi, the grandson is named after you.
> O Antwi-Boasiako, you carry the gun.
> You suffer due to brave deeds.
> You brought fire into this world. In this grandson
> you come, you show yourself, do not return,
> Nana Antwi-Boasiako. (Here the elder pours libation,
>   then dips his or her forefinger into the drink and
>   says to the child:)
> *Se wo se nsa a, na eye nsa ampa!*
> When you say rum, it should be rum. (The elder
>   repeats this three times. Then the elder dips his
>   or her finger into the water and says:)

Se wo se nsu a, na eye nsu ampa!
When you say water, it should be water. (The elder
    repeats this three times.)

The elder may also add: "When you say black, mean black; when you say white, mean white." In other words, this is the first moral lesson in telling the truth. Since right speech and social sensitivity are very important to the Akan, this ritual contains deep signification. To become a member of a clan, one must be upright, honest, and hardworking.

After this, the father, through his elder, gives the child and the mother gifts. The linguist takes some of the drink around to each guest to offer a toast and to pronounce the child's name. The meal, even if it is breakfast, follows like a dinner banquet, with fufu, soup, and beer.

The Ga of Ghana have a more elaborate ritual, as reported by Kofi A. Opoku (Opoku 1978). The elders are more numerous and the head elder recites a more detailed moralistic libation prayer.

The names of children among other peoples of West Africa seem to be more meaningful than the names the Akan give their children, except for such names as Nyamekye (Gift of God, like the Greek names Theodore or Dorothy). However, a note of caution is in order here. While Nyamekye (female form: Nyameama) seems to be a nice name, among the Akan it sometimes implies that the father is not known or that the father refuses to name the child (Sarpong 1974).

Many of the names Achebe gives his fictional characters are both traditional as well as functional for the purposes of his story. The Yoruba and the Igbo have only four days to their week. The Igbo call them *Nkwo, Eke, Oye,* and *Afo.* So, like the Akan, boys and girls are named and dedicated to a day spirit of the week. The hero's name of *Things Fall Apart,* Okonkwo, is a combination of the masculine prefix *oko* and the Nkwo market day. If the parents do not wish to stress the sex of their child, they will, like Nwoye, call him Oye's child. Some Igbo and Yoruba names are expressions of a philosophy of life, of praise, of the time of life of the parents or their happy or difficult situation when the child was born, of religious import, and so on. The names express the dignity of a human being or the joy at having a child. Yoruba names include:

Omololu	Children are supreme
Omoleye	Children confer glory
Ibidun	Childbirth is sweet
Owotomo	Money is not as valuable as children
Omotoso	Children are enough adornment

Some Igbo names are:

Mma'du	Let goodness exist. (Actually the word means "human being." When God, Chukwu, said: "Let goodness exist," the first human being came into the world.)
Maduka	The human person is the greatest
Ndubuisi	Human life is first
Nwabuisi	Children are supreme (Ehusani 1991, 151)

Similar names exist among the Efik, Ibibio, and Ebira in Nigeria.

In Achebe's novels some names apply to the *ndichie*, the titled elders and initiates into the *ozo* society. Their title was *ogbuefi,* killer of cows, because the initiation required the killing of a cow to entertain the members of the society (Ogbaa 1992). Praise names are achieved and awarded later in life, and, like our achievement awards, are elitist. Priests are called praise names related to their ritual offices and the deity they serve, the prefix being Eze (priest), followed by the name of their shrine deity, such as Eze-ulu, Eze-ani, or Ez-idemili. In *Arrow of God* even the British officers have names, like Captain Winterbottom, called also Wintabota in pidgen, who was known as Otiji-Egbe, Breaker of Guns (Achebe 1974).

Among the Akan twins are special children. A twin, *ata,* with brother or sister is regarded as a potential helper at the royal court. Identical boy twins *(ntafo)* become the elephant tail swishers at the king's court, while identical girl twins become potential royal wives. Ata always appears in the name of the person. Similarly, the person born after twins is named Tawia. The Ga believe that twins, *haadzii,* are associated with certain sky spirits. Shrines are erected in homes to honor the twin spirits in their midst. Families perform all twin rituals on Fridays. In Ghana the third-, sixth-, and ninth-born children are special and considered lucky. So the names Mensah, Nsia, and Nkrumah often remain as prestigious names.

We began this chapter by discussing the African sense of life, the belief that each human being bears the spark of God's own breath. The Igbo have a saying: *Nduka,* "Life is supreme." Killing a clansman is an abomination. Okonkwo went into exile to his mother's land just for accidentally killing a kinsman. Unborn children are protected and abortion is taboo. There are sacred trees and animals that one does not kill or abuse, like the royal python. Blood is life. Spilled blood is an abomination to Mother Earth. Suicide is never permitted. The hanged Okonkwo was torn down to be carried off like a dog. The sacredness of life explains the importance of virginity, so that the first blood was dedicated to new life. Hence, the personal name of an Ebira, Ehusani reports, could be an expression of an African philosophy: Ozovehe, "The human person is life" (Ehusani 1991).

The dance and the drumming discovered that life as a human being is precious. Life is celebrated every time the clan gathers for festival—to dance, to drum, to sing, to pour libation, to tell the stories of life. But death lurks around the corner. Although the ancestors are revered most after God, the passage to becoming an ancestor is not a journey one eagerly looks for. In the next chapter we shall look at the Akan notion of death, its celebration, and the veneration of ancestors. But we shall also look at another force, like death—the evil force.

BIBLIOGRAPHY

Achebe, Chinua. *Arrow of God*. New York: Anchor Books/Doubleday, 1974.
————. *Things Fall Apart*. New York: Fawcett Crest, 1989.
Adler, Peter, and Nicholas Barnard. *Asafo!: African Flags of the Fante*. London: Thames and Hudson, 1992.
Appiah, Kwame Anthony. *In My Father's House: Africa in the Philosophy of Culture*. New York: Oxford University Press, 1992.
Boahen, A. Adu. *Topics in West African History*. Burnt Mill, Essex, U.K.: Longman House, 1966.
Christensen, James Boyd. *Double Descent among the Fanti*. New Haven: Human Relations Area Files, 1954.
Ehusani, George Omaku. *Ozovehe: An Afro-Christian Vision, Toward a More Humanized World*. Lanham, Md.: University Press of America, 1991.
Ephirim-Donkor, Anthony. *African Spirituality: On Becoming Ancestors*. Trenton: Africa World Press, 1997.
Mbiti, John S. *African Religions and Philosophy*. 2d ed., revised and enlarged. Portsmouth, N.H.: Heinemann Educational Books, 1990.
————. *Introduction to African Religion*. 2d rev. ed. Portsmouth, N.H.: Heinemann Educational Books, 1991.
Mensah, J. E. *Asantesem Ne Mmebusem Bi*. Kumasi, Ghana: Kumasi Catholic Press, 1992.
Obeng, J. Pashington. *Asante Catholicism: Religious and Cultural Reproduction Among the Akan of Ghana*. New York: E.J. Brill, 1996.
Ogbaa, Kalu. *Gods, Oracles, and Divination: Folkways in Chinua Achebe's Novels*. Trenton: Africa World Press, 1992.
Opoku, Kofi Asare. "Aspects of Akan Worship." In *The Black Experience in Religion*, edited by C. Eric Lincoln, 285-299. Garden City, N.Y. : Anchor Books/Doubleday, 1974.
————. *West African Traditional Religion*. Accra, Ghana: FEP International Private Limited, 1978.
Rattray, R. S. *Religion and Art in Ashanti*. London: Oxford University Press, 1954.
Sarpong, Peter. *Ghana in Retrospect: Some Aspects of Ghanaian Culture*. Tema, Ghana: Ghana Publishing Corporation, 1974.
————. *Girls' Nubility Rites in Ashanti*. Tema, Ghana: Ghana Publishing Corporation, 1977.
Yankah, Kwesi. *Speaking for the Chief: Okyeame and the Politics of Akan Oratory*. Bloomington, Ind.: Indiana University Press, 1995.

STUDY GUIDE

1. Discuss and relate each of the spiritual elements of the Akan psychology to the social relationships an individual has, for example, the relationship of the *sunsum* to the father's *ntoro* grouping and to his water deities.

2. What is the significance of a matrilinear clan relationship in West African societies as exemplified in the Akan cosmology?

3. What is the *chi* in Achebe's novels? Explain the meaning of guardian spirit and how it can be "worshiped." What moral implications can be derived from the concept of the *'kra*?

4. Discuss the notion of the *kradin*, the "soul-name," and the relationship of the person to God and his or her destiny.

5. Compare the Yoruba notions of the *emi* and the *ori*. How do they differ and how are they similar to the Akan notions of *'kra* and *sunsum*? Explain the notion of the *sunsum* as a personality as well as the person's "double," which can roam about at night. Compare the Mandinka *ni* and the Hausa *kurwa* with *'kra* as life principle, and the Mandinka *dya* and the Hausa *iska* with the Akan *sunsum* as a person's "double" that can leave the body during sleep and become visible in another form (consider the Scottish "wraith").

6. What is the significance of the *ntoro*? How do the paternal groupings among the Akan relate to the father figure in the family and to naming?

7. Discuss the *mogya* and how blood relationship is set up in the clan and in the lineage. Show this from the history of the Asante Nation.

8. What is the *asafo*? Research the significance of the *asafo* flags.

9. Chart the social hierarchy of Akan society, with the *omanhene* at the top. How do the traditional chiefs line up for battle formation? What are their titles?

10. Discuss the marriage customs of the Akan. What is the role of women in the clan? Discuss the role of the queen mother and the other female heads. Why is the role of women so significant in the matrilinear system?

11. What are the moral implications behind the nubility rites of the Asante for motherhood and for a good relationship between husband and wife?

12. Class project: Write a ritual for the outdooring and the naming of an Akan baby. Do a class presentation with a narrative and a performance in full dress of the ceremony. You may be eclectic but try to be as authentic as possible. To make it more local, refer to local river or lake or ocean deities in the libation.

13. Discuss the role of boys and men in a matrilinear society. What is the role of the *wofa,* the uncle?

14. Discuss African names from West African ethnic groups, such as the Yoruba and the Igbo. Why is context important for understanding the names and naming?

15. Go through Achebe's *Things Fall Apart* and *Arrow of God* and list the names of the characters and the villages and relate them to the different ways names are given, such as dedicatory names, praise names, metaphoric names, and other names that refer to lineage in the matrilinear society of the Igbo. A good source for this is Kalu Ogbaa's *God, Oracles, and Divination.*

16. Discuss the symbols of the naming ritual: clear water and alcoholic drink, the similar sounding *nsu* and *nsa,* the other gifts, and so on. What implications does this ritual have, especially considering what was said about the importance of discreet speech and how the Akan admire the wise use of proverbs and other figures of speech? Read chapter 4 of Yankah (1995). There Yankah discusses the meaning of the naming ritual and the meaning of speech in Akan culture, including the use of proverbs.

17. Discuss the fictive forms of marriage. From other sources discuss their meanings. Why are they misunderstood by outsiders? The linguist or king's spokesman is sometimes called the king's wife. He even celebrates rituals similar to marriage. If the king dies, the linguist must pass through a period of ritual widowhood. Discuss the meaning and implications.

18. Anthony Ephirim-Donkor discusses the Fante viewpoint of the Akan personality in his book *African Spirituality: On Becoming Ancestors.* However, he does so in terms of developmental psychology. Note his version of the myth of the Old Woman pounding fufu. Chapter 2 discusses various theories concerning the spiritual elements, which indicate a wide variety of witness from the elders the researchers consulted. The reader should be cautioned that the author refers solely to Fante terms with a Fante emphasis, which may differ somewhat from the other Akan groups. It therefore does not always address the approach of all Akan people, just as this book does not represent every detail of Akan spirituality. Ephirim-Donkor does present some Fante details worth noting, such as the concepts that relate a child to his or her father.

4

Every Spirit Is Reflected on Earth

THE PHYSICAL AND SPIRITUAL WORLDS

From dance to talking drums, from language to ritual prayer and symbol, from storytelling to proverb and wit, the Akan cosmos reflects a traditional system of life replete with rituals, beliefs, behavior, and worldviews, that we in the West call religious. Akan religion is so different from the highly moralistic and dogmatic notions we have inherited from Christianity, Judaism, and even from Islam that much of what is described is dismissed as mere superstition, primitive, or simply weird. The reader may be tempted to think that we are studying anthropology but not religion. We need to emphasize that religion is a system of symbols, as Clifford Geertz reminds us (Geertz 1973).

Akan and much of West African traditional society is permeated with symbolism in major as well as the most banal of activities. Ritual and visual and audio symbolism define relationships among persons, between living persons and the ancestors, on the one hand, and between those same living human beings and other spiritual entities that are simply presumed to exist. The relationships are holistic. They define a certain order without questioning how or why something is done or used in the ritual. As Appiah notes, the ancestors are the sources of the tradition, but they are not around to question (Appiah 1992, 111). We could make up our own stories about the symbolism of a ritual, he says, but a symbol is always somebody else's symbol, and, to say that it originates from the decree of some unknown ancestor is good enough reason to accept it as religious and part of the overall cultural baggage of the Akan, even if we (meaning all non-Akan observers) think it is not religious and/or is perhaps primitive. Religion and its ritual overflow into other areas of life. We have noted how the art of conversation oils the wheels of society like palm oil flavoring yams. The handshake and the snapping of the fingers on the palm of the hands are relational rituals. I have not attended a single fund-raiser or social activity in Ghana that did not require the appointment of a chairperson to preside and a master or mistress of ceremonies to conduct the function, from a highly ritualistic opening with libation or prayer to a final "vote of thanks." The easy flow from "nontraditional" ritual structures, such as strict adherence to Robert's Rules of Parliamentary Order, to the more traditional pouring of libation or effusive words of respect bestowed on the honored guests, does not in any way contradict the Akan worldview. If the ancestors were around, they would certainly do it this way.

What is important is that ritual is coupled with beliefs and fundamental assumptions that the physical world reflects in exact order a spiritual world. Things here on earth reflect in some way the spiritual world. Akans perform activities and make symbols and say things on the authority of the ancestors and ultimately on God. When the rituals and symbols are accumulated, they constitute what anthropologists term *culture*. But culture is not static. It changes with contact with other cultures and with the exigencies of the times; however, it is always buttressed with the traditional mode of ritual "as it was in the beginning." Appiah remarks that "though there is a religious component in the installation of a chief, as there is in any ceremony in Asante, that does not make the installation an essentially religious act" (Appiah 1992, 113). The installation ritual is a religious act because of the relational activity the ceremony implies with regards to the ancestors and the spiritual order of the Akan universe. To quote Appiah: "Ritual entails symbolism" (Appiah 1992, 113). If the symbolism derives its meaning from the ancestors' authority, then it is religious in its deepest sense. It is "derived from the conception of relations between people and spirits as relations between persons" (Appiah 1992, 114). Appiah compares notions about what is religious with Islam and Christianity, each of which has its corpus of doctrines that one needs to profess in order to convert to that religion. Akan religion, however, has no similar doctrine. It is a system of ritual, practice, and belief that we call religious. The contrast is sharply drawn, says Appiah, quoting from a remark of Chinua Achebe's: "I can't imagine Igbos traveling four thousand miles to tell anybody their worship was wrong!" (Appiah 1992, 114). The same could be said about Akan religion or any other African Traditional Religion.

We remarked that culture is dynamic, not static. Traditional culture, as a way of life and a way of coping with the exigencies of time and place, changes and is not closed. Yet it is fundamental. An Asante, a Fante, an Ewe, or a Ga, in Ghana, for example, who is educated in the former colonial language, or has acquired a degree in law or science, or is even is a member of the Christian clergy, does not find it at all contradictory to follow traditional beliefs and rituals along with those of Christianity. Later on, we shall discuss where Christianity or Islam diverge from Traditional Religion in actual practice.

For the Akan, as for the rest of Sudanic West Africa, culture is anthropocentric. The living and the living dead form a unique community. Mbiti has declared that in the African context "to be human is to belong to the whole community and to do so involves participation in the beliefs, ceremonies, rituals and festivals of that community" (Mbiti 1990, 2). The religious context of the cultural complex centers first of all on the ancestors and then on the problem of evil or those forces that disrupt the equilibrium of community. Kwesi Dickson, a Ghanaian theologian, remarks:

> The African sense of community requires the recognition of the presence of the ancestors as the rallying point of the group's solidarity and they, being the custodians of law and morality, may punish or reward in order to ensure the maintenance of the group's equilibrium. (Dickson 1984, 70)

The ancestors form a part of the extended family. After death they live in proximity to God the creator. They "have clout" with God. They sanction the moral life of each and every person as well as the entire community by reward or punishment. They can relate to other spirits, both benevolent and malevolent.

The Akan cosmos includes Onyame, God, the creator of every creature spiritual or material. God bestows the *'kra* on each human being and sustains everything and everyone, as the adinkra symbol *Gye Nyame,* "Only God," suggests. The Akan recognize two poles in the spiritual order. There are the river spirits, who are male, the ancient tutelar deities, the *tete abosom,* whose task is to protect the villages, towns, and traditional states from any evil. They are the *ntoro abosom,* the father spirits, from whom every Akan receives a name on his or her father's side of the family. At the other pole there is Asase Yaa, the Earth Goddess, God's consort. Earth is not strictly a deity, but rather a force to be reckoned with; it has its own taboos and demands. After all, one is buried in the ground, where one becomes an ancestor.

But there are other forces, such as those spirits brought into Akan land from northern Ghana, the *abosom brafoo,* such as Tigare, Kune, or Nana Tongo, who can be influenced to kill or bring sickness upon one's enemies (Opoku 1974). This leads us to consider bewitchment and sorcery, the manifestations of evil through which the African deals with whatever deprives one of unity and harmony within society.

The evil all must encounter, but also the door through which one "crosses the river" from this life to the life of an ancestor, is death. While we deal with the ancestral beliefs and with the problem of evil as central to the Akan religious cosmos, we shall discuss in this chapter dying and death and funeral rites. Then we shall investigate the ancestral beliefs and practices. Finally, we shall define in general what is meant by the "evil force."

FUNERAL RITES *(AYIE)*

Birth is regarded by the Akan as a death in the spirit world. A spirit mother is bereaved, for she has lost her child to a mother in the physical world. The Akan do not therefore regard a newly born baby to be settled in this world until it has lived for eight to ten days. It is considered only a visitor from the ancestors' world *(samando)* until "it has come to stay." If the child should die within the eight days, it is given a rather summary treatment, as we noted in chapter 3. Among the Fante the body of such a child is called *kukuba,* "pot-child." The relatives place the body in a clay vessel and bury it on the trash heap outside the village. The parents do not mourn publicly, and their purification ritual is kept to a minimum (Christensen 1954, 68; Bame 1991, 120).

The burial of a pre-adolescent child or even of a younger teen is not elaborate. Christensen notes that it is difficult to generalize about the burial of a late teen. It may depend on the wealth of the father, whether or not the youth was a Christian, or whether he or she was a well-respected student at school by the other youth (Christensen 1954). I have observed during the burial rites of a late teen secondary school student in the Kwahu traditional area, the son of a reigning local village chief, much beloved by his fellow students, and a Catholic by the name of Martin Osei, that the celebration was very elaborate in both the traditional rituals and in church. I have noted in other youth burials that the body was even taken out on the soccer field to play one last game before the family took the body for burial.

There are two dimensions of the entire ritual of death: the burial rites, and the funeral or final obsequies, as they are called in English. The burial usually occurs within a day of the death. The various funeral rites take place from a week to a year after the burial. The death of an adult is observed solemnly by the *abusua* at its expense.

When it is apparent that a patient is about to breathe the last breath, an elderly female relative gives the patient a drink of water with a little prayer that he or she depart peacefully and take the water for the "journey." Death is regarded as a trip "across the river." As on any trip, a person takes some water both at the start and at the end. Asante elders are normally accompanied by a blood relative on trips, just in case they should die while on the road. The maxim says, "The one without a blood relative dies thirsty."

There are a number of rituals performed after death before mourning is permitted. The body is washed by women from both the mother's and the father's side. Once the family has been informed and everyone is in agreement about the arrangements, the body is laid in state with the best clothing on the bed, usually on the left side facing east.

Since health, illness, and death are more social and cultural than biological in African contexts, the disruption of the ordinary through death is a highly social event. The family is first informed of the death, and then the public gets to know of the event through drumming, wailing, and the shooting of guns. The wake is formally begun and the mourners enter to wail for the grief of the family. Adults fast from food. Among the Akan there is much heavy drinking of alcoholic beverages. Women sing dirges. The people arrive in their mourning adinkra and other somber wrappers. Some relatives wear red bands on their heads or arms and dance a sorrowful dance. Other relatives shave their heads, and the hair is piled up at the entrance of the compound. The larger the size of the heap, the greater the number of children and grandchildren the deceased had in a long life. Small children smear red clay on their shaved heads and run up and down the central street of town proclaiming that no fasting need be done, implying that such a father or mother was so distinguished in life, having had so many descendants, that everyone should rejoice for having one like that for an ancestor (Bame 1991). The children seem to honor the dead already, while back at home the professional mourners incessantly cry and moan, reciting stereotyped verses. When a woman loses her husband, she sometimes wears a raffia twig on her elbows to signify that she now has no one to support her. Another relative wears some leaves, or bites a twig of leaves in his mouth, to indicate that he has no one to support him and is reduced to wearing leaves (Sarpong 1974).

The wake lasts from the evening to the dawn of the next day, called the *nsaguda,* the libation-pouring day. The *abusuapanyin,* the head of the blood relatives, performs the rituals. With a calabash or glass of schnapps or rum he stands at the head of the gathered relatives to offer the first libation to the *saman* or spirit of the deceased. He tells the ghost that he and the family wish to say farewell and to make certain that the *saman* is escorted safely to the abode of the ancestors. He makes a lengthy speech, stopping from time to time to pour a few drops of the liquid on the ground, while a family linguist addresses the gathering with a word of approval, such as *Ampa!* "That's true!" or *Hwiem!* "That's right!" In the meantime, the gravediggers from both sides of the family have poured libation to the earth and ancestors to prepare the grave. They have secured a coffin, which in some cases is designed according to the deceased's wishes, perhaps like a boat, if he had been a fisherman, or a luxury car, if he always wished for one, or even an airplane, probably to "cross the river" in style.

After the libation the family places the body in the coffin and lays other objects there, including some gold dust or money, some food, and a little drink. A maternal relative releases the *'kra* from the lineage, and a paternal relative leads the procession to the cemetery, followed by children and relatives and guests. The drummers and other mourners make more sorrowful noises. The children lower the coffin into the ground and libation is poured once more when they cover the coffin with soil.

The solemn mourning sometimes lasts for two more days, while the relatives gather to take stock and to settle accounts for the deceased and for the funeral. Purification rituals are performed and the burial service comes to a close. The subsequent funeral rites take place on the eighth, fifteenth, and fortieth days, and at the first anniversary. The Fante and other Akan continue to remember their dead through libations and festivals. The elders say: "The funeral of the royal blood never ceases." This means that all who are of free-born ancestry, *odehye,* are considered royal or patrician, as opposed to strangers and slaves (Christensen 1954).

Widows and widowers go into mourning for one year, often wearing black or red clothing or bands. Widows isolate themselves and are attended by elderly women. At the end of three months of mourning both the Fante men and women perform ritual ablutions in the ocean, if it is convenient, because they believe that the sea spirit, Bosompo, is very powerful and can restore things to normality once more (Christensen 1954).

THE ANCESTORS *(NANANOM NSAMANFO)*

Death is an evil that disrupts the harmony of the family. The gathering of the relatives and friends and the proper observance of the burial and funeral rituals express the belief that harmony is restored during the time of family stress through the correct passage of the deceased to the abode of the ancestors *(samando).* Intense preoccupation with death and the rituals of dying and burial seems to outsiders to be excessive. But the Ga have a proverb: "Plenty meat does not harm the soup." In other words, more is better than less. The more people involved and the more time consumed with the right ceremonies, the more effective will be the total restoration of harmony in the community. This principle applies to other rituals and applications of religious activity undertaken to solve problems that have created confusion in one's personal and communal life. We shall return to this later.

Once the deceased is properly escorted into the abode of the ancestors, he or she joins the revered forebears of the clan. The *mogya* turns into the *saman,* or ghost, which now is a *sasa,* a spiritual power, which can influence the living for good or for bad (Bame 1991). The ancestors, *nananom nsamanfo* (the Igbo call them *indichie*) are venerated, but not worshiped. They are very powerful in their own right because of the close relationship they continue to enjoy with the living and, because now joined to the spiritual side of the cosmos, they have earned clout with God and with other spirits. Formerly, when West African society was totally oral in its tradition, one learned everything about one's language and culture from the parents and elders. The living elders are the link with the ancestors, who have already crossed the threshold of death. The ancestors are thus the bearers of tradition, the link with the past of one's clan and ethnic group. They reach to the mythical point of the foundation of the nation and state with the common ancestress. The ancestors are the bond for the present generation with its past, for all who hold tightly to their dancing, drumming, proverbs, folktales, myths, symbols, art, and all the other signs of tradition. The justification for certain modes of behavior is placed on the customs handed down from time immemorial. We have noted above that certain rituals are performed because the ancestors have decreed them to be so. What the symbolism means is not always clear, except that certain things are done as signs of respect and rituals are carried out simply because "that's the way it has always been done" (Wiredu 1991, 213; Appiah 1992, 111).

One of the reasons for the daily reference to the living-dead, as Mbiti calls the ancestors, is that they will continue to be concerned with the problems of the family and clan to overcome all forms of evil in the world. The living defer to them in the hopes that one of them will reincarnate in one of their children to bestow blessing upon the family. The living listen for their instructions and obey their authority, for they have knowledge about life and its problems. If one should return to this world, life's problems can be surmounted.

The story of Okonkwo in Achebe's *Things Fall Apart* is one of failure to care for and honor his ancestors, especially his own father. In some ironic fashion Okonkwo becomes the first modern Igbo even though he still lived in the traditional society just before things began to "fall apart." Achebe notes that "age was respected among his people, but achievement was revered" (Achebe 1989, 12). As a young man Okonkwo achieved wealth and titles, but he would commit several blunders that derived from his fundamental lack of respect for his father, Unoka, whom he declared a failure without achievement. Even though Okonkwo enjoyed wearing the mask of the ancestral founders, the *egwugwu,* of the nine villages of Umuofia, his crimes against them and against the Earth Deity, Ani, eventually brought about his downfall by suicide. Okonkwo's ambitions to succeed worked out contrary to his own traditions, as prophesied by his living elders, Uchendu and Obierika. While attempting to become an ancestor himself and to be reincarnated in his Igbo world, Okonkwo fared worse than his own father, "to be buried like a dog." He used his religious practices as a pretext to pursue his private ambitions, and so he worked against the unity of his fellow villagers and clansmen, even while he lamented his own son's conversion to the white man's God and the future empty ancestral shrines. As the first modern, he rejected the traditions of his forefathers and was cursed with failure and useless death. Like Ezeulu, Okonkwo tried to fight the fight of the gods instead of simply acting as an "arrow of god" (Ogbaa 1992).

Okonkwo's tragic story elucidates for us that not every Igbo qualifies to become an ancestor and in this way a candidate for reincarnation. Indeed, he may have become a spirit that inhabited the "evil forest" or that was reincarnated as *ogbanje,* an evil spirit that attempts to torment mothers with babies born only to die again, as was the case of Ezinma. Such spirits have to be exorcised by powerful medicine men, who exhume the *ogbanje*'s "evil stone," the *iyi-uwa,* to neutralize the spirit (Achebe 1989).

Every West African wishes very much to live well and in the end to die well in order to qualify for membership among the ancestors. Among the Akan one must live a life worthy of emulation; one must live normally to a ripe old age and have had children and grandchildren. Death by accident, by tabooed causes, and by infectious diseases all disqualify a person in Akan, Yoruba, and Igbo societies (Assimeng 1989). In contemporary Akan society, where heavy drinking at funerals and fasting for days weaken the drivers' perceptions, more funerals result from accidents on the road home. One wonders if exceptions are now made for so many otherwise noble people coming to such untimely deaths. Those who suffer from leprosy or from dropsy are said not to qualify. However, since the causes of illness and death are attributed to witchcraft and sorcery, recourse to divination and oracles seeks the underlying solution to the problems. We shall return to this topic later on.

Ancestral beliefs underscore the following basic beliefs about the Akan worldview.

1. There is a strong understanding about life after death. Human relationships cannot be broken even with death. One remains a family member. One is never alone.
2. The living-dead are expected to continue to protect and guard the living with their increased power.
3. When things go so bad for the clan or lineage, especially when the living cannot provide effective leadership in a time of crisis, the ancestors will send one of their own to lead the people at the appropriate time. A charismatic person is often said to be the very reincarnation of the revered ancestors. Such a person is called Nana (grandfather or grandmother), even as a child.
4. The ancestral beliefs act as a form of social control by which the moral behavior of individuals and groups in the community is regulated. The constant reminder of the glorious deeds of the ancient ones recounted in the rhythm of the talking drums, in the enactment of the myths, in the telling of the folktales, and in the wise use of the proverbs spurs one to imitate them. The reminder that those who lead an immoral life will not be admitted to the ranks of the great ancestors serves as a goad to right living (Opoku 1978, 38-39; Wiredu 1991, 212-13).

The Akan honor the ancestors, particularly the royal ancestors in every traditional area and town where royalty are sitting on the stools of their ancestors. We have referred to the rituals of the Adae Festival every month, when the king or local chief enters the royal stool house to venerate and recall the great deeds of the royal ancestors. The stools represent the ancestors. (*Ote nananom akonnwa so,* "He sits on the ancestral stool.") During the Adae days, the king and his elders go to the stool house to perform rituals of purification. The blackened stools receive the offerings of blood and food. While the king sits in state to receive his subjects on this day, the court poet *(kwadwumfo)* recites the magnificent activities of the past kings, whose stools are preserved, so that the reigning king will follow in their footsteps and himself be revered as they are. The king is supposed to be holy in the sense of being set apart but also in the sense of a good moral life. He is accorded the utmost respect, but he also must exercise self-restraint; his least sign of annoyance may unleash extraordinary forces that no one wants to encounter.

At the end of the ninth Adae a new year is ushered in with great festivity in honor of the ancestors. Most Akan celebrate the Odwira or Great Purification Festival at this time. This festival has always been taken seriously as a time for stocktaking of the year just ended and as a period of spiritual cleansing. At the end of the eighth month the ritual of *adaebutuw* is performed; it calls for the ancestors to rest and all other religious rituals to be suspended for the next forty days. It is a time for quiet and meditation. The drums are retired, and sometimes the head drummer *(asokwahene)* dismantles the drums for repairs. Most elders leave for their villages, and practically all traditional administration is suspended. Even elaborate funerals are not permitted during this time since the elders themselves, not to say the ancestors, are not to be disturbed. At the end of the forty days the festival is celebrated (see chapter 1). They bring out the new yams for the first time, and the elders once more offer libations and thanks to the ancestors, who are awakened from their month-long slumber.

Among the Yoruba and Igbo the ancestors control the ordering of the local town and village through secret societies or ancestral cults. The Yoruba have the Egungun and Oro cults, both regarded, according to Kofi Asare Opoku, and used as "instruments of discipline and execution" (Opoku 1978, 47-48). The Egungun are masked figures who dance through the streets on festival days and speak in a high pitched voices, which, it is believed, is the way people in the ancestral world speak. Where among the Akan the kings perform priestly functions and lead the veneration of the ancestors, the Yoruba Egungun perform sacrifices to honor the dead at the planting season. Afterward the masked men appear in the streets, drumming and dancing, as they proceed to the chief's house. The Egungun cult is a way for sons to continue contact with and to honor their dead fathers. Neglect in the honor of the dead is a very serious offense. So, the Egungun cult becomes a way to ensure that their honor is not forgotten. The rule of the ancestors is brought upon society, such as upon stubborn youth and criminals, through the actions of the Egungun, which is enough to chill even the hardest heart. Even wayward, despotic kings fear possible removal and banishment or worse.

The masks are distinctive, along with the peculiar costumes and cloths. Many of the masks are plays on the supposed attributes of the red savanna monkey, which, according to the foundational myth of Egungun, was the neglected dead father of a king who returned from the dead to be buried with the correct rites (Drewal 1992). Part of Egungun activity is simply to have fun and engage in horseplay as well as to honor the dead.

The Igbo in eastern Nigeria honor their dead with the Mmo ancestral society. At seasonal festivals the men appear with white painted masks to give the impression that they are spirits. The Mmo is divided into age sets, beginning with boys about eight years old. One stays with the age set throughout life, and together they advance from one rank to the other. The more physically fit belong to a branch group called the Ayaka society (Opoku 1978, 48). Achebe recounts that Okonkwo was a member of one of those age sets. The hero was moreover a member of the nine-man *egwugwu,* the founding sons of Umuofia. Their head was Evil Forest, who wore a smoking mask. But Okonkwo himself looked horrifying. "He looked terrible with the smoked raffia body, a huge wooden face painted white except for the round hollow eyes and the charred teeth that were as big as a man's fingers. On his head were two powerful horns" (Achebe 1989, 85-86).

In addition to the masks the Igbo use other ancestral symbols, including the *ofo* stick used by the family head as a symbol of authority. Libation is sometimes offered to the ancestors through the *ofo.* Another type of wooden stick is the *okpensi,* about 6" to 18" long; sometimes men carry it around, but they also hang it in the hut with the *ikenga* or personal ancestor (a kind of benign power that enhances personal advantage). Finally, there is the ancestral stool, the *okposi,* where the ancestors sometimes reside (Opoku 1978). Achebe mentions several of these in *Arrow of God:*

> Ezeulu rose from his goatskin and moved to the household shrine on a flat board behind the central dwarf wall at the entrance. His *ikenga,* about as tall as a man's forearm, its animal horn as long as the rest of its human body, jostled with faceless *okposi* of the ancestors black with the blood of sacrifice, and his short personal staff of *ofo.* (Achebe 1974, 6)

The incident where Akukalia split Ebo's *ikenga* in two was an abomination, as if the latter had already died and joined his ancestors. The symbolism of these so-called fetishes was indeed great in traditional society. They were, as we have noted, relational symbols, which kept people in contact with the spirit world but were not worshiped in themselves. They assured the worshipers of some measure of comfort in a world hard to comprehend where evil lurked around every corner.

THE EVIL FORCE

Death and the causes of dying and death are central concerns for the peoples of West Africa. While there is a strong belief in life after death and while the role of the ancestors is prominent in the religious life of the clan and lineage, the West African is not eager to attain the distinctive title of ancestor just yet. In prayers to the ancestors at libation pouring the person asks for health, long life, children, and prosperity in this life. No one ever prays for future happiness in a life after death. Once a person is dead, every minute detail of the burial and funeral ritual is meticulously followed. For the good of the clan and society, everyone makes certain that the departed family spirit sets out on the journey to the ancestral world. Sarpong reports how a mourner cries out to the deceased during the wake: "Farewell, you priest!" "When you start out, do not tarry, O Prince!" "Receive condolences and proceed!" (Sarpong 1974, 22). The deceased takes gifts for the journey, and then is almost shoved on the way lest the living be tainted by the death.

The ancestor is a revered spirit; nevertheless, West Africans regard death as unjust. Death is a ruthless oppressor that delights in stealing away one's spouse or parent or friend. The proverb notes that death is almost personified as an evil force: "When death overtakes you, you do not say to it: 'Look, there is an old woman; take her first.'" At the time of mourning at the wake the bereaved often shout out to death itself or to the departed to take the surviving dear ones along with them: "Father, come and take me away with you!" Of course, such exaggerated pleas are not to be taken seriously. As the saying goes, so truthfully and rather cynically: "'I will come with you,' or, 'I will go with father,' is only said to deceive a deceased person" (Sarpong 1974, 22).

The West African knows that death is unavoidable. Ultimately, he or she knows that God is the author of death. On the other hand, since God is good, merciful, and kind, the West African refuses to accept that God is the immediate cause of illness and death, except for a notorious criminal. In that case, the death was a blessing on society. The maxim says: "If the Almighty has not killed you, but a human kills you, you do not die." Other than punishment of a very evil person, no death is considered natural. Death is the result of some evil force—a broken taboo; a terrible misdeed, conscious or not; the activity of witches or sorcerers. Such a death seems to a dear relative or friend to be a cruel punishment. Death finally is determined by fate, which God decides or even one's own *'kra* establishes before birth. While bad diet, disease, anxiety, hostility from other persons or groups, and so on, may be noted as the real causes of death, they are always precipitated by other equally real personal and social malevolent forces. In traditional religious culture one does not ask "Why?" for the causes and diagnosis of some personal problem. One instead asks "Who?" "Who is the cause of my illness? Was it I or someone else?" (Masamba ma Mpolo 1991, 24, 81).

Traditional African Religions are constantly dealing with death and its causes. They are religions of fear, anxiety, and constant ritual activity employed for the systemic control of evil. The frequent ritual observances of problem solving as a means of liberation are indulged in, including libation, traditional medicine, observance of totemistic practices, taboos, divination, and charms. The evil force that confronts African religious systems sometimes means evil divinities, but in many societies, including the Akan, they are not clearly defined. In the Akan cosmos the spirit forces are the sources of witchcraft, sorcery, and ritual manipulation (magic). They are not, however, personified like a devil or evil spirit. God does not have any evil rival. Max Assimeng refers to a single evil force as the symbolic term for the unseen, unpredictable, vitally pervasive force, which he calls in Twi the entity of *honhom fi* (Assimeng 1989).

Assimeng translates the term variously as "dirt, pollution, danger, or evil, not in the ordinary sense, but in a ritual, spirit-charged sense" (Assimeng 1989, 62-63). Not all misfortunes are attributed to the work of *honhom fi,* he says, and many elders recognize this. Evil, such as death, may be turned for the prestige of the family, which is often done among the Asante and other Akan during funerals. The display of wealth with the kind of coffin they purchased, the drinks they supply, the funeral clothes they wear, the bands they hire to drum and sing, the firing of guns, the gifts brought by relatives—all enhance the corporate image of the lineage in the local community (Bame 1991). Some misfortunes, such as the headache of a single person, may be looked upon as an ordinary sickness curable by any medicine. But an epidemic of greater proportions in a village—for example, a large number of children coming down with chicken pox—normally is considered inspired by witchcraft. A diviner is called for immediately. That is what is meant by *honhom fi,* an evil that is out of the ordinary, for which they say, *ennye kwa.* The remedy is proposed, which usually consists in various rituals; in the use of medicine found in herbs, roots, and leaves; or in charms or talismans.

It was because Africans seemed to place so much significance in charms and amulets and in other ritual objects that African Traditional Religions were labeled fetish or juju. The mistaken notion that Africans were infatuated with the objects and worshiped them as gods contributed to the notion that African Traditional Religions centered around the objects. If Africans themselves refer to Traditional Religions as "fetish," and the shrines and their priests are "fetish," and their rituals as "juju," it is simply because of their own assessment of their gods as minor and the objects only as means to an end, namely, to overcome evil wherever it is found or known to exist. If the gods do not produce the goods, as it were, they and their ritual objects are treated with ridicule. One does not act that way with God or the ancestors. They are serenely and sublimely good, while the gods and other objects that represent them can be tainted with the evil they propose to eradicate.

In the last analysis the purpose of communal dancing, drumming, singing, telling of folktales, dramatization of myths, the spicing of speech with proverbs and riddles, and the whole cult of the ancestors is to ward off death as long as possible, to enjoy good health, and to find happiness in this life on earth through the prevention or avoidance of any evil force a person or a community should encounter. It is only with this insight that we now turn to the study of the totems and taboos, the use of charms, the meaning of magic and witchcraft, the role of the deities, and ultimately the place of God in African Traditional Religions.

Religion, to recapitulate, is life in West Africa. Without the correct understanding of the religious basis of reality, we cannot begin to grasp the West African worldview and the intense desire to succeed in life. When there is evil on hand to deal with, the West Africans will, through a bending with the wind, as it were, make the most of a bad situation and wait patiently for the solution to the problem. For "if Nyame has brought the sickness, he will also provide the right medicine."

BIBLIOGRAPHY

Achebe, Chinua. *Arrow of God*. New York: Anchor Books/Doubleday, 1974.
————. *Things Fall Apart*. New York: Fawcett Crest, 1989.
Appiah, Kwame Anthony. *In My Father's House: Africa in the Philosophy of Culture*. New York: Oxford University Press, 1992.
Assimeng, Max. *Religion and Social Change in West Africa: An Introduction to the Sociology of Religion*. Accra, Ghana: Ghana Universities Press, 1989.
Bame, Kwabena. *Profiles in African Traditional Popular Culture: Consensus and Conflict*. New York: Clear Type Press, 1991.
Christensen, James Boyd. *Double Descent among the Fanti*. New Haven: Human Relations Area File, 1954.
Dickson, Kwesi A. *Theology in Africa*. Maryknoll, N.Y.: Orbis Books, 1984.
Drewal, Margaret Thompson. *Yoruba Ritual: Performers, Play, Agency*. Bloomington: Indiana University Press, 1992.
Geertz, Clifford. *The Interpretation of Cultures: Selected Essays*. New York: Basic Books, 1973.
Masamba ma Mpolo, Jean. "Kindoki as Diagnosis and Therapy." In *African Pastoral Studies/Etudes Pastorales Africaines*, ed. Jean Masamba ma Mpolo and Daisy Nwachuku, 74-99. New York: Peter Lang, 1991.
Mbiti, John S. *African Religions and Philosophy*. 2d ed., revised and enlarged. Portsmouth, N.H.: Heinemann Educational Books, 1990.

Ogbaa, Kalu. *Gods, Oracles, and Divination: Folkways in Chinua Achebe's Novels*. Trenton: Africa World Press, 1992.

Opoku, Kofi Asare. "Aspects of Akan Worship." In *The Black Experience of Religion*, ed. C. Eric Lincoln, 285-99. Garden City, New York: Anchor Books/Doubleday, 1974.

————. *West African Traditional Religion*. Accra, Ghana: FEP International Private Limited, 1978.

Sarpong, Peter. *Ghana in Retrospect: Some Aspects of Ghanaian Culture*. Tema, Ghana: Ghana Publishing Corporation, 1974.

Wiredu, Kwasi. "Morality and Religion in Akan Thought." In *African-American Humanism: An Anthology*, ed. Norm R. Allen Jr., 210-22. Buffalo: Prometheus Books, 1991.

STUDY GUIDE

1. What is the difference between the Western mode, centering as it does on ideology or philosophy, and the African mode, centering as it does on ritual and symbolism? Since there is a difference, does this require Westerners to change our method of studying African Traditional Religions? How?

2. What is the meaning of culture? How is culture dynamic? How does ritual feature in African cultures to build up those cultures? How does religious symbolism permeate the whole of the African cultures?

3. How do the ancestors control the systems of social control in African societies? Does community solidarity revolving around the ancestors ensure security? How?

4. What is the role of the *ntoro abosom?* Who are the *abosom brafoo?*

5. Explain the importance of the funeral rituals from childhood to adulthood. What is the significance of the burial rites and the funeral rites?

6. Describe the meaning of the rituals of burial.

7. How does the death of a clan member disrupt the equilibrium of society? How does the clan handle the disruption?

8. How did Okonkwo refuse to honor his father? What was the spiritual revenge he ended up enduring?

9. Describe the ancestral beliefs. What is the meaning of reincarnation in the African sense?

10. How does the Adae Festival give honor to the royal ancestors among the Akan? What is the purpose of the Odwira Festival?

11. What is the meaning of the Egungun among the Yoruba? How do the men honor their ancestors with this society?

12. Compare the Egungun with the Mmo society among the Igbo. What is the social function of these societies?

13. Explain the "evil force." What explanation does Assimeng give?

14. Show how the cult of the ancestors and the preoccupation with the various appearances of evil are central to African Traditional Religions.

15. Note the funeral preparations in Achebe's *Arrow of God*. Why were the obstacles placed by Ezeulu regarded as extreme?

16. Look up articles dealing with the Ghanaian art of coffin carving, with costume designs of the Egungun and Mmo societies, and with mask making. Note the manner of decorating around cemeteries.

5

"The Mouth of the Elder Is More Powerful than the Amulet"

THE LAND

When the African dances, especially the male, he firmly stomps his feet and grinds them into the earth. Connectedness with the earth here and now affirms the this-worldliness of African religions and cultures. Punishment and reward due to life on earth are meted out in this world. The highest form of reward is return to this life. And so the dead are quite alive in the spirit world. They have the power to punish and to haunt the living if their last wishes and the burial rites are not carried out correctly and profusely. Once the rituals are carried out, the living can live in peace and the dead are assured that one day they may return to this world.

Life affirmation and connectedness to the earth above the grave still admit to roots and origins from within the earth. We saw that in the myths of clan origins. The common mother of the clan rose out of a cave deep in the earth. Interestingly enough, the trickster animal of the folktales, often called the wayward son of God, is the owner of mystical knowledge having to do with the riches of the earth. Among the Akan, I think that Kwaku Ananse is not only sometimes the manifestation of Onyame, but he is the link between the living and the ancestors with their knowledge of culture and life. The ground-dwelling spider comes out of its burrow, where it has lived in close proximity to the ancestors. Like the crab, another symbol of earth and sea, digging out of the sand, the spider crawls out with a message from the ancestors.

The possible foundation of common West African ancestral beliefs and the link with the earth may have originated in the continent's first agriculturist sedentary communities in the area known today as the Sahara some seven or more millennia before the rise of the Nile Valley civilizations (Farrar 1993). As the Sahara suffered increasing desiccation from 4000 B.C.E. onward, the Saharans migrated in different directions southward to the west and the east to search out pasturage and water resources. Those who settled West Africa developed the farming of the tropical staple grains millet and sorghum in the savanna and the African yams and the oil palm in the forest belt (Farrar 1993). The West African neolithic farming system developed between 4500 B.C.E. and 1500 B.C.E. Toward the end of this early period, around 1500 B.C.E., a forest people established an early urban society in an area not far from modern Kumasi in Ghana; archeologists call this the Kintampo culture site of Boyasi Hill. There they have discovered the remains of an architectural tradition that antedates the pre-colonial Asante civilization (Farrar 1993). We have also mentioned the Nok culture that developed in Nigeria's Jos Plateau region, the first known iron working culture from around the mid-first millennium B.C.E. Over all, the ancestors had built up West African spiritual and material cultures beginning with the development of the land. As each group separated from an original group and settled in new areas, the group discarded some old ways of coping with the environment and events and developed new ways, often unique to the area.

The land developed by the traditional group or clan and inhabited by it belongs to the ancestors. The living are merely the custodians of the land; they are not permitted to sell the land but only to use it or to lease it. The land and the water areas within it become the symbols of the relationship the living have with the spiritual world, the basis for the different ways individuals and groups learn to cope with the evils that hide within and behind the perceived world and for the various beliefs that teach the living how to maintain an equilibrium in their world.

While there are common elements in West African cultural baggage, there are also many different elements as well. And while it is recognized that there are cultural differences among linguistic groups, it is not appreciated that there are in many cases cultural differences *within* linguistic groups. Hence the development of symbolic systems for the ordering of the world upon the land, while holding to common elements attesting to the common origin in ancient times of these people, have vast and complicated differences as well. So, we are forced to generalize sometimes and then to point out distinctive aspects, especially of the Akan, at other times. The differences between the Asante and the Fante among the Akan are well recognized. The influence of the Akan languages and cultures is noted in the case of the Ga in southern Ghana. A common element through all is the origin of the land. The myths of creation state that the land was created by the sky-god. The Yoruba, for example, explain the origin of Ife from the myth of Olodumare and the establishment of the Yoruba urban culture at the center of the earth. Yet the land of the ancestors and its use are also governed by another spiritual force, the Earth Spirit. In every society this deity is a woman.

THE EARTH GODDESS

We expect an earth-oriented culture to declare that the earth contains divine qualities. Among the Akan, earth is a goddess, Asase Yaa; the Fante show their difference in naming her Asase Efua. In either tradition the goddess is the consort of Onyame. She is sometimes called Aberewa, "old lady." The Akan erect no shrines to her, and she does not have a priesthood. She is not an oracular deity whom people consult in critical moments. In fact, Earth is not even a deity in the sense of the spirits below Onyame. The Akan elders say: *Asase nye bosom, onkyere mmusu,* "Earth is not a deity, she does not interpret evil things" (Opoku 1978).

In contrast, the Igbo regard the Earth as very central to their belief. She is Ani, sometimes called Ala, Ana, or Ale, the giver of every good thing. She is regarded as the daughter of Chukwu, the Creator, and the goddess of fertility, who herself gave birth to a host of other deities. The Igbo gave her a priesthood, but they erected for her temporary shrine-like huts, called *mbari*, which housed sacred sculptures of her and other deities and human beings and animals. Women came to her to beg for children.

Achebe in *Things Fall Apart* notes the significance of Ani at the feast of the new yam:

> It was an occasion for giving thanks to Ani, the earth goddess and the source of fertility. Ani played a greater part in the life of the people than any other deity. She was the ultimate judge of morality and conduct. And what was more, she was in close communion with the departed fathers of the clan whose bodies had been committed to the earth. (Achebe 1989, 37)

The statement Achebe makes about Ani being the ultimate judge of morality and conduct brings us back to the relationship the people have to the land. Although we noted that rituals and customs are derived from the traditions handed down from the ancient ones, the ancestral rules of behavior have as their authority the Earth Goddess, embodied by the land as the womb where the ancestors lie and where a baby's umbilical cord is buried. In another sense *land* means the community, which is ruled by a paramount king together with other kings and chiefs representing the ancestors, the true owners of the land. And so the whole system of rules of behavior is land-centered. There are customs, totems, taboos, and medicines derived from the land, based on the ancestral codes concerning respect for the land. Among the matrilinear Akan, some of these areas of behavior are found in the clan systems, especially when carried out by the kings and other rulers. But these overflow into the patronymic groups, where the river deities as part of the land are worshiped, including their shrines and oracles. For the present we shall refer to the taboos of the land, and then to the other taboos relative to groups in general and to special persons. We will then mention the totems as they are expressive of taboos. The actual evils Africans encounter are discussed in terms of bewitchment and sorcery in their social context. Finally, we shall discuss the diagnosis of the evils through divination and the cure through the use of social palaver, medicine, and amulets.

TABOOS AND TOTEMS

A taboo *(akyiwadie)* is something that is bad, because a nonhuman being or force considers it bad and so one needs to avoid it. No other reason is offered for why a thing should be avoided except that noncompliance will bring disaster (Wiredu 1991). Some taboos are really customs or what we sometimes in the West call superstitions; for example, the Akan believe that if you sing while bathing, you will lose your wife or your mother; or if you cut your nails just after having your evening meal, you bring bad luck (Sarpong 1974). A genuine taboo is much more sacred than this.

A genuine taboo includes those things forbidden or required always because they are offenses against the ancestors and Asase Yaa (Efua). For example, it is strictly forbidden to till the soil on Thursday (or Friday among the Fante). To do so would bring dire consequences not only upon the individual but upon the entire community. Moreover, when a farmer is about to plow the soil before planting, he must offer sacrifice to Asase Yaa with chickens and scatter the blood over the ground to be plowed under. Or before a grave is dug, the deceased's children pour libation to Earth and the ancestors. More specifically, taboos against the land and therefore against the ancestors and Asase Yaa include these:

1. To swear by hitting the ground is not permitted.
2. To have sex in the bush, on the farm, or on the bare floor is not allowed.
3. To kill by shedding blood upon the ground is forbidden.
4. To commit suicide is an act against the Earth.

The prohibition against sex in the bush also seems to be quite common among other West African ethnic groups. Even to have sex with one's own spouse in the bush is extremely obnoxious to the Earth Goddess, and she will visit her wrath on the entire community by destroying the crops (Wiredu 1991). We have noted earlier that such offenses are what the Akan term *musuo*. To avoid a disaster after such an offense, the principals of the offense must provide ritual blood sacrifices to appease the deity concerned. It is interesting to observe that killing by shedding blood on the earth through murder or even by accident must be appeased by shedding the blood of a sheep or cow on the very spot in order to avoid similar crimes there. The land is purified by sacrificial "gathering" of the spilled blood.

Taboos admit of degrees of importance. It is morally wrong to commit adultery with another man's wife. But it is an evil sin to commit adultery with the chief's wife or to insult the chief or to steal from a deity's property. In fact, the latter prohibition is viewed in terms of a disruption of the social fabric, and that makes it more serious than a taboo forbidden by a deity.

To return again to the prohibition against sex in the bush (meaning the farm land or forest), the elders and the wise men *(anyansafo)* would say that the wisdom behind such a taboo is clearly meant to issue a stern warning to sex-starved men who may be tempted to rape an unsuspecting maiden in the unpoliced fields (Wiredu 1991). Similarly, the taboos against cutting yam tendrils on another's farm or changing land boundaries at night are rules regulated today by public legislation to protect the economic life of the community. Even a taboo against fishing in a sacred river or hunting in a sacred grove was in some fashion meant to protect the environment and wild life.

Certain taboos apply to special persons. For example, the *asantehene* and some other high-ranking kings and chiefs may not touch the ground with the soles of their feet. During solemn festivals a number (depending on the chief's rank) of attendants carry spare sandals just in case the ones he is wearing break.

A priestess of a shrine or a trainee is forbidden to do or eat certain things during periods of ritual liminality. For example, the trainee during her novitiate may not eat sweets, or drink alcohol, or eat *kenkey* (a cornmeal dough ball) on days sacred to her deity, and so on (Opoku 1978). A menstruating woman may not cook for her husband or have sex with him during her menses. We have noted that the ban on sex while a woman is pregnant and during the period of lactation was one of the incentives for polygamy.

In Achebe's novels about Igbo traditional culture references are made to certain persons who have themselves become taboo to the rest of society, partly by custom or "ways of the land" *(omenani)* and partly by the decrees of oracles (shrines of deities) that they have become an abomination. Twins are abandoned in the bush (Achebe 1989) and their mother is ostracized. The oracle pronounced Unoka an abomination to Ani because of his "swelling sickness" and because of it he "could not be buried in her bowels" (Achebe 1989). Even Okonkwo's suicide met the anger of Ani as he himself had so many times in his life and he was "buried like a dog." Worst of all was the cruelty handed out to an *osu*, an outcast slave to a deity. He was an *efulefu*, a useless person. The convert explained what an *osu* was to the Christian missionary:

> He was a person dedicated to a god, a thing set apart—a taboo for ever, and his children after him. He could neither marry nor be mar-

ried by the free-born. He was in fact an outcast, living in a special area of the village, close to the Great Shrine. Wherever he went he carried the mark of his forbidden caste—long, tangled and dirty hair. A razor was taboo to him. An *osu* could not attend the assembly of the free-born, and they, in turn, could not shelter under his roof. He could not take any of the four titles of the clan, and when he died he was buried by his kind in the Evil Forest. (Achebe 1989, 146)

In *No Longer at Ease* Okonkwo's grandson, Obi Okonkwo, could not marry Clara because she was an *osu*. Representatives of Umuofia in Lagos and even his parents (both devout Christians) back home rejected the marriage proposal on that account and because of an ancient oracular pronouncement.

Related to such personal taboos are the animal taboos and totems. A totem is more than a mascot. It is usually an animal—rarely a plant, except perhaps the baobab tree—that is associated with the clan or the patronymic group, like the *ntoro* among the Akan. Such animals are considered sacred to the particular group, and therefore it is taboo to kill or to eat the animal. It represents a certain character often illustrated in the folktales. Sculptures of the totems sometimes appear on the linguists' staffs. Other animals and plants are simply considered taboo but not sacred in the same way a totem is. For example, the totem *(atweneboa)* of the Bosompra or the Pra River *ntoro* group is the leopard. Taboo *(akyiwadie)* for this group includes eating of a white-feathered chicken, the wateryam, and the drinking of palm wine on Wednesday. The Bosomuru group has the mouse for its totem. Its members are forbidden to eat or kill the cow, the fox, the dog, the monkey; to eat maize on Tuesday; and to drink palm wine on Tuesday. Why? Ask the ancestors.

Like the ground-burrowing spider mentioned above, these animals have human characteristics and feature in the folktales. In a sense they are like the living shrines of the ancestors and are one of the means ancestors use to communicate with the living. Diviners (discussed below) take the dog for their totem because they learn to sniff out the problems of their clients. The trickster hare and the slithering python are admired and therefore respected.

WITCHCRAFT AND RITUAL POWER (MAGIC) OR SORCERY

Striving to live successfully on this earth is often thwarted by many obstacles that will eventually lead to death. The *honhom fi*, the evil force, lurks within every shadow in the village and in the forest. Observing taboos and respecting totems are ways to preserve the harmony of the community. But other forces both within a person or family and outside them are evident in illness, infertility, and other misfortunes. Among other things, such as breaches of taboos or even contact with a corpse or a leper, the causes that precipitate illness—aside from recognized natural ones, such as death in old age—are witchcraft and sorcery. Earlier we discussed how a person with a "light" *sunsum* could easily become victim of an evil force and come down with an otherwise unexplained disease. We also noted that most often the question asked for why one becomes ill or suffers from some other mishap in life is not "Why?" but "Who?" What is sought in every illness, whether physical or mental, is its symbolic meaning or significance. And that usually points to some human factor within or without the afflicted person and the clan or lineage. The diagnosis and the cure of the patient through divination by a seer with herbal medicine and by the use of amulets often points to a person in the social fabric of a family or clan who has caused the problem, usually a witch or a sorcerer.

Among the Akan witchcraft may be good or evil. Usually it is evil. The word for witch is *obayi,* which comes from *oba,* child, and *yi,* to take. In the Caribbean, the word became *obeah,* and the "obeah-man" was the good doctor who countered the evil. The name means that a child is taken from birth, usually a female, to become a witch. Either the child inherits witchcraft *(bayie)* from its mother or it acquires the ability from her mother's bathing in the river after a witch had bathed there and washed herself of nocturnal filth before returning home in the early morning (Opoku 1978). The witch's power is a psychic force residing in her *sunsum,* which she can call forth merely by wishing it. She may own a pot of oddities, such as human hair or nails, fish, cocoa, kola nuts, and herbs, but these are not really the source of her power, which increases as she grows older. Witches are said to make nocturnal visitations in groves and even on top of the baobab or silk-cotton trees. Their *sunsum* flitters here and there freely while the body of the person lies asleep. They are said to ride on spider webs, on the back of toads or rats. Some can change themselves into snakes, leopards, or antelopes. They emit flames from their eyes, nose, mouth, ears, and armpits. They walk on their heads. The Yoruba believe that witches move about while flying on the spirits of birds. The Igbo say the witches turn themselves into night birds, like owls or bats, or into insects, like mosquitoes or beetles (Opoku 1978). Whatever happens to the animal at night happens to the witch. So if the beast is killed or captured, so is the witch.

The common belief is that witches "eat" their victims. The *sunsum* of the witch consumes the victim's *sunsum* with bodily effects, for example, ulcers on the legs, boils, infections, severe headaches, or even "holes" in the pockets that cause the victim financial loss. The eventual evil worked by bewitchment is the victim's death.

Another evil deliberately concocted by human beings is sorcery or ritual power, usually termed black medicine. It is countered with white or moral medicine, also a form of ritual sometimes called magic. In either case visible means are used, usually referred to as *suman* (amulet) or *aduru* (medicine) by the Akan, such as charms, amulets, herbs, or ritual incantations, to generate mystical forces into action either for evil or for good of individuals or groups. At this point we are discussing the form of sorcery that consists in the manipulation of symbolic forces to cast evil effects on others. This is the type of African religious practice that is sometimes defined with the terms *fetish* or *juju.* The practice of magic for evil or for good is usually described with the classical definitions first proposed by James Frazer: the law of similarity and the law of contact or contagion. The law of similarity operates when a magician makes an object or image to resemble the victim. Whatever he or she does to the object analogously is done to the victim. So, to burn the object or to prick it with thorns is intended to cause burns or pains in the body or mind of the victim. This is the classical image one gets of *juju,* which literally means "a doll." The law of contact or contagion works on the principle of contiguity, where things that have been in contact with the victim's person can be manipulated to cause harm to the person until the contact is broken. For example, hair, nails, underwear, jewelry, even footprints, are manipulated through rituals, prayers, damage done to them, and so on, to cause harm to the individual, such as impotence or infertility (Opoku 1978).

While the evil force is at work everywhere, it is not the sole source of every misfortune. West Africans recognize natural causes too; for instance, when termites eat through roof timbers and the ceiling falls down, or when people grow old and die. God is the cause of such problems, and no one raises a question why. But when a roof caves in faster than normal or when one dies prematurely, then questions are asked and reasons are sought out because these phenomena are out of the ordinary, *ennye kwa* (Assimeng 1989). At this point sometimes frantic running from one question to another occurs in order to search out the mystical force behind the misfortune. This is where we start to look for the diagnosis and the cure.

SOCIAL PALAVER, DIVINATION, MEDICINE, AND AMULETS

If Onyame is the reason for the misfortune, then because "If God caused the sickness he provides the cure," if the situation worsens no one can do anything to change it. After that, the victim or the household head tries various means of discovering the cause of the illness or bad luck. The origins of the problem may be the ancestors, the Earth Goddess, one of the local deities, one of the "spirits of the wild," or ultimately bewitchment and sorcery. Sometimes the problem arises simply from intra-family or village conflicts. We shall discuss the deities and their shrines and oracles and the "spirits of the wild" in the next chapter. Here we concern ourselves only with the diagnosis and cure.

From the African point of view, physical or mental illness is not merely biological but is more appropriately psychosocial in both etiology and diagnosis. Misunderstanding of this viewpoint by colonial governments and Christian missionaries has resulted in ineffective denouncements of sorcery and traditional medicine as pagan and unscientific. However, as Jean Masamba ma Mpolo remarks, elaborate and advanced African traditional medical and mental health systems have long existed. "The babalawo tradition among the Yoruba, the usenakpo, specialized in solving emotional problems among the Ibos; the Sikidy in Madagascar; the ngamba-ngombo and nganga-mbuki among the Kongo of Central Africa, are some of the traditional systems and institutions specialized in contributing to health and healing through guidance, diagnosis, counseling, divination, telepathy, etc." (Masamba ma Mpolo 1991, 12). Africa was not devoid of physical ailments. Nor was there a lack of emotional stress and phobias in traditional societies due to required rituals, taboos, socio-ethical codes, and familial conflicts resulting in various neuroses and forms of psychoses. Sometimes severe mental disorders are allowed to persist if no cure is found. I have encountered mental patients walking on the streets of Cape Coast (perhaps escapees from the nearby Ankaful Mental Hospital) or Tema who were totally naked and unconcerned about their appearance. These cases are tolerated and are considered harmless. Of course, contemporary rapid urbanization and industrialization have produced their own forms of "Western" illnesses. But urbanized Africans still view many of their problems in terms of the violation of traditional norms and seek out the cure accordingly.

Seeking the welfare of the community and lineage is the basis of the social and political life. Moral obligations are rooted in social life. So a person's worth is measured in his or her personal and social relationships, which assure him or her as an individual of success in life, good health, and potency or fertility. Both wealth and health mean primarily well-being in mind, body, and spirit. While the family and community are central to this equilibrium for wealth and health, individual achievement is the mark of a life well lived. For that reason, when illness does strike, the individual suffers, but normally not alone. The sick person turns to those who live together with him or her in the same or nearby household. Relatives are usually consulted who rally around the patient to provide comfort and to suggest remedies. Elders are summoned who first observe if the sickness can be cured with the herbs or the "white man's medicine." This first stage is called the *social palaver.* The elders decide what other steps are needed to secure the diagnosis and cure and how to provide for the needs of dependents. The kin group shares the expenses of the treatment. In some cases the entire kin group, usually the lineage, might undergo some form of dietary or ethical taboo for the sake of the sick person. As Kofi Appiah-Kubi observes, the kin group is like an "extended patient" (Appiah-Kubi 1981). If there is no other apparent reason for the illness, and it is not too serious, the elders apply their own remedy, for most people have a store of the common herbal remedies. Since many villages are remote, people know of the herbs and roots needed for common ailments such as malaria. Recall how Okonkwo diagnosed his daughter Ezinma's fever, *iba,* and went into the bush to collect leaves and grasses and barks of trees to make a medicine for her (Achebe 1989).

If home remedies fail, there are several types of healers the group might appeal to. Appiah-Kubi lists first the herbalist, the person knowledgeable in all natural medicines. Then there is the diviner or diagnostician, whom we shall discuss next. There is the traditional midwife, a woman who attends childbirth but who also has skills in other family medicines, especially dealing with women's problems and children's sicknesses. There are those who are skilled in bone-setting and problems of the joints, such as arthritis. Finally, there is the exorcist, popularly known as witch-doctor or medicine-person *(duyefoo),* often a priest of a shrine familiar with both herbalism and the use of charms and other spiritual powers (Appiah-Kubi 1981, 35-36). The latter type of healer is sometimes regarded a magician or sorcerer for good rather than evil, though some say such healers also perpetrate evil.

From the types of healers, one may surmise about the categories of medicine. There are the general remedies known to all. There are family secret remedies handed down from parent to child. There are the methods of diagnosis known only to initiated diviners, the real problem solvers who recommend going to the next step. The last type are the specialists, initiated into the arcane secrets of very special remedies, the gathering of which is often accompanied with special rituals (Appiah-Kubi 1981). We shall refer to the shrine priests in the next chapter. They are often diviner, doctor, and priest combined in one person. Sometimes the priests of the "spiritual churches" fulfill a similar function. Here I wish to discuss the role of the diviner and the various forms of medicine.

Divination is a type of diagnosis of all types of problems with regard to the community and the individual. The problem to be solved touches on all areas of social and private difficulties in life where no apparent solution is at hand. The diviner is a trained interpreter of cultural and social change who attempts to diagnose the root problem and therefore eventually to recommend the type of solution a group or a person may resort to. Even today, when rapid social change confuses those accustomed to tradition, divination remains for most of Africa a source of vital knowledge for decision making.

Divination is therefore a system of knowledge, sometimes quite complicated and related to an oral tradition, like the Yoruba Ifa Odu, where set verses accompany the type of throws of kola nut or cowrie shells. In Akan the diviner is called from the *omusu kyerefo,* the removers as well as the interpreters of mischief or misfortune. In many ways divination stands at the heart of an ethnic group's worldview, with all its cultural knowledge spread out before us, the "outsiders," so we can arrive at a "thick description" of each ethnic culture. Philip M. Peek rightfully declares:

> The situating of a divination session in time and space, the cultural artifacts utilized (objects, words, behavior), the process of social interaction, and the uses made of oracular knowledge all demonstrate the foundations of a people's world view and social harmony. Divination systems do not simply reflect other aspects of a culture; they are the means (as well as the premise) of knowing which underpin and validate all else. Contemporary Africans in both urban and rural environments continue to rely on divination, and diviners play a crucial role as mediators, especially for cultures in rapid transition. (Peek 1991, 2)

People with all sorts of problems seek out the diviner, who tries to discover the roots of the problem and the solution, whether sacrifice, medicine, or rituals. The diviner as mediator often refers the client to other specialists, such as the shrine priests. The diviner, moreover, might point to a particular witch as the real cause for the disharmony one suffers, whether as an individual or as a member of a clan or village. In other words, the diviner, starting from scratch with precise methods of questioning and in concert with the spirit world, attacks not only the symptoms but the underlying problems.

Kofi Appiah-Kubi relates the following story:

> Akosua and Amma were very good friends. Akosua started flirting with Amma's husband, and the result was an unexpected pregnancy. Akosua was embarrassed but could not bring herself to confess to her friend. When Akosua was in labor she became very wild. The doctors helped her deliver her baby, but after her delivery Akosua became more violent and uncontrollable. The doctors diagnosed a mental breakdown (psychosis) and advised she must go to a mental hospital. After some weeks of observation and treatment, Akosua was getting worse and worse, and the family removed her to a traditional healer. Through divination, Akosua was brought to confess to the infidelity. Akosua's parents were told to pacify her friend and ask for her forgiveness for the offence. Amma, at this stage, had no alternative but to forgive her friend. A sacrificial meal was prepared and Akosua and her friend Amma, with a few of her relatives, shared a meal. Akosua was purified of her pollution, and peace was made between the two friends and the families. Akosua is now back to normal. (Appiah-Kubi 1981, 75-76)

This story indicates that Western medicine does not always adequately deal with deep-seated needs of Akan patients. This is why sometimes Akan and other Africans utilize both types of medicine, the "white man's" for the individual and the African's for the social and religious implications of illness. The familial and social dimensions of the Akan practice of medicine are clearly more pronounced than the more impersonal Western method.

Many African societies resort to divination before hunting or fishing, and especially before warfare. In these situations types of medicine belts are divined before the activity to determine if they will be effective. The medicine in this case is preventive, an aid against the evil forces lurking in the forest or savanna. The medicine protects the hunter or warrior from being killed or wounded. In any case, the problem-solving technique is a religious and a cultural experience.

A person's own sins and breaches of taboos are internal factors the family and elders need to discover. The disfavor of the ancestors or deities and the hatred or evil thoughts of others, usually in one's very own family or among friends, are the two outside forces believed to precipitate illness or bad luck on the field or in the forest. What Western doctors and counselors among African peoples must learn are that the social and cultural implications of the perceptions of a bewitched or troubled person should be a vital part of the diagnosis and therapy.

Finally, we end here by returning to the land. The medicines, whether in the form of a powerful object containing a spirit, usually a charm or amulet *(suman)*, or in the form of a vegetable-derived medicine, like roots, barks, leaves, seeds, and juices or oils, all are earth related. Whatever means necessary to restore equilibrium to the body, mind, and society somehow are a return to the earth-endowed values from the things the earth produces. If a human makes an object, he does so in order that a spirit possess it. The African world is cosmic, and so disease or other misfortune derives from a broken society. The individual's cure is relative to the cure of the disequilibrium in society. The Akan have a proverb: *Obi nko obi abusua mu nkoyere,* "No one goes to another clan to bewitch people." The evil worker is not far away. The medicine that caused the harm is close by, just as the abode of the ancestors is near under the earth, and not far away is the medicine growing out of the earth to effect the cure. Even if the concept of bewitchment could be explained in terms of rejection in family relationships, the medicine and the cure restore the relationship. But the herbs of the earth are nonetheless effective where there is real physical and mental illness.

Appiah-Kubi lists some of the herbs and the mixtures needed to cure certain diseases. For example, the cure for heart attack is to grind the leaves of the *bomaguwakyi* on a grinding stone, add the white of one egg, and mix this to put in a glass for the patient to drink. This should be repeated until the patient is normal again (Appiah-Kubi 1981). A cure for dizziness is to squeeze the juice out of cassava leaves and place the drops in the eyes. Each culture has preserved its oral tradition in the field of medicine. Before we dismiss such remedies as hoaxes, we need to recall that aspirin was first found in the bark of the willow tree, and quinine came from the Andean cinchona tree. Africans too have their remedies against everything from impotence and infertility to measles and stomach ache.

But whatever may be the "real" reason for the problem, the advice of the elders is needed. Even if the amulet or medicine is powerful, the advice of the elder is always the last word. As the proverb says, "The mouth of the elder is more powerful than the amulet."

A corollary to our discussion of the land concerns the dislocation of the African from the land. Since the land belongs to the ancestors, to leave it, in particular by force, as was the case in slavery, was to deprive the African of contact with the ancestors. A consequence of the removal of human beings to new land was to place them in a strange land where they could not reach the abode of their living-dead. They could not pour libation to them, they could not consult them through divination, they could not find cures for their many anxieties. Likewise, colonialism produced a strange new dislocation of many peoples from their land by possession and sale of their ancestral lands. Colonialist policy of the division of the peoples with new national boundaries and new allegiances still disrupts inter-ethnic group activities and has led to wars between peoples in Liberia, Rwanda, Burundi, Angola, and so on. When Africans arrived in the various American colonies, their only solution was to create a new ambience of religious life. With great imagination and resilience they established the "Invisible Institution" as Christian churches in the "hush arbors" and hollows deep in the plantations. And they still stomped on the earth hard enough that the ancestors far away had to hold their ears, the holy noise was so loud!

BIBLIOGRAPHY

Achebe, Chinua. *Things Fall Apart*. New York: Fawcett Crest, 1989.

Appiah-Kubi, Kofi. *Man Cures, God Heals: Religion and Medical Practice among the Akans of Ghana*. Totowa, N.J.: Allanheld, Osmun & Co. Publishers, 1981.

Assimeng, Max. *Religion and Social Change in West Africa: An Introduction to the Sociology of Religion*. Accra, Ghana: Ghana Universities Press, 1989.

Farrar, Tarikhu. "Afrocentric Scholarship and Models of History and Culture Growth." *The Afrocentric Scholar* 2, no. 2 (December 1993): 56-69.

Masamba ma Mpolo, Jean. "A Brief Review of Psychiatric Research in Africa: Some Implications to Pastoral Counselling." In *Pastoral Care and Counselling in Africa Today*, ed. Jean Masamba ma Mpolo and Daisy Nwachuku, 9-33. Frankfurt am Main: Peter Lang, 1991.

Opoku, Kofi Asare. *West African Traditional Religion*. Accra, Ghana: FEP International Private Limited, 1978.

Peek, Philip M. "Introduction: The Study of Divination, Present and Past." In *African Divination Systems: Ways of Knowing*, ed. Philip M. Peek, 1-22. Bloomington: Indiana University Press, 1991.

Sarpong, Peter. *Ghana in Restrospect: Some Aspects of Ghanaian Culture.* Tema, Ghana: Ghana Publishing Corporation, 1974.

Wiredu, Kwasi. "Morality and Religion in Akan Thought." In *African-American Humanism: An Anthology*, ed. Norm R. Allen Jr., 210-222. Buffalo: Prometheus Books, 1991.

STUDY GUIDE

1. What is the relationship between the land and the ancestors? In particular, note the significance of the king or chief among the Akan as the representative of the ancestors and the custodians of the ancestral or stool land.

2. Note the archeological findings in West Africa that establish a long tradition of agricultural practice peculiar to the region and developed by the people who settled there. Read Tarikhu Farrar, "Afrocentric Scholarship and Models of History and Cultural Growth, in *The Afrocentric Scholar* (December 1993), 2:56-69. Recent studies show that West Africans developed forms of agriculture and architecture distinct from those developed in the Nile Valley. Comment.

3. How are the ancestors and the Earth Goddess interactive in African rituals and practices? Note the difference between the Akan and the Igbo beliefs with regard to the Earth Goddess. How does Achebe describe the sometimes cruel oracles proclaimed in the name of the Earth Goddess?

4. What is a taboo? How does the taboo admit of degrees of importance? Illustrate this in the case of the Akan taboos. Explain the significance of the major taboos of the Akan and their sanctions. What are some of the practical meanings of the taboos? Give examples.

5. What is a totem? How does a totem describe the cultural self-understanding of an ethnic group?

6. How does bewitchment symbolize and even realize the brokenness of a society? What are the psychosomatic implications of witchcraft and sorcery?

7. What is the origin of the Akan word for witchcraft? How was this term carried to and modified somewhat in the Caribbean area?

8. Explain the Akan understanding of what a witch is and does.

9. Explain the classical understanding of magic and sorcery. What is wrong with the word *magic* to describe rituals in various world societies?

10. Explain the Akan conception of problem solving in their culture.

11. What is the role of the elders and of the family in problem solving? How was this illustrated in the story of Akosua and Amma?

12. What is the great significance of divination in African cultures? Discuss the Ifa Odu of the Yoruba.

13. How is medicine discovered and how is it applied in Akan society? Do you think that in such an environment it is possible for someone to become a hypochondriac?

14. What happens when the African is deprived of the ancestral land? Since even divination has as its purpose to cope with change, as does all ritual, how has the African succeeded adapting to the harm done by slavery and colonization? How failed?

15. Albert J. Raboteau, in *Slave Religion: The "Invisible Institution" in the Antebellum South* (New York: Oxford University Press, 1978), discusses the elements of African Religions preserved among the African slaves. Note what he says about medicine, root work, the myth of High John the Conqueror, and conjuring. Why does he say that the "gods died"?

6

"You Consult the Spirit Three Times"

MANY GODS?

For the Akan and for most West Africans, religion consists in the means available to counteract evil in all its manifestations and to reinforce life through proper precautions against any destructive powers (Appiah-Kubi 1981, 12). There are enough of the forces around which account for all the wickedness, tragedies, and misfortunes of life. We have noted that divination is one of the ways of discovering what may have caused an individual's sickness. Most of the time the disease or mishap is due to some antisocial behavior such as the individual's own immorality or another's vicious machinations by means of witchcraft and sorcery. However, the spirit world is suspect and divination might point to the ancestors or the deities, who want something from an individual.

Among the ambivalent spirits are those which protect and heal and those which cast spells and disease and other unfortunate problems on persons. Beside the ancestors we can count among the spirit world all the deities and their cults and the so-called "spirits of the wild." We have alluded to them earlier. In chapter 1 we discussed the religious functions of dance, such as the *Akom* dance as a type of corporate worship and spirit possession of a priestess at a deity's shrine. Moreover, we examined briefly the annual festivities where the ancestors and spirits are honored, such as the Apoo Festival at Wenchi in the Brong Ahafo Region of Ghana. Both of these forms of worship, whether at shrines or in the form of state festivals, fall under one of the following classifications, according to Sarpong (Sarpong 1974, 14).

1. There are the major divinities worshiped by one ethnic group, relatively few in number, called the tutelar deities, the *tete bosom* of the Akan, whose function is to protect the state and its towns and villages from any harm. Such are the river deities, all male, very ancient, and associated with the peoples who inhabit the river banks and fish and transport goods along the alluvial highways through the forest regions. Among the Akan these

spirits are the manifestation of the *ntoro* groups with their taboos and names. In Ghana the river Tano, which flows through the traditional states of the Brong and Asante, and empties into the Gulf of Guinea in Fante traditional areas, is the name of a powerful spirit who is regarded as the second son of Onyame. Tano has a major shrine and many minor ones throughout the land. Another river and cult at Antoa in the Asante area is Asuo Nyamaa, a watch-god of moral behavior and mighty in meting out severe punishment in the form of illnesses. Thieves, murderers, and other criminals are required to confess their sins openly and perform various rituals as soon as possible lest they die quickly (*tutuw-bo* is the process of public exposure of a criminal). The Lake Bosomtwe is the abode of the spirit Twe, who has many taboos. The bodies of water are the places where each *ntoro* washes and acquires its taboos and titles.

2. There are spirits of the inhabitants of certain towns and villages. These are local divinities, and they are numerous. Many of these minor deities are connected to small streams and tributaries of the major rivers in Akan traditional areas. Some of them attain broader fame outside of their town or village because of the healing powers of the spirits made manifest through noted shrine priests. For example, at the top of the Kwahu escarpment in the Eastern Region of Ghana lies the sleepy town of Kwahu Tafo. Just outside the town, on the road to the River Afram, stands a tall phallic rock said to be the abode of many spirits. The shrine at the town's edge is called Brukuso, and it is famous throughout Ghana for its healing powers. Its chief priest *(okomfopanin)* wears his office like a paramount king. He is the instructor of other shrine novices as well as diviner and healer of many illnesses. I have lived in proximity to this shrine for several years and witnessed some of its festivals and rituals. Down the escarpment on the road from Nkawkaw to Kumasi near Kwahu Praso is another shrine to a stream deity, Afenasu, at Aboagyekrom, similarly famous for its healing powers through its priest, Kofi Osei, known to his people as Kramo (Appiah-Kubi 1981).

3. Smaller sections of communities and lineages, as well as *asafo* groups, have their spirits and shrines. I have already remarked how the *asafo* military groups among the Fante display mystical forces on their flags and temples (chapter 3). Their spirits are protectors of both the Fante *ntoro* or the *egyasunsum*, the father's ghost and of the local state, which is matrilinear.

4. Finally, there are the spirits worshiped by individuals and by households. These spirits are privately owned and most often are the imported deities of more recent times known as the *bosom brafoo* or the *suman brafoo*, brought from northern Ghana (possibly from Côte d'Ivoire), among which are Tigare, Kune, and Nana Tongo. While they were brought to southern Ghana for protection against witchcraft and other moral evils, they are competitors of the traditional tutelar deities, who were considered weakened by

the arrival of Islam and Christianity. The newcomer spirits can be influenced to kill or bring sickness on one's enemies (Opoku 1974). Sometimes individuals attach themselves to a single shrine and take home a *suman* or amulet or other visible representation of the deity to set up a household shrine before which they offer daily acts of worship in the form of libations, offerings of kola nuts, or an occasional animal sacrifice and the sprinkling of blood on the object. I have recently visited a shrine dedicated to Tigare at Asamankese in the Eastern Region of Ghana and viewed such an object, which looked very much like a blackened coconut. The purpose of such a shrine is protection of the individual and the household. One has to keep oneself morally upright and observe certain dietary rules and other taboos. Infringement of these rules nullifies the effectiveness of the talisman and usually results in punishment of the devotee. However, as we have said, once a deity is weakened, many devotees leave it to look for other remedies to problems, possibly at other shrines. Some deities simply die out from lack of business.

Among other peoples of West Africa the cosmic arrangement of mystical powers varies. Some say the Yoruba have four hundred deities, some say they have five hundred, and some say as many as seventeen hundred spirits in various shrines all stemming from Ile Ife, the mythical center of the earth. The name for deity among the Akan is *obosom,* probably derived from *obo,* "stone," and *som,* "to serve." It is a name applied only to the spirits listed above and never to Nyame or Asase Yaa. Among the Fon of Benin the word for deity is *vodu* (perhaps *vodun*), from *vo,* meaning "set apart," hence sacred (or maybe? "to rest"), from which we get the word *voodoo.* The Yoruba say *orisha* for deity, any of those many deities with their shrines. The Ewe, who inhabit southeastern Ghana and part of Togo, believe in three sky deities (beside God, Mawuga): a thunder deity, his wife, and a spirit of wealth (Nelson-Adjakpey 1982). The earth deities are called *trowo;* beside the Earth Goddess, there are ancestral deities, the *togbuitrowo,* much like the Akan tutelar spirits, and the *dzo,* or fire spirits, the medicine deities much like the Akan *bosom brafoo,* and lastly the personal guardian spirit or *aklama.* The Krobo of eastern Ghana probably attribute more prominence to their deities, the *dzemawei,* than to their ancestors. They are agrarian or land deities the Krobo invoke to help the people root out all evil among them so that the land after the planting will produce its crops. There is a causal relationship between evil and guilt for immorality and crop failures on the farms (Marfo 1978).

The characteristics of West African spirit worship include the following:

1. The deities all have shrines and priesthoods. The priests usually are experts at divining and healing, as well as at the required rituals and taboos with respect to their shrine. Some priests are magicians or manipulators for evil purposes. In any case, the priests are ritual leaders.

2. Spirit possession of both priests and patients; the deity inhabits the body of human beings usually by riding the head. During liminal periods the possessed person speaks in tongues and delivers oracles through a linguist.

3. The use of animal sacrifice, such as goat, sheep, or chicken, and votive offerings, for example, libation in food or drink, and the splitting of kola nuts.

4. Peculiar patterns of drumming, dancing, and singing, even special types of drums for each deity and festival (a point often missed by Western adaptationists); for example, the Krobo at the planting festival engage in ritual hooting and trampling of *koda,* the evil force that negates a bountiful harvest.

5. The use of talismans and charms *(asuman)* as representations of the spiritual powers of each deity, including objects and medicine, such as white clay, flour, and grain and yam products.These items taken from plants or even animals are the so-called fetishes; they contain certain spiritual powers manipulated through ritual to ward off evil or to cause harm to another for the advantage of the owner.

Although each of these characteristics deserves development, we shall discuss only sacrifice, spirit possession, and oracles. After that we will discuss elements of African Religions brought along from the motherland to the Americas.

SACRIFICE

Like libation and prayers *(mpae),* sacrifice in the form of killing an animal and offerings of food, drink, and money abolishes any disharmony existing in the cosmic order of the religious and social fabric of a society. The quality of the sacrifice depends on the deity and the reason for the sacrifice. Here we should include sacrifice offered to ancestors. Sacrifice from ancient times is related to the offering of blood as a symbol for life (note the prescriptions regarding sacrifice in the Old Testament). Analogous to blood letting of an animal is the pouring of other objects, such as libation, and other food offerings, like eggs, at the shrines. The normal sacrifices at household shrines consist in food and money offerings. But sacrifices that must be done for the infringement of a deity's taboos and prescriptions as well as sacrifices offered to ward off misfortune, for example, personal illness or community epidemics, are usually determined by the oracle in the form of animal sacrifice.

In former times among the Akan human sacrifice was required of a royal prince to rejuvenate the *sunsum* of a deity. The annual Aboakyer Festival at Winneba in the Central Region of Ghana at one time required the royal sacrifice of a prince to keep the deity Penkye Otu satisfied. Later, the deity through its oracle accepted instead a leopard, and when leopards became scarce, the deity settled for the blood of the bush buck, which is why every year now the annual deer-hunting festival is observed amid great rejoicing and fun while the various *asafo* groups vie with each other for the prize. Still feared today is the death of a great paramount king among the Akan. On this occasion several young men's heads must roll in order for the dead *omanhene* to take a few slaves with him to the abode of the ancestors. I recall how a young man, the subject of the Kibi (Kyebi) traditional area, took refuge in my (mission) house while the funeral celebrations of the king were observed at Kibi. And my place at Akim Ofoase was many miles distant from the center, even in a distinct traditional area. The fear was still very much alive.

SPIRIT POSSESSION

Appiah-Kubi did extensive field research for his book *Man Cures, God Heals,* published in 1981. He concluded that when a shrine priest or a client is possessed by his god riding on them, he is not unbalanced or insane, or even possessed by a demon. He says the Akan "employ divination to determine whether an individual is having a vision or supernatural experience or is just mad. With the help of divination it is ascertained whether the individual involved is required by a deity to perform such useful functions as healing; whether he is possessed by an evil spirit that has come to destroy him; or whether he is simply insane, as the result of misconduct against a god, an ancestral spirit, an individual, or a community" (Appiah-Kubi 1981, 27). Appiah-Kubi illustrates his point in a narrative about Kofi Osei, a Christian educated at the Catholic school in Kwahu Tafo. At the age of twenty-two Kofi started to act strangely, to talk to himself, and sometimes to strip himself naked. At such times he became unusually strong and difficult to restrain. His family elders tried treatment at the local church-operated hospital in Nkawkaw, where the doctors recommended sending Kofi to the mental hospital at Ankaful in the Central Region. For a year and a half Kofi underwent Western psychiatric treatment with no sign of improvement. Eventually the family removed him from there and brought him back to Kwahu Tafo, where they carried him, in the face of scandal, to the Bruku shrine, even though he was a devout Catholic. Before they could speak to the priest at the shrine, he (the priest) glanced in Kofi's direction and divined that the young man was not mentally ill but possessed by the powerful spirit of the stream at their village Aboagyekrom. The spirit, Afenasu, wanted the young man to be his priest, and unless he did so no amount of treatment would do any good. So Kofi and his family yielded, and he trained to be a priest at the Bruku shrine until he took over at the Afenasu shrine and became a very popular and powerful priest of his deity, expert in dealing with psychiatric and emotional problems and other "modern illnesses"

(Appiah-Kubi 1981). As Kramo, the priest of Afenasu, Kofi cured individuals with financial problems and alcoholics. He advised prominent business people and students. He helped people get jobs and restored relationships between estranged husbands and wives. The priest encouraged his patients to lead a morally good life and to believe totally in God as their helper.

This story illustrates that God has commissioned his messenger deities to do his work of helping human beings to cope with the changing world. It also shows us that the person who was believed to be insane himself became the helper of those with similar symptoms. Possession by a deity, therefore, normally occurs for the good of a broader spectrum of society. Finally, the case indicates that the cultural dimension influencing a person's perception of himself or herself and of the environment should be taken seriously both for the diagnosis and for the therapy. Kramo's capacity to share his patients' worldview helps them to move on to another level of interpretation used by the foreign religions, Islam and Christianity, and by Western medicine. So, one may ask, was the possession genuine? The answer is yes. The skeptic and the pragmatist may not agree, but then they are far removed from the culture described. On the other hand, this is not to say that traditional possession episodes are themselves totally holistic either. They do not help the patient to advance toward a greater self-awareness and emotional and spiritual growth. Always, as we have said before, a "thick" description of any culture is needed for "outsiders" to understand it very well.

ORACLES

Oracles and divination are closely related and often confused. Divination is the method or the act of discovering the reasons for things through the casting of cowrie shells and the like, for example, while oracles are the actual signs or omens of some divine or spirit revelation. Sometimes the oracle is localized in the priest or in the shrine. Divination is therefore the means of discovery of what the oracle signifies. There are usually two forms of oracles, one being involuntary and the other consultative. Involuntary oracles are simply beliefs in signs, omens, and premonitions. Every Akan clan believes in the *asenkyerenee* (good luck sign). For example, for anyone in the Aduana clan or lineage at Offinso in the Ashanti Region it is a good omen to meet a dog or have a frog bump the leg while setting out to farm or to hunt. Dreams are oracular. If a hunter dreams of an animal while in the forest it presages a successful kill. A dream of a dead relative ordering certain things to be performed needs interpretation and therefore divination or consultation to learn the meaning of the demand. Other oracles are consultative, usually at shrines of the gods. Not every verdict of a divination is an oracle, but many are. Sometimes occasions for certain dreams are set up in order to find a solution to a problem. Before major trips by drivers or traders, before building a new house, before starting a new cocoa farm, or before school examinations, dreams are sought from the priests or elders to predict a good outcome of the activity. The Akan use chicken divination to determine the prediction of oracles. They slaughter a chicken and let the body loose after the head is severed. The body flops around until it stops, literally dead. If the chicken dies body upward it is considered a good sign. If otherwise, they repeat the creation of a good sign or oracle, for, as the proverb says: "You consult the spirit three times" (Appiah-Kubi 1981). Most of the time the oracles are pronouncements of the gods when the priests at their shrines have danced themselves into a trance to speak in tongues and deliver messages to clients, prescribe medicine, and give other advice. Among the Akan most shrine priests have specific times when they are possessed by their oracle, very often in cycles of forty-two days (as do the Akwasidae).

We have already noted how Achebe in his novels exploits the belief that literal and slavish obedience to oracles may lead to major calamities. The entire fate of Okonkwo runs from the first oracle against the burial of his father due to "the swelling sickness," through the murder of his adoptive son, Ikemefuna, and two other murders, to his own suicide, all related to "the Oracle of the Hills and Caves." Achebe extends the power of the oracle against the *osu* from *Things Fall Apart* to *No Longer at Ease* and himself considers how sad it is that the divine decree should reach into the twentieth century to touch the fate of a grandson of Okonkwo's marriage to Clara (Achebe 1978). Similarly, in *Arrow of God* Ezeulu suffers because he is obedient to perfection to the god Ulu. Achebe tries to be nonjudgmental about divination and oracles, but he does seem to point out that sometimes the will of the spirits can be manipulated to force the will of human beings upon the characters of his novels, mostly for their harm.

SPIRITS OF THE WILD

The deep, dark, forbidding forest in West Africa contains frightening monsters and magical spirits that form part of the coherent cosmic system. The Akan know of two kinds of spirits that inhabit the trees and rocky places of the jungle. The closest spirit to the devil of Islam and Christianity is the *sasabonsam,* literally the "evil spirit." Village hunters at Akim Ofoase in the Eastern Region of Ghana claim to have encountered this evil spirit sitting in the odum tree, looking like a wild animal with long black hair and a long beard, a flaming mouth, and a tail ending with a snake's head (Opoku 1978). The *sasabonsam,* always evil, are said to be dead witches, who associate with witches at night. The proverb describes this in this way: *Sasabonsam ko ayi a, osoe obayifo,* "When the evil spirit attends a funeral, it lodges with the witch" (Opoku 1978, 73).

Other "spirits of the wild" are the dwarfs, the *mmoatia,* which are not wholly evil, although they inflict punishment on those herbalists who have not followed their directions. Witnesses have reported individuals being kidnapped by the dwarfs, and have noted their size. They are like humans, but one foot tall, with curved noses, yellow skin, and feet pointing backward. They whistle at each other and eat bananas. They live in rocky places in camps. They sometimes capture lone wanderers in the forest and sometimes teach them their secrets about herbs and cures. But anyone they capture they set free and send back home. The *mmoatia* are often associated with the Muslim jinn (genies), which attach themselves to a diviner who conjures them up to discover cures for various maladies. They are not oracles for really serious problems.

THE GODS IN THE AMERICAS

Achebe introduced us to Ulu, a manmade deity, whose oracle seems to reflect the will of the people often opposed by his priest, Ezeulu. The Yoruba have elevated ancestors to the level of divinities. Among them the most prominent is Shango, the *orisha* of thunder, and to a lesser extent, Ogun, the *orisha* of iron. They have a great following among African descendants in the Americas.

Shango

According to Akinwumi Ishola, the popularized myth of the human origins of Shango, the fourth *alaafin* or king of Oyo, who in the end abdicated and hanged himself but was divinized by his faithful followers, is all a falsification perpetrated by a Christian missionary in the 1940s (Ishola 1991). According to the myth incorporated in school books in Nigeria and elsewhere in West Africa and immortalized in the folk opera *Oba Ko So* by Duro Lapido at the University of Ibadan, Shango was the hot-tempered fourth king of the Oyo kingdom, versed in the art of medicinal charms. In a failed attempt to eliminate at least one of two of his war lords the tables were turned against Shango and the king killed many of his own people. In frustration, he abdicated and fled with some of his followers and his three wives. In the end, everyone deserted him, including his favorite wife, Oya. Shango hanged himself (*obaso* in Yoruba) in a fit of depression. His close friends, however, planned a cover-up. They traveled to a distant town and obtained some thunder flint stones and rained thunder on Shango's enemies. They spread instead the story and the saying *oba ko so,* "the king did not hang." According to Ishola's research, this story has become popular throughout Nigeria. But it was the work of a missionary by the name of Hethersett (Ishola 1991).

Historically the story does not match facts about the fourth king of Oyo, who was Babayemi Itiolu, or about the two war lords, who lived earlier in Oyo's history. Second, the popular phrase *oba ko so* should read *obaa Koso,* "king of Koso." According to Ishola's research, Shango's origins are traced back to the mythical foundation city of Ile Ife, where the Ifa or Yoruba divination oracles also originated. According to the Ifa poetry, Shango was in fact a deity fond of dancing. He was also a womanizer and seduced the wife of Ogun. He is the deity who hates liars, but who also helps kings to withstand revolts with his symbol of the two-headed axe. Flint stones found on the farms in Yoruba country became symbols of thunder bolts. When the founding king of Oyo, Jegbe, migrated to where the city stands, he brought Shango with him as his guiding deity. Starting with Jegbe, every king of Oyo was regarded as the personification of Shango. When on the throne the king incarnates Shango. When dead, the king is deified and "becomes" Shango. On account of this, there has been a proliferation of Shango stories and sites of Shango shrines. So, in this sense the fourth king of Oyo may have been Shango (Ishola 1991).

These various kinds of Shango stories were carried along with captive Africans to the New World and survived in predominantly Catholic colonies in a syncretized version of the original rituals, where Shango was identified with a Catholic saint, for example Santa Barbara, the patroness against fire. In Brazil there are variations of the cult of Shango. In Rio it is called Macumba, in Bahia it is Candomblé, in Recife and Porto Alegre it is Xhango. In Cuba, and from there to Cuban centers recently in the United States, it is known as Santeria, the cult of the saints. Other versions are found in Haiti, Grenada, St. Vincent, Trinidad, and Puerto Rico. The devotees in these areas, as well as in contemporary Yorubaland, through trance dances "become" Shango when the deity "mounts" them. Other devotees call these possessed persons *orisha.* Women in particular are regarded as priests of Shango; they worship the god with their breasts lifted in their hands. Where men become the deity's priests, they dress like women to qualify as his wives. The cult of Shango in the Caribbean and in Brazil has served as a way for lower-class people to gain some degree of prestige. In the years of slavery these variations served (disguised as saints' fiestas) to preserve their Yoruba and other African rituals of worship of the deities. With the passage of time, however, Creoles, East Indians, and others have joined the cults, and they have now evolved into New World religions distinct from their original rituals in Africa.

Ogun

Another popular Yoruba *orisha* is Ogun, the spirit of iron and war. Ogun's origins probably reach back to the dawn of the iron age, when blacksmiths were highly respected as mediums for divine revelation and power. The power of iron over stone itself expanded Ogun's influence with the emergence of other crafts and arts, including leather work, wood carving, barbering and tattooing, even surgery and circumcision. In a sense, Ogun in Yorubaland and in the New World is a spirit of many themes. The trance dances of Ogun evoke images of power, masculine strength, and violence. When women are "mounted" by Ogun, their appearance transforms them into male-like figures. They might boldly expose false penises from beneath their wrappers.

Ogun is the first receptor of all sacrifice, since the animals are cut with knives. Ogun is also the overseer of justice in courts. Hence a Yoruba takes an oath on a piece of iron. If a witness should give false witness, he may be visited with horrible punishment from the deity.

In contemporary practice the cult of Ogun is usually found wherever Shango is worshiped. Ogun is the patron of taxi drivers and practically anyone who uses metal. Ogun's symbol is an iron pot containing nuts and bolts, guns and knives, and anything else made of metal.

There are two Yoruba cultural elements related to the use of the blade worth mentioning here. They are the practice of scarification and the nude art. Scarification or tattooing among the Yoruba and other West Africans is often a mark of identification within an ethnic group or clan as well as a mark of beauty. I wish to add parenthetically that among Akan a person is not thought of as complete unless he or she has all the body parts. Some strict traditionalists maintain that even circumcision is taboo. No king or chief may remain on the stool if he loses any part of his body through accident or surgery. Those few Akan who have facial marks are considered to be reincarnated ancestors who were marked after birth to avoid possible return to the ancestral world (Appiah-Kubi 1981). But among the Yoruba scarification of the face of males and the lower parts of women creates works of art. A herbalist makes an incision in the body with a knife and places some herbs in the cut. Sometimes the skin rises over the herbs to leave an embossed form of scar that tickles the sensuous imagination of admirers.

The art of wood carving is similarly dedicated to Ogun among the Yoruba. The knife cuts into the wood or ivory eventually to emerge with a human or divine figure. In Yoruba art, nude figures symbolically represent the "naked truth." Before the advent of Islam and Christianity, which both frowned upon nudity as sinful, Yoruba artists were the cartoonists of their day. They exposed exploitation and misuse of power by their own rulers and by the European slave traders and colonizers through their statuary. The Yoruba appreciate wearing fine clothing. To be exposed naked for stealing was therefore one of the best sanctions. If the rest of the body is nude, at least the genitals are covered. Instead of mentioning the word for the male and female genitals, usually one says the word for buttocks, *idi*. So, the nude in art is literally the truth—everything is exposed, even the genitals. And that is what Ogun stands for. In contemporary art the Yoruba have returned to nude art to protest against poverty and the inequality that exists in Nigeria due to the oil industry and the control of the south by the northerners (Okediji 1991).

To conclude, the deities are not simply spirits languishing and sensuously lying in the shade of the trees in the forest. They have remained very much alive in many areas. Yet they are also losing their followers as the worship of their God is emphasized in different ways by Islam and Christianity. The distant dance of the "no-gods" and the ancestors is now changed to a new dance and a new song sung in honor of God in an epiphany that has changed the religions in West Africa. This is where things have begun to fall apart.

BIBLIOGRAPHY

Achebe, Chinua. *No Longer at Ease*. London: Heinemann Educational Books, 1978.

Appiah-Kubi, Kofi. *Man Cures, God Heals: Religion and Medical Practice among the Akans of Ghana*. Totowa, N.J.: Allanheld, Osmun & Co. Publishers, 1981.

Ishola, Akinwumi. "Religious Politics and the Myth of Shango." In *African Traditional Religions in Contemporary Society*, ed. Jacob K. Olupona, 93-99. New York: Paragon House, 1991.

Marfo, Kofi. *Essays in West African Traditional Religion*. 2d ed. Cape Coast, Ghana: University of Cape Coast, 1978.

Nelson-Adjakpey, Ted. "Penance and Expiatory Sacrifice among the Ghanaian-Ewe and Their Relevance to the Christian Religion." Dissertation, 221. Rome, Italy: Academia Alfonsiana, 1982.

Okediji, Moyo. "The Naked Truth: Nude Figures in Yoruba Art." *Journal of Black Studies* 22 (1991): 30-44.

Opoku, Kofi Asare. "Aspects of Akan Worship." In *The Black Experience in Religion: A Book of Readings*, ed. C. Eric Lincoln, 285-99. Garden City, N.Y.: Anchor Press/Doubleday, 1974.

————. *West African Traditional Religion*. Accra, Ghana: FEP International Private Limited, 1978.

Sarpong, Peter. *Ghana in Retrospect: Some Aspects of Ghanaian Culture*. Tema, Ghana: Ghana Publishing Corporation, 1974.

STUDY GUIDE

1. What is the primary function of the deities?

2. List and comment on the different classes of Akan deities. Note the importance of the tutelar or ancestral deities with regard to the father's side of the family. How can local village deities attain a certain prominence?

3. Who are the *suman brafoo*? How did they come into southern Ghana?

4. What is the purpose of sacrifice in relationship to any particular deity?

5. What is the difference between an oracle and divination? Describe each.

6. How does a spirit take possession of a devotee?

7. How have oracles shown the negative side of Traditional Religions, as described by Achebe?

8. Who are the "spirits of the wild"? How have they contributed to human society, according to local belief?

9. Discuss the influence of African Religions on religious practices in the Americas. How has Shango come to be worshiped? Explain the various forms of the modified African Religions in the Western Hemisphere.

10. Discuss scarification among certain African groups. What was the purpose of tattooing?

11. Describe West African nude art and its meaning.

7

"Except for God"
Gye Nyame

By this time it should be clear that *religion* as discussed in these pages is an analogous term to the *religions of the Book.* Nonetheless, African Traditional Religions are truly religions in their own right. It would be wrong to compare a liturgy or gathering of people for a service in a Christian church with a session at the shrine of a deity like Tano or Shango. In the latter case there are no ordered congregations gathering with hymn singing and scripture readings every week or so. Yet it would be equally wrong to think that, because so much time and effort are expended dealing with the ancestors and the deities, that God, by whatever name God goes in any given language, is not uniquely supreme and the sole Creator as much as Yahweh is, or Allah, or "God and the Father of Jesus Christ." Yet, as in the case of other religious realities, there are differences. The approach taken here is an African Religious Traditions study "from below," beginning with the visible and audible sources of Akan religious practice. The central preoccupation of these traditions is concerned with human beings, living and the living-dead, and with how to overcome the evil forces that may impede one from living a fully integrated life on the land God gave his people. Even as Mbiti has noted, God is above and below, creating and sustaining. God is the force or power for the creativity referred to in chapter 2, where we noted Amadou Hampate Ba's comment that the power of God's word is manifest in the activity of the waly, the wise man, and in the professions of blacksmith, weaver, and farmer or shepherd. The castes of the leather workers and of the griots or bards established that God was within reach. The rituals combined with skills evinced God in the world. The smith was a sorcerer, a worker of good or evil, depending on the context. But none of that power could be utilized without God. Not even the horrendous works of Sumanguru, the smith-sorcerer-king, the antagonist of Sundiata, could be all that evil since in the end he was praised as the "King of Yesteryear" (McNaughton 1995).

Yet Muslim traders and invaders into the Wolof or Soninke societies at first thought the bards were talking nonsense or something satanic. Christian explorers, slave traders, colonialists, and missionaries simply thought the West Africans had no notion of God, or, if they did, that they had borrowed it from Muslims or the Christians themselves. Historically, as Lamin Sanneh remarks, the Christian mission arrived in West Africa in the fifteenth century along with European expansion based upon the desire to circumvent Islam and reach the Orient to search out other areas for Europe's economic markets (Sanneh 1990). The need to spread the gospel established the notion that Africans did not know about God. However, the missionaries soon discovered they had to master the language of the local people and thereby to ask questions about their religious beliefs. It turned out that Africans knew about God. They could describe God eloquently in proverbs and in story, and they revered God in worship and in sacrifice (Sanneh 1990). However much the Europeans tried to suppress the people and convert them to "civilization," as if European culture and progress meant something better, the efforts of missionaries to translate the scriptures into the local languages meant for the Africans a written sanction of their religious heritage. The God of Abraham, Isaac, and Jacob, and the God and the Father of Jesus Christ, was assimilated with the God of the ancestors. Only there was a difference: The God preached by the foreigners was a jealous God, who did not tolerate lesser gods, a God who promoted intolerance and wars. On the other hand, the God of the Africans was a hospitable God, who was mediated through lesser deities (Sanneh 1990). The process of the Africanization of Christianity commenced almost immediately with the replacement of the exclusive notion of Western Christianity with the inclusive rule of African Religious Traditions. Sanneh remarks that by embarking on the translation of the scriptures and other Christian texts, the missionaries stimulated a pluralist ethos of the gospel in Africa (Sanneh 1990). We shall return to this phenomenon in chapter 9.

The judgment made by the missionaries, and later by anthropologists, was that the God of the Africans was a vaguely deistic, distant God, who, once he created the world according to the various myths, left it alone to lounge languidly in his heaven. The Africans did not give their Supreme Being due honor and worship, the outsiders thought.

Responding to this claim, at first some missionaries themselves and then African scholars asserted that they could discover homologies between Western-type philosophies and theologies and African modes of thought. The first to write about African philosophy was the Belgian missionary Father Placide Tempels with his work *La philosophie bantoue,* based upon his

observations of the Shaba Baluba of Zaire (Belgian Congo). We cannot enter into a discussion of his "Bantu ontology," but we can at least comment
on his notion of God. Basically, Tempels regarded God as the creator of a
vital force in all things, even inanimate objects. In so saying, Tempels was
simply endorsing the philosophy of Henri Bergson and his notion of *élan
vital*. It was a question of metaphysics or the study of being. God enters the
scene as the principal force or being. Yet Tempels, while claiming some
similarities with Western philosophy, nonetheless reduced the Bantu notion
of being and therefore of God to a form of "primitive, unscientific" mode of
thought (Masolo 1994). Hence, the Bantu must advance to a superior and
therefore more fulfilling form of humanity by accepting Christian civilization (Masolo 1994). African writers like Fabien Eboussi Boulaga (Eboussi
Boulaga 1984) and V. Y. Mudimbe (Mudimbe 1988) have challenged these
notions as outsiders' "inventions of Africa."

More closely aligned to a theology of African religions are the works of
the Yoruba Methodist clergyman and theologian E. Bolaji Idowu and the
Kenyan Anglican scripture scholar John S. Mbiti. Idowu attempted to reject
the patronizing concept of a remote deity, a God removed from the world:

> Western scholars created an "inferior" god for (to them) "inferior"
> races of the world. It became complicated when he "created" not just
> two gods—one for his race, and one for collective batch of "the primi-
> tives": he retained his own one god and gave his imagination rein to
> overrun the world of "the primitives" with "high gods" of all descrip-
> tions. (Idowu 1975, 65)

One of the ideas abhorrent to Idowu is that God is a "hidden God" or that he
is remote from Africans. Idowu criticizes nineteenth-century missionary
Noel Baudin and scholar Dietrich Westermann for maintaining, among others, that African religions are polytheistic or have lost the idea of a true God
(Idowu 1975). Instead, Idowu—making use of a concept ("refracted monotheism") borrowed from E. E. Evans-Pritchard in his study of Nuer religion
in eastern Africa (the Nuer are a Nilotic people) (Evans-Pritchard 1956)—
introduces "diffused monotheism" or "implicit monotheism" as terms that
adequately define at least the religious systems of the Yoruba, if not perhaps of the whole of sub-Saharan Africa (Idowu 1975). By "diffused monotheism" he means that there is only one God, who creates all the other gods
and spirits, through whom he manifests his creative purposes to the world
of human beings. Thus Olodumare the creator has commissioned his arch-
deity, Orisha-Nla, to create the world at Ife. All other gods, even Shango
and Ogun, when they receive worship and sacrifice, give it to Olodumare.
While Idowu has rejected the notions of those scholars he criticizes, such
as Westermann, he has in fact worked out a theology of the Yoruba belief in
one God in the terms of his nemesis as "the purest expression of religious

thinking" (Shaw 1990, 345). In so doing he may have fallen into the trap of the "inventors of Africa," forgetting that God is also called Olorun, a name Idowu claims is too much influenced by evangelism, but one earlier writers use to describe God as "Master of the blissful abode of the dead" (Onwubiko 1991). Failing to accept this point is perhaps a failure to recognize that Traditional Religions are not always centered on God but on the ancestors, even among the Yoruba, who have such a huge pantheon. Idowu is sometimes driven to exaggeration in his attempt to homologize Yoruba religion with the biblical faith. For example, the Yoruba have a four-day week traditionally, as do the Igbo. In trying to create a day of rest for the gods, Idowu claims they are worshiped on the fifth day (Onwubiko 1991). Onwubiko quotes from the ancient texts of Ifa to make his point about four days of creation rather than five, contrary to Idowu:

> Ifa is the Master of today
> Ifa is the Master of tomorrow
> Ifa is the Master of the day after tomorrow—
> To Ifa belong all the four days the divinities created
>   on earth.
>   (Onwubiko 1991, 79)

The Yoruba tradition not only fails to mention a fifth day of rest for Olodumare, but creation was the work of more than one divinity, Olodumare and his divine agents. Only in the act of creation itself is there any analogy between the biblical and the Yoruba myths.

While Idowu attempted successfully to "contextualize" his study by limiting himself largely to Yoruba religious traditions, he did try to harmonize the various aspects into one mold of Yoruba religion and then to Christianize it, religion to religion. He then extends it to apply to the rest of sub-Saharan Africa. John S. Mbiti, on the other hand, in his several studies— *Concepts of God in Africa* (1970), *African Religions and Philosophy* (1969), *Introduction to African Religion* (1975), and *The Prayers of African Religion* (1975)—has attempted to study in detail some three hundred peoples' religions all over Africa outside traditionally Christian and Muslim communities (Mbiti 1990). He states that his approach is ontologically centered on the concept of time (Mbiti 1990), for which he has met his own share of criticism (Onwubiko 1991). Mbiti respects the local culture of all the societies he has studied. Yet, he does not hesitate to state: "In all these societies, without a single exception, people have a notion about God. . . . One should not expect long dissertations about God. But God is no stranger to African peoples, and in traditional life there are no atheists" (Mbiti 1990, 29). Mbiti perhaps has in mind those earlier European explorers and missionaries who claimed all Africans do not have any notion of a God. Yet Mbiti, who has studied proverbs from many African cultures, quotes the Akan proverb "No one teaches a child about God" and interprets it literally to mean that everyone in Africa has an innate knowledge about God. We have noted in our discussion of proverbs that, although proverbs such as this indicate a belief in God, they do not intend to teach what they say. In context this proverb means that some adult person, who did or said something stupid, should have known the obvious. The speaker sharply reminds the person of his or her mistake. Mbiti's implied pan-Africanism, while supposedly respecting the plurality of African Religions, negates his good intentions. Okot p'Bitek, in a monograph long ignored entitled *African Religions in Western Scholarship,* declares that African scholars, such as Jomo Kenyatta, J. B. Danquah, K. A. Busia, W. Abraham, E. B. Idowu, and John S. Mbiti, claimed that African peoples knew the Christian God long before the missionaries told them about God (p'Bitek 1970). Mbiti has used the method of James Frazer in the style of the *Golden Bough* to perhaps Hellenize and so to Christianize an African deity, forgetting that Frazer's purpose in his monumental work was to discredit Christianity by proving that the resurrection of Jesus was analogous to notions found in pagan religions (p'Bitek 1970). Masolo remarks that "for Mbiti, it would seem, Africans need no conversion to Christianity. They already live the Christian message. They need no teaching on the 'life to come' because they participate in that life as part of the present" (Masolo 1994, 119). Mbiti and other authors have applied the final blow to the traditional gods through their advocacy of monotheism by squeezing many African religious concepts into monotheistic conceptual frameworks (Masolo 1994).

The purpose of African scholars of religion has been to demonstrate one way or the other that African Religious Systems are the *praeparatio evangelica,* the preparation for the gospel. On the other hand, there are the secularists, even Okot p'Bitek, who have been influenced by the atheism or at least the agnosticism of social anthropology in general. The nineteenth-century reductionism of Freud and Marx—that all religion can be reduced to the primitive stages of humanity—was assumed by Edward B. Tylor to mean that the earliest stage of religion was animism, where human societies believed in a spirit-inhabited cosmos and developed through stages ending with monotheism. Frazer, Durkheim, Malinowski, and others referred to African Religions and other "primitive" forms of religious activity simply to discredit religion and especially Christianity. It was against these that the Christian scholars of African Religions wrote. But the African secularists and nationalists followed suit. Influenced by expressions of thought originating in the diaspora, such as the Harlem Renaissance and the negritude movements, one school of thought wrote about the return to Africa and African consciousness, as Leopold Senghor did. This was just another way of writing in the manner of the African scholars of religions. The other school, assuming that culture is monogenetic, advocated, against Western arrogance and boasts of cultural superiority, that all human civilization and progress originated in Africa and indeed in Egypt. Such notions are the basis of contemporary Afrocentrism found in the writings of Cheik Anta Diop and Henry Olela (Masolo 1994). Diop has certainly contributed a major focus to contemporary discourse that knowledge can be utilized to marginalize certain groups of peoples. In this case, Africans and those of African descent in the diaspora have suffered the pretensions of Eurocentrism, which claims that Greece founded modern civilization. Diop's objective was to demarginalize Africa by placing it at the center of human evolution and controversially joining the monogenetic theory of human origin (that all humans descended from the same parents) to geographical culture precedence (Masolo 1994). In a similar manner Diop postulated that monotheism has its roots in Egypt. By extension, all of Africa receives its culture, agriculture, science, and religion from Egypt. By further extension, the rest of humanity receives all these things from Africa. Olela goes a step further by advocating that the cradle of civilization moved from black Africa northward to engulf both Egypt and the surrounding regions of the Mediterranean (Masolo 1994).

The point behind this lengthy discussion of scholars' views on African Religions is that practically all of them either (1) reduced African Religions to a form of primitive animism and thus placed them on the lowest stage of human evolution; or (2) one way or the other constructed African religious philosophies and theologies based upon an explicit or implicit Islamic-Christian template. Either way, monotheism along the lines of Islam or Christianity is the norm and is considered the highest form of religion. In this book the approach "from below" is followed; cultural homogeneity and philosophical monogenetical origin are rejected. The mere reversal of chapters from the usual approach is not disguised evolutionism. We write about the "ethnographic present," which is synchronic; that is, we take the cultural text as we observe it here and now with all its historical influences from the past along with present-day implications. The model proposed in chapter 3 based on Mbiti—that human beings, living and living-dead, are at the center of the universe—is the one we have tried to follow. God is there, both creating and sustaining the human world. But this God is not defined or even described. Still, in the contemporary situation—for example, my own field research in Ghana—the influence of the monotheistic religions, Islam and Christianity, has deeply engraved itself on the beliefs and thoughts of modern Akan people about what they think concerning God, the deities, the ancestors, and traditional ritual practices. While I have attempted to present Akan religious systems from within (the *emic* approach), indicating that even among the Akan there are differences, I show that there are also similarities there, which overflow into other religious systems, for example, among the Yoruba and Igbo. These cultures also express differences as well as similarities. Moreover, as Jacob Olupona and other contemporary scholars have written (Olupona 1991), modern life and intercultural exchange have helped African Traditional Systems to refine their own vague notions about God and their spiritual universe. What follows will be a discussion of God among the Akan followed by comparative titles and attributes among several other West African religious systems.

ONYAME IN AKAN LIFE

Ananse Kokroko (the Great Spider) is really Onyame in disguise. Half-and-Half are always fighting each other, resisting union, forever creating turmoil and distress. Ananse sneaks up on them, slams them together, and the two become the first human person. One of the few stories of the creation the Akan have, this folktale not only explains why there is division in every human person but asserts that God is the Great Ancestor. Like the bore-hole spider, Ananse comes from the abode of the ancestors, the *samando,* himself the first one, to create people, who will become the bearers of tradition. It is perhaps a more ancient version of creation that connects Onyame with the ancestral abode and with the land. The first human person is the creation of the ground-dwelling deity. Probably because the first human who emerges from the primal cave is a woman, the mother of the people, her *'kra* and her destiny were to establish the first clans, who were destined to set down the traditions and rituals that future generations were to emulate. The centrality of the land and the relationship between Nyame and Asase Yaa, his consort, explain the closeness of God to the people and the sacredness of the land. That Nyame is later associated with the sky is brought out in the myth of separation, which tells of the Old Woman pounding fufu and hitting the nose of Nyame with her pestle. In order to avoid being further abused by the Old Woman, Nyame ascends higher in the sky. This explains why Nyame is no longer close to the people but lives in the sky. He nonetheless is at all times available to anyone who needs him, since, as the adage says, "If you want to talk to Nyame, say it to the winds."

The English word *God* is both specific, referring to the Supreme Being, and generic, referring to various spiritual forces. The latter is usually written in lower case—god. The Akan system of languages makes no such distinction, nor does it speculate about Onyame in a philosophical sense. Some African authors, p'Bitek and Masolo, for example, object to the term *Supreme Being* because it is derived from Socratic, Platonic, and Neo-Platonic philosophies, which are concerned with the transcendental notion of a unified reality at its highest level over against the problem of the many. The Akan term *abosom* refers to the greater and lesser deities we have discussed in chapter 6. We have noted that the term does not apply to Asase Yaa. It certainly does not apply to Nyame. Generally Ghanaians translate Onyame (or simply Nyame) as "God." The title Onyakopon is usually translated either as "God" or as "Almighty." Some have attempted to break down both words to arrive at an etymological meaning, but I believe that to be unnecessary. The suffix *pon* always means "one who is great." So, Opoku explains *Onyakopon* to mean "Nyame who alone is the Great One" (Opoku 1978). Moreover, Nyame is called Nana, a title given to kings, chiefs, elders, and especially the ancestors, something like Grandfather. Nyame is therefore on a different pedestal from all other gods but is the chief of the eldest of the eldest. The Akan say: *Onyame ne hene,* "God is king or chief." Nyame is therefore head of all clans, the One who settles family disputes and who has the last word. He is Nyaamankose, the Confidant, a trusting counselor in times of trouble. He is Tweduapon, the One who listens to our problems, decides wisely and whose decision gives us comfort (Opoku 1978). From this discussion of names given to Nyame, one can readily grasp the fact that it was a misconception to claim that this African God was aloof, a deist God. Rather, Nyame is the Great Ancestor, the Founder and Builder of community, of which he is the Head. Nyame is not selfish and aggressive but tolerant and all-embracing. He makes life within family in the large sense. The other spirits are never in competition with Nyame. He rules over all for the sake of his human children.

The centrality of human life derives from Nyame. We have already noted how the *'kra* may be called the "spark from God." Nyame bestows on every human person born in the world a destiny, which reports back to him at death. The proverb emphasizes human dignity: "All people are Nyame's children; no one is the child of the Earth."

Opoku tells another creation myth. Odomankoma, Creator, first made the sky and the sun and the moon and the stars. He then made the land, the rivers, and the plants. Finally, he made human society and the animals. But to protect the human family from elemental evil, Nyame placed spirits in the rivers, the forests, and the rocks. The spirits exist solely for the good of human persons (Opoku 1978). Again, the myth tells why human beings are so important in Nyame's scheme of things.

Opoku, as we noted in our discussion of the talking drums, recounts the drummer's version of creation, reflecting the order of the king's court. "Odomankoma created the *Esen* (herald), then the *okyerema* (drummer), and finally *Kwamu Kwabrafo* (executioner)" (Opoku 1978, 22). The meaning of this brief account is that as there is order with officials in the king's court, so the Almighty has created order in the world. Each person and thing has its purpose and duties. Each functionary displays skills particularly associated with conveying messages from, to, or about the king or chief. Each of these must be adept at demonstrating proper etiquette in the forum of the king or chief and hold knowledge about court ritual and speech. Similarly, in Onyame's creation, every creature displays appropriate reverence toward the Almighty with ritual and word. The *abosom* ("no-gods") and the ancestors link human beings with Onyame and with one another. Nyame does not have a human priesthood. Neither do the ancestors have priests to serve them except the kings and chiefs themselves, who represent the ancestors as holders of the stool lands. The deities, however, have shrines and intermediaries, the priests *(akomfo)*, who transmit and receive messages between human beings and the spirit world. Even though anyone may address *mpae* (prayer) to Onyame, formal speech and honorific titles referring to Nyame's attributes are abundant.

Some titles of address bestowed upon elders, chiefs, and other dignitaries are not uncommon when one prays to Nyame. Nana is a common title used to speak to a chief or to a grandfather or grandmother or especially to an ancestor. Not unusual is the reference to Nyame as a great king or chief *(otumfoo)*, Almighty *(osagyefo)*, similar to the biblical notion of Savior at war; and the Most Generous One *(daasebre)*. We noted that God is better than any parent or grandparent in his generosity, and so the Akan call upon him as Tweduampon, Most Dependable. Because the weather affects the crops, farmers call upon Onyame as Amosu, the Rain-Maker, and Amowia, the Giver of Sunshine. Dependence upon Onyame is often expressed in speech with expressions such as, *Se Onyame pe a . . . ,* "If God wills it," or *Onyame ma kwan a . . . ,* " If God grants me."

Earlier we discussed the proverbs and their use in public discourse at length. Traditional ancestral wisdom triggers the use of old proverbs in new situations. Reference to Onyame usually refers to the ancient belief in divine providence and guidance, expressed both in contemporary society and individuals through their problems. While proverbs state one truth, they are always spoken within a wider context. Still, the basic truth contains a meaning one cannot ignore. Proverbs about Onyame express a deep-seated belief not only in God but in God's most notable traits; for example, "It is Onyame who drives away the flies on a tailless animal." Although through some mishap a certain animal lost its tail, which is used to drive away flies, God takes care of his creatures. In a given human context the proverb could mean that one should not complain of one's difficulties but trust that eventually they will go away. Sometimes sickness is not due to social and family stress but is a sign perhaps of God's wisdom and direction. One must look to God for a clue to the problem in this proverb: "If Onyame has given the sickness, he will provide the medicine." Sometimes criminals get away with their crookedness and human justice cannot ferret them out. In such moments of distress the wise person refers to this proverb: "Since Onyame does not like wickedness, he gives every creature a name." And if human beings are malicious in their treatment of the poor and the widow, divine providence will make all things right in the end: "If Onyame gives you palm wine and someone kicks it over, Onyame will fill your cup again."

Graphic designs are a particular talent of the Akan. The Asante Nation's kente and adinkra cloths are especially suited to convey messages in proverbial style. The adinkra symbols on fabrics, buildings, and gold weights for Onyame are classic. Since Onyame has no temple or shrine, no priesthood, and no festival days, his relationship to ancestral custom is emphasized in the custom of erecting a symbol of him, the *Nyamedua* ("God's tree") at the compound yard's entrance. It is a branch with three prongs at the top with the base planted in the ground. Within the fork a pot of rainwater is placed, called "God's water." It symbolizes God's providence. Ancestors may visit at night and drink some of the water. The water is used at times to sprinkle members of the household to give them divine blessing. The adinkra symbol, *Nyamedua,* means the same thing. Nyame, the most dependable, takes care of his people. Most famous of all, *Gye Nyame* stands for total dependence on Onyame. Sometimes translated to mean "Except for God," or "Only God," the symbol refers to God's great power. Another symbol is a long prayer, *Nyame, bribi wo soro, na ma no mmeka me nsa,* "Onyame, there is something above, let it fall into my hands." The prayer and the symbol request blessings, especially prosperity in this life now. It is an expression of the Akan this-worldliness in outlook. A final symbol we note here is *Nyame bewu na mawu,* which means "If Onyame should die, I will die." In fact Onyame does not die. Because of the *'kra* in me, God's spark, as it were, I too will not die. This refers to ancestral belief. God, the Ancient One, leads us all into the land of the ancestors, the ancient ones.

Akan religious beliefs are not dogmas but really maxims about life. In a society that values tradition and antiquity, the present has meaning only in relationship to the past. But the past is not dwelled upon so as to become affixed to the old ways. New proverbs and new views lead society toward the future and its own set of problems. As rapid industrialization and communication systems invade Akan land today, these ancestral beliefs must bolster society to face the new challenges. That is why religious expressions, the *tete kasa* (archaic speech patterns), and proverbs about Nyame still appear in wax prints and in "High-Life" songs. Geertz may have said that the observer should describe a culture "thickly" from the inside, but long before him the elders said of the speech of ancient days: *Emu pi,* "It is thick."

OTHER WEST AFRICAN EXPRESSIONS ABOUT GOD

Comparisons with other West African religious systems reveal both similarities and differences in the divine reality. For example, the Ewe-speaking people in eastern Ghana and in Togo have been largely influenced by the Akan, since many groups of them were subjugated by the Akwamu and Asante. The Ewe learned the art of kingship from the Asante. Still, the words used for the Supreme God vary somewhat. Mawu can mean both a supreme celestial deity as well as a title given to three deities of the sky—Mawu-Sogble, Mawu-Sodza, and Mawu-Sowlui—according to Nelson-Adjakpey (Nelson-Adjakpey 1982). Hence, to distinguish these deities from the Supreme God, the Ewe sometimes use the term Mawuga. Authors have sometimes confused the worship of the sky gods with Mawuga because of the similarity of names. Aside from a peace-making ritual in which peace is bestowed upon quarreling family members with a green leaf and water in Mawuga's name, there is no direct worship activity in Mawuga's honor (Nelson-Adjakpey 1982). In order to gain favor with Mawuga, the Ewe turn frequently to the *trowo*, the lesser spirits, who have shrines and priesthoods. The Ewe depict Mawuga in myth and story as the creator of all things in sky and on earth, including all of the deities, who are subservient to him. Sometimes the praise-names given to Mawuga confuse researchers, like Mawu-Lisa. But this name implies that, similar to the chameleon, which can change its colors to get what it wants, Mawu is wise and powerful (Nelson-Adjakpey 1982). The Ewe have the same myth about the separation of Mawu and the human world as the Akan, the story of the Old Woman pounding fufu in the evening. But the world of the sky fascinates the Ewe, who otherwise, like the Akan, are earth- and human-centered. The rolling of the thunder from one end of the heavens to the other is a sign of the sky deities' wreaking vengeance upon the world. But human beings can appease them through their rituals and sacrifices.

The Ewe of southern Ghana and Togo, the Ga and the Ada of Ghana, the Fon of Benin, and the Yoruba of Nigeria are in many ways related and share one another's worldviews. In fact, the Ewe regard Oyo in Nigeria as their ancestral home. It is called by them Amedzofe, the original home of humans, or Mawufe, the Home of Mawu. It should be no surprise to find similar ways of regarding the spirit world among these peoples.

The Yoruba call God Olodumare very often and also Olorun, which means "Lord of the abode of the dead." In the work of creating the world and human beings Olodumare enlisted the aid of his arch-deity, Orisha-Nla. The latter went down to the earth, which was a marsh-like waste, with a snail's shell full of dirt. He took with him a hen and a pigeon, which he used to scatter the dirt around on a wide, flat area to make it solid. After his work was done, Orisha-Nla reported to Olodumare that he had accomplished his mission. God sent a chameleon to inspect the work; after two trips the chameleon told Olodumare that the world was wide and flat. This explains why the foundation area is called Ife by the Yoruba; *ife* means "wide" (Opoku 1978). The earth became a home as much for Olorun, who would make it the abode of the dead, as for the human beings he was to create through Orisha-Nla.

In southeastern Nigeria the Igbo, the people of Achebe's novels, have lived out their religious convictions for centuries before the advent of Christian missionaries. There are at present two names for God: Chukwu, which seems to be the more recent term, and Chineke. They are used interchangeably under the influence of the Christian theology of the Creator. According to Donatus Ibe Nwoga, Chukwu was the name of a very powerful oracular deity of the Aro branch of the Igbo, who traveled extensively throughout

Igbo territory in the seventeenth century engaging in trade, including slavery with Europeans. The Aro promoted their oracle of Chukwu so successfully that soon shrines sprang up in many villages and Chukwu's word was regarded as final on many matters. Children were named after the god when they were born after their parents had consulted the oracle. So, when missionaries arrived and looked around for a word for God, they adopted Chukwu (Nwoga 1984). This name now dominates all other names among Christian Igbo. It is derived from *chi,* the personal spirit, and *ukwu,* meaning "great." Nwoga believes the name therefore means some sort of a universal *Chi* from which every personal *chi* is derived.

Chineke is the older term. It clearly contains the word *chi;* the second syllable is *eke,* which, according to Nwoga, denotes division. So, Chineke is not "God the Creator" in the biblical sense, but Soul who recognizes the two to be one. Both *chi* and *eke* are said to be "the same." Something like Ananse Kokroko, who slaps together Half-and-Half, Chineke appears with "two-and-two" in expressions where duality is present (Nwoga 1984). Instead of "two-and-two," Chineke is "One-and-two." Chineke is the One who divides to make reality as it coexists, for example, in the sky and earth, in man and woman, in hot and cold, and so on.

To conclude, West African Religious Systems are not at all comparable to Muslim-Christian models. Yet the God of these systems is not a deistic and lazy God. The myths of separation, which explain how sky and earth were next to each other at first and then separated so that God went way up above, are not stories of a "fall." In West African mysticism the more the divinity is distant, the more he is longed for and every effort is spent on finding ways to get to the divinity. But it is always on the earth that this happens, not in the sky. God's place is still on the earth. He gives human beings, the living and the dead, free rein to work out their human condition. They need to dance out their trances in order to get in touch. The ancestors return to the land of the living, if need be, to rejuvenate the clans. The divinity allows these things to transpire without interference.

We have noted that God embraces the world of human beings by creating them and sustaining them. But the human beings are not so much interested in the creating as in the sustaining. They see themselves at the crossroads between the sky, which fascinates them, and the earth, which they know all too well. The circle of life is centered in the human universe, where humans in their society and each one as a spark from God work out their destiny, the plan God has given to their *'kra* or *chi.* The dance, the drumming, the ritual, and the words of prayer all have as their purpose to control the universe, visible and invisible. Even the deities respond and come to the earth in the village circle. The human is the thing, and the spirituality is human-centered.

For the individual in community, especially after a liminal experience where a person becomes consecrated, if one may say so, through dance and ritual, he or she develops a certain self-esteem and self-control. Such an attitude leads to respect for others, because, as the proverb says: "Every person is a child of God; no one is a child of the Earth." The rest of creation matters little. The name is the thing.

Finally, let me close with another proverb: "It's when you get closer to the shore that you can hear the crab's cough." There is nothing like authentic traditional lore for grasping the ways of the people, free from any religious or socio-historical notions "outsiders" may want to superimpose on a culture. This discussion about God in West Africa illustrates this perhaps more than any other topic we have discussed. Tradition, language, and speech-making all are learned from God through the media of revelation—Ananse, the Old Woman, the blacksmith, the artisan, the waly, the drummer, the griot, and so on. The means to create a culture, a body politic, a society, all have religion as a root metaphor, the symbol par excellence. Looking back over the last seven chapters, we can see where this golden thread is woven into the tapestry of Akan and other West African cultural symbol systems. As we glance ahead we shall glimpse where a new weave has changed things with the advent of Islam and of Christianity. What will change and what will not? We shall see . . .

BIBLIOGRAPHY

Achebe, Chinua. *Things Fall Apart*. New York: Fawcett Crest, 1989.

Eboussi Boulaga, F. *Christianity without Fetishes: An African Critique and Recapture of Christianity*. Maryknoll, N.Y.: Orbis Books, 1984.

Evans-Pritchard, E. E. *Nuer Religion*. New York: Oxford University Press, 1956.

Idowu, E. Bolaji. *African Traditional Religion: A Definition*. London: SCM Press, 1973; Maryknoll, N.Y.: Orbis Books, 1975.

Masolo, D. A. *African Philosophy in Search of Identity*. Bloomington: Indiana University Press, 1994.

Mbiti, John S. *African Religions and Philosophy*. 2d ed., revised and enlarged. Portsmouth, N.H.: Heinemann Educational Books, 1990.

McNaughton, Patrick R. "The Semantics of 'Jugu': Blacksmiths, Lore, and 'Who's Bad' in Mande." In *Status and Identity in West Africa*, ed. David C. Conrad and Barbara A. Frank, 46-57. Bloomington: Indiana University Press, 1995.

Mudimbe, V. Y. *The Invention of Africa: Gnosis, Philosophy, and the Order of Knowledge*. Bloomington: Indiana University Press, 1988.

Nelson-Adjakpey, Ted. "Penance and Expiatory Sacrifice among the Ghanaian-Ewe and Their Relevance to the Christian Religion." Dissertation, 221. Rome: Academia Alfonsiana, 1982.

Nwoga, Donatus Ibe. *The Supreme God as Stranger in Igbo Religions*. Ekwereazu, Nigeria: Hawk Press, 1984.

Olupona, Jacob K. "Major Issues in the Study of African Traditional Religion." In *African Traditional Religions in Contemporary Society*, ed. Jacob K. Olupona, 25-33. New York: Paragon House, 1991.

Onwubiko, Oliver A. *African Thought, Religion, and Culture.* The Christian Mission and Culture in Africa Series, vol. 1. Enugu, Nigeria: SNAAP Press, 1991.

Opoku, Kofi Asare. *West African Traditional Religion.* Accra, Ghana: FEP International Private Limited, 1978.

p'Bitek, Okot. *African Religions in Western Scholarship.* Nairobi, Kenya: East African Literature Bureau, 1970.

Sanneh, Lamin. *Translating the Message: The Missionary Impact on Culture.* American Society of Missiology Series, no. 13. Maryknoll, N.Y.: Orbis Books, 1990.

Shaw, Rosalind. "The Invention of 'African Traditional Religion.'" *Religion* 20 (1990): 339-53.

STUDY GUIDE

1. Why must we keep in mind the use of analogy when speaking about God in different religions?

2. Although African Religions are not "religions of the Book," how do they still have a form of writing about God and other aspects about religion, as exemplified in Asante culture?

3. What were some of the misconceptions of missionaries and other Europeans about African religious beliefs?

4. Why did both European and even African religious writers look for homologies between Western theologies and philosophies and African religions? What was the result? Show how this was done in the case of Tempels and Idowu.

5. What criticisms can be made of Idowu and Mbiti? What positive contributions have they made to the discussion about religions in Africa?

6. What were some of the reasons of the non-religious African writers for their approaches to African Religions? Discuss Diop and Olela.

7. How is Nyame connected with the earth? How did it come about that he is associated with the sky? Is Nyame really distant?

8. What are some of attributes of Nyame? How do the proverbs assist us in understanding Nyame?

9. Compare Akan belief with that of the Ewe and Yoruba.

10. Compare the concept of Shango with that of Chukwu. How did missionaries influence them? Go into detail (see Achebe 1989, 165).

11. How can Chineke and Olorun, like Nyame, be connected with the earth and the ancestors?

12. Discuss the scientific notion of the origin of human beings from Africa. Recall the myth of the woman rising out of the primal cave. Or recount the myth of the Old Woman *(aberewa)* trying to pound fufu for her children while hitting Nyame in the nose. What may be said about God and the Old Woman, at least in a matrilinear system such as one finds among the Akan? The Old Woman taught her children something about God and about achieving some relationship with God. How have we shown where the tradition comes from? Why do the elders in council say that sometimes they have to go and consult the Old Woman?

8

Dar al-Islam of West Africa

The rolling thunder of Arabian stallions was no longer the sound of drums and of dance in 640 C.E. Under 'Umar, the first successor of the Prophet Muhammad, the conquest of Africa for Islam and its expansion westward across to the Maghrib (the "West," ultimately Morocco) began in earnest at Alexandria. The occupation of the dockyards marked the initiation of former desert nomads into the art of naval military science. Both by land and by sea, except for a brief resistance by the Berbers, Islam had spread across North Africa by 698 and into Spain and by 721 as far north as Toulouse, where it was checked at the battle of Poitiers in 732.

The first contact from Morocco with the peoples of West Africa south of the Sahara was probably in the eighth century, not through conquest but along the trade routes. Slave trading, long practiced among the Arabs, was now encouraged among the North Africans. The aim of the intrusions was twofold: to obtain slaves for the growing Muslim ruling and merchant classes; and to garner the best element of all: gold. The ancient kingdom of Ghana and the Kanem-Borno territory were areas the Muslims staked out for the next two to three hundred years.

From its inception Islam was divided into the Sunnis, who regard the community as the guardian of the Islamic truth; the Shi'ites, who regard the imam or caliph as the true interpreter of the Qur'an; and the very conservative Kharijites, who believe that anyone who is a non-Muslim or one who has denied the faith can be pillaged, enslaved, or put to death. While Sunnis and Shi'ites also entered the area of West Africa in the Sahel, many Kharijites belonging to the Ibadiyya or Sufriya sects were the first to enter the territory. (The first West Africans who embraced Islam were therefore unorthodox Muslims.) Once in West Africa, however, the Kharijites' fiery zeal abated. Even though later eleventh-century movements attempted to rectify the situation by jihads, holy wars, the Africanization of Islam had begun.

At this point we need to establish a few guidelines for our remarks about Islam in West Africa. First, in any study of Islam in West Africa it is necessary to realize that Traditional Religious Systems were the norm prior to the invasion from across the Sahara. Second, the acceptance of Islam was gradual, for the most part, so there was ample time for the mutual influence of one religious system on the other. And third, as mentioned above, the form of Islam that first encountered West African Traditional Religions was unorthodox.

We have noted the presence of Muslim chroniclers in the Introduction. They, mostly north Africans or Arabs, have had their own perceptions of Islam, while the Sahelian African insiders, such as the Muslim leaders and modern commentators, have their own approach. Western historians, therefore, have not always provided a true interpretation. According to David Robinson there are three distortions manifest in historical literature about West African Islam. The first is the orientalist approach, typical of the North African or Arab view, which presupposes knowledge of Arabic and all the literature written in that language. It suggests that unless Islam is as orthodox as that of North Africa, or more especially of Arabia itself, it is not truly Islam. Authors attempt to force this orientalist version of Islam on the peripheries of Islamic influence, such as West Africa, and to maintain that it is present when that is not altogether the case. The second, or Sahelian, approach reinforces the orientalist bias by limiting itself to Arabic literature and traditions and especially to legitimatizing forms of writing stemming from the Islamic tide of the nineteenth century. For example, the primary documentation of the Sokoto Caliphate in that era attempted to legitimatize its use of jihad as a received tradition from the Prophet. Thus the great reformer, Usman dan Fodio, his brother Abdullah, and his son Muhammad Bello, justified their expansion into new territory. Historians have had to sift through this material to discover the true nature of the Islamic revolution but have not always succeeded. Africans "Arabize" themselves so far as to claim relationship to the Prophet. The third distortion arose from the colonial powers, mainly France and Britain, who wished to distinguish the African peoples into Muslims and "pagans" (Robinson 1991). The colonials appreciated the politics and military prowess of the Muslims more than that of the "natives."

It is perhaps useful to recall that from the inception of Islam into West Africa, starting with the ancient kingdoms of the Sahel from the eighth century onward, there were some aspects of Islam that were not so orthodox, as noted above, such as the Ibadite branch. In West Africa we discover Muslims who are not as orthodox as North Africans would like. Some are not as learned. And there are differences between the city dwellers and the rural or bush inhabitants (see below). Finally, some Muslims were pacifists and scholarly and spiritually quietists, while others were militants; one need only recall the militant fuming of Seku Amadu of Masina against the pietists of Djenne in the nineteenth century.

Islam did not take hold suddenly. Tradition was very strong. After all, how could the God of all forbid reverence to the ancestors? How could God denounce the other gods he had made to serve human kind? Maryse Conde, in her novel *Segu*, has perhaps captured the sentiments of the Bambara in the Sahel when they were surrounded by Muslims yet deeply desired to remain faithful to their ancestral customs:

> He [Dousika Traore] was temporizing because he knew the kingdom of Segu was becoming every day more like an island; an island surrounded by other countries won over to Islam. Yet the new religion had advantages as well as disadvantages. To begin with, its cabalistic signs were as effective as many sacrifices. For generations the mansas of Segu had availed themselves of the *mori* of the Somono families— the Kane, Dyire, and Tyere—and they had resolved the kings' problems just as satisfactorily as the priests. Furthermore, these signs made it possible to maintain and strengthen alliances with other peoples far away, and created a kind of moral community to which it was a good thing to belong. On the other hand, Islam was dangerous; it undermined the power of kings, according sovereignty to one supreme god who was completely alien to the Bambara universe. How could one fail to be suspicious of this Allah whose city was somewhere in the east? (Conde 1987, 41)

For the elder Dousika, it was unheard of for the Traore to turn their backs on the protectors of his clan. The Muslim profession of faith, "There is no God but Allah, and Muhammad is his Prophet," was an outrage and brought down the fury of the spirits and the ancestors upon his people.

Yet, sub-Saharan Africa was not alone in preserving its traditions. Even in northwest Africa, in what is today Morocco, customs long held sacred by the people continued in the form of institutions in Islam. Clifford Geertz has classified three institutions that also permeated other West African Muslim societies. The first of the institutions he terms, in Arabic, the *siyyid* complex, "after the name given both to dead saints and to the tombs in which they are thought to be buried" (Geertz 1968, 49). The cult of the saints preserved in the respect given to their male descendants was a hidden form of ancestral practice preserved in the Islamic concept of the *baraka,* the mystical wisdom handed down from master to disciple.

The second institution is labeled the *zawiya* complex, which indicated the brotherhoods with their lodges, their founding sheikhs, and their peculiar practice, or *dhiker*, handed down from one leader to the next. Both these forms of male-centered Islam preserved the patriarchal systems in terms of Islamic traditions, but with a hidden agenda that knit together certain groups, if not clans, around the deceased. The focus in both institutions was the holy man, the marabout or waly. A prime example of such leadership is the separatist movement in Senegal founded by Ahmadu Bamba in the early years of the twentieth century: the *Muridiya,* or the Murid Movement. The marabouts were the supposedly "venal" Muslim teachers that the great fifteenth-century Muslim commentator on Islamic law, al-Maghili, and the nineteenth-century jihad leader, Usman dan Fodio, and other more orthodox West African Muslims attacked for peddling a corrupt version of Islam in return for a livelihood. To be sure, there were fake marabouts. Sembene Ousmane, in his short story "The False Prophet," tells of Mahmoud Fall, who pretended to be a descendant of a great patriarch from Mauretania, Aidra by name. This opened all doors to him. He became a respected imam and gathered much wealth until he himself was robbed while dreaming about Allah. In the end he lost his faith, because he was always a thief. "With his *boubou* flapping in the wind he ran off. He had just realized that there is no need to believe in Allah in order to be a thief!" (Ousmane 1985, 7).

Geertz's third label for the Islamic institution is the *maxsen* complex. This means that local kings, now emirs or sultans, could consolidate their authority and power by claiming descent from the Prophet. The sanctity of the royal office of king stemmed from its ancestral authority. Once the veneration of the ancestors gave way to the sole worship of Allah, the kings lost their basis for authority, as the character Traore mused in Conde's novel *Segu*. However, under Islam the king performed all his duties in the name of Allah. And the name of the sultan was invoked at the pronouncement of the Friday sermon, when judges were appointed, and when holidays were declared (Geertz 1968). Here religion and statecraft were joined together so forcefully that no one would question the divine right of the monarch. "The law of the sultan is the law of the country"; so goes the Muslim saying. In West Africa, as elsewhere in Muslim countries, the power of the state is mystically and institutionally bound up with the very reading of the Qur'an in that it is legal discourse. This experience was new for African societies. Those who resisted were eventually crushed under the rule of the persistent wave of the jihad, especially in the nineteenth century. It was precisely at Segu, the former Bambara capital on the Niger Bend, designated the "capital of paganism" by Muslim zealots such as Al-Hajj Umar (ca. 1796-1864), that national shrines were publicly destroyed and new Muslim palaces erected. Segu became the capital of militant Islam in the western Sudan. The former quiet erosion of Traditional Religions under the marabouts was replaced with the violence of those who claimed a divine and ancestral right from the Prophet himself. We have noted above that the legitimization of jihad as from the Prophet himself was simply a way of continuing the ancestral principle. On the other hand, the Prophet Movements under the marabouts evinced a rather more pacifist mode of enunciating the same principle, perhaps in a more distinctly African manner than the former. The marabout was a prophet in his own right. While both approaches to Islam affirmed the authority of the Qur'an as their foundation, the Reform Movements sought to be more orthodox by espousing the Arabization of society while Islamizing it. Indeed, as Lamin Sanneh emphasizes, the retention of

Arabic deeply influenced culture change. The Prophet Movements, however, introduced versions of the Qur'an in regional languages and so adhered more firmly to African cultures (Sanneh 1990).

Contemporary West African Islam utilizes both approaches. Historically, they have evolved depending on the power base of the territories Islam aspired to possess and its own power to subvert existing authorities. While earlier historians, basing themselves on vague Muslim chronicles on ancient Ghana, believed that the Almoravid Movement from northwest Africa had subdued Ghana during its attempt to rectify heretical Muslim beliefs there, later historians have concluded that there is sufficient evidence to suggest that the zealous Muslims worked in concert with Ghana for their mutual benefit (Clarke 1982). The gold trade, in fact, was not interrupted but increased during the eleventh century. Trade and the influence of Muslim slaves had more to do with the spread of Islam than any other factor, including invasion or jihad.

In 1973 Humphrey Fisher and David Conrad formulated a three-level historical paradigm to explain how over time Islam penetrated West Africa: the quarantine, the court, and the reform levels (Robinson 1991; Clarke 1982). The first level is evinced in the capital of ancient Ghana, Koumbi-Saleh, as attested by the eleventh-century Muslim chronicler from Spain, al-Bakri. The quarantine period is marked by the Berber traders living apart on their own side of the town, quite considerable in size, with twelve mosques. The king of Ghana and his people dwelled on the other side, the "pagan" side, where only one mosque had been built. The king, even before his own and his court's conversion, utilized the resources of the Muslims for finances and for an understanding of the law and academics. Later, in the Asante Kingdom, the *asantehene* made extensive use of Muslim wisdom and technology without himself being converted. The Muslims, who remain a minority in modern Ghana, still live on their own side of town in Kumasi and elsewhere, an area called *zongo*.

The classic example of the court level is found in the writings of Ibn Battuta (named the "Prince of Travelers" in a 1991 edition of the *National Geographic*). A Moroccan by birth, a Muslim by faith, Ibn Battuta for some twenty-nine years crossed North Africa to Mecca for his hajj (pilgrimage), and then went on to traverse southern Asia, logging some seventy-five hundred to eight thousand miles, three times the distance logged by Marco Polo. Having returned from his major journey and having written down everything about Asia and Islam in those foreign parts, his sovereign at Fez, the Sultan Abu Inan, requested one final exploration by camel across the Sahara in 1352 to determine trade links with the Bilad as-Sudan, the "Negro Lands" (Abercrombie 1991). After a treacherous journey of twenty-five days, Ibn Battuta arrived in Mali, the empire along the Niger River Bend that succeeded Ghana. He described the ruler, Mansa Sulayman, the grandson of the lavish Mansa Musa, who had distributed so many gold coins in

Cairo on his way to Mecca that he depressed the gold market there. The grandson, in contrast, Ibn Battuta reported, was miserly, though extremely competent. As an "outsider," Ibn Battuta was impressed with the great number of men who attended the mosque on Fridays. He observed that they wore very clean clothes to the service. He noted how the parents made sure their children learned the Qur'an by heart in Arabic. In one place a Muslim judge chained his own children until they learned to memorize their lesson. Ibn Battuta furthermore recounted that the Muslims in Mali practiced *zakat,* almsgiving, one of the five pillars of Islam (Clarke 1982).

However, Ibn Battuta observed, most of those who professed Islam were members of the royal court and of the merchant class. Even then, they followed many, in his opinion, un-Islamic practices and customs. He fumed that the women went about with a great deal of bare-breasted nudity (Abercrombie 1991). The subjects prostrated themselves before their king, a practice, according to orthodox Muslims, only permitted at prayer to indicate submission to Allah (*Islam* means "submission"). Divination was quite widespread in Mali. And the matrilineal system of succession and inheritance continued among the royalty long after they had converted to Islam. After all, one could determine one's mother but not surely the father! Traditional titles were bestowed upon government officials at court rather than Arabian honors. For example, Mania Must had instituted the Order of the Trousers. Whenever a knight achieved new successes in battle, he received from the king a pair of ample trousers. The more exploits, the wider the seat. Islamic law was not thoroughly enforced, although many Muslim scholars (*'ulama*) and lawyers, experts in the *Shari'a* or systematized codes based on the Qur'an and the *hadith* (traditions), were on hand from Morocco. Yet security in the capital was excellent, crime was not even a reality. On the one hand, the court provided many philosophers, scholars, and marabouts; on the other hand, the king was wont to surround himself with the griots and the traditional priests and diviners of Traditional Religion. Ibn Battuta noted that on traditional festal days the griots would stand (mind you!) before their king and, in a preachy voice, recount the great deeds of past kings, no doubt reciting once more the epic of Sundiata. They admonished their sovereign to go and accomplish similar deeds (Clarke 1982). In conclusion, the reliable witness of Ibn Battuta attested to the practice of Islam among the courtiers in Mali and among the upper classes of merchants. However, this Islam was mixed with a considerable amount of Traditional Religion and culture.

The third stage, according to the Fisher scheme, was the reform movement of the eighteenth and nineteenth centuries in West Africa. This period in history was marked by European expansionism in North and South America, the slave trade, and eventually occupation of many African territories, the later halt to Islamic expansion, the establishment of European colonialism, and the exploitation of natural resources in Africa. For Muslims, as early as the sixteenth and seventeenth centuries, a religious geography was provided by the renowned Timbuktu scholar Ahmed Baba, which divided territory into Muslim and non-Muslim peoples. The Muslim, the *dar al-Islam,* provided a protectorate for all inhabitants, while the non-Muslim, the *dar al-Harb,* permitted the slave trade and enslavement of the peoples (Robinson 1991). While conceived in the Songhay period, the *dar al-Islam—dar al-Harb* dichotomy was rather limited in scope and was oriented to the trans-Saharan trade from the Niger River Bend to areas south from the savanna to the forest regions, including the emergent empires of the Mossi and of the Asante.

The Muslims of the period under discussion were well aware of their Islamic identity and concerned with orthodoxy and therefore with the spread of Islam beyond the earlier boundaries of court, city, and savanna. Zeal for Islam expressed itself in two ways: the quietistic mode of the marabouts, the legal and economic scholars, who through trade and the furtherance of education sought to move into new territory; and the military mode of the jihad, the use of conquest and force to increase the territory of *dar al-Islam.* The first mode of activity simply carried out what had occurred over the last several centuries, gradually penetrating through the savanna into the forest regions, as we shall note below. The second mode, however, was effective in such areas as came under the influence of the Fulani or Fulbe from modern Senegal to Nigeria.

History records four Fulbe movements from the early eighteenth century, beginning in Futa Jalon, through the late eighteenth century in Futa Toro, to the early nineteenth century under Fulbe leadership in Hausaland. The nineteenth-century movement occurred at first under the leadership of Usman dan Fodio and his brother and son. Later, the movement was spurred into action in Sokoto and beyond under Seku Amadu, a Fulbe cleric originally from Djenne on the Niger Bend. Legitimization through manipulation of texts in the case of dan Fodio and Amadu provided links with the past and the great leaders of Islam. The result was that by the time the European powers arrived on the scene in West Africa at the end of the nineteenth century, the *dar al-Islam* had established itself in the minds of most of the inhabitants of the savanna region, perhaps more firmly in the Central Sudan, but rather less decisively in the West Sudan due to infighting among the Muslim leaders. At any rate, in the West the fragmentation of truly Islamic states turned to the advantage of both France and Britain, who trained their sights on Muslim as well as "pagan" leaders, defenders of their territories from any further invasions by the reformers of Islamic societies.

The penetration of Islam in West Africa was uneven. Traditional practices did not always intersect well with Islamic beliefs and devotions. While rulers favored Islam because of trade relations with peoples to the north, literacy, accurate accountancy, and cosmopolitan diplomacy, they did not easily abandon all traditional practices due to the strong relationship they wished to maintain with their ancestors, in order to retain the loyalty of their subjects in their clans, and on account of their land. In other words, Islam presented practical implications on a wider scale, while traditions subsumed all other religious and social concerns on a more local ethnic scale. This was so to a large extent in the Sahel regions, even where Islam was most successful. In urban areas Islam did in fact penetrate much of society, even to the lower classes. More people learned to read the Qur'an in Arabic and to pray in that language. Strict monotheism was adhered to, and the veneration of the ancestors was practically abolished. Where Islam was the religion of the majority, the sultan or emir consolidated his reign in terms of Islamic law and around Muslim festivals, where he himself offici-ated, leading the prayers. In rural areas however, and in areas where Islam was not in the majority, traditional religious practices were mixed into Is-lam. The marabouts encouraged the translation of the Qur'an and other Muslim works into the local languages. The cult of personality centered around the *malams* (*malam* is Hausa for the Arabic *'ulama*, Muslim liter-ates) and dead Muslim leaders and their tombs. In this way the veneration of ancestors was continued. The use of symbols and emotional experiences prevailed more often than respect for abstract words and rules (Clarke 1982).

The Yoruba in the nineteenth century present a classic case in point. Many converted to Islam due to jihad from the northern Hausaland. But many others returned to their homeland after escaping from slavery in Brazil or in Sierra Leone as converted Muslims. Yet they accommodated themselves to many elements of Yoruba traditional religious and cultural practices. Their influence and numbers gradually increased, especially in Lagos. Their knowl-edge of Portuguese and English added to their influence, especially as they confronted colonialism and the Christian mission (Clarke 1982). In the twen-tieth century, Islam in northern Nigeria has succeeded very well in the old Hausalands of Kano, Borno, and Sokoto. Perhaps more than half of the Yoruba in the south are Muslims. In both areas Islam merged with Western capitalism to establish a modern entrepreneurial class and a Muslim intelli-gentsia. The Yoruba, however, have retained a large number of their regional cultural and religious practices at the shrines of their many deities. And the Yoruba also have preserved various forms of Christianity, including syn-cretic forms such as Xango, Candomblé, and Santeria, brought from Brazil and the Caribbean, as well as indigenous "independent" types, such as the Aladura Church, which will be discussed in the next chapter. The Igbo, on the other hand, were converted to a large extent to Catholicism, which Achebe has commented on in his novels.

In Akan areas, especially during the height of the Asante Confederacy just prior to the British capture of Nana Agyeman Prempeh I in 1896, Mus-lims from the northern regions of the Asante territories and beyond enjoyed a special place at the court of the *asantehene*. The Muslim leader served as the *asantehene*'s physician and adviser, while the imam, the prayer leader, served in the court as a scribe. The Asante were interested in trade with the north, selling their gold, kola nuts, ivory, and timber in return for cattle and leather, imported silk from China, brocades from Arabia, and, most important, salt. Between the palace of the king, Manyhia Palace, actually a complex of residences, offices, and ceremonial halls, and the Kumasi market, in the *zongo* or strangers' ward, dwelled many Muslims who were not Asante— Hausa, Mossi, Dagomba, and people from further north—but more lately also Asante converts, the *Asante Nkramo*, dealers in cattle and traders. Instead of the former trans-Saharan caravans that passed through the savanna, and, then, often by boats along the rivers or by foot, now by truck, through the forest regions, the *Asante Nkramo* have played an important role in Asante economic life. They, along with others who live in cosmopolitan Kumasi, such as the Ga, the Ewe, and Fante, pay their respect to Otumfo Opoku Ware II, as they did in August 1995 during the twenty-fifth anniversary of his reign as *asantehene*. He himself practices the rituals of Asante culture and religion while professing Christianity as an Anglican.

To conclude, we may note the following concerning the appropriation of Islam by West Africans, including those who live in Akan areas:

1. God, by whatever name in local languages, became the sole religious spirit with the Arabic name Allah. The Muslim call to prayer and the various holy days have become the armature for all events in traditional life, including puberty rites and ancestral festivals. The introduction of Arabic as the *lingua franca* and of Arabian personal names implied a condemnation of local tradition and culture (Sanneh 1990).

2. The cult of the ancestors was gradually replaced in urban areas but not in the rural towns and country. Still, ancestor veneration remained a threat to Islam. The hierarchy of the spiritual order represented a danger to the political structure of Muslim society. No intermediary was needed to stand in the way of community interests.

3. Similarly, lesser deities were anathema, since the very first of the five pillars of Islam is the "bearing witness," the *shahadah,* the first words a child hears: "There is no God but Allah, and Muhammad is his Messenger." Anything else is *shirk,* association with other gods.

4. Polygamy, practiced in most Traditional Religions, remained in force, permitted according to the Qur'an.

5. The question of the evil force is still problematic. Here the solution of divination assumes a new form. The Qur'an, along with literacy, introduced the concept of linear time to African societies. Non-Muslim concern was over past or present misfortunes, and perhaps over the future if one did not change his or her ways. Muslims learned preoccupation with future, unforeseen events. The past had been controlled by the ancestors, from whom all tradition was derived; the future was controlled by human beings. The new ancestors are Muhammad, Jesus, and the prophets. Their words in the Qur'an formed the basis for the new revelation, which gives direction in

life. They are not, however, new mediators as were the blood ancestors, who receive sacrifices and handed down proverbs in an oral tradition. What was formerly achieved through sacrifice and offerings to the ancestors or at the various shrines of deities is now accomplished through Islamic daily prayer, the Friday service, almsgiving, fasting during the month of Ramadan, the following of the law, and perhaps pilgrimage to Mecca, the center of world Islam. Not only the sultans but the griots claim origin in Arabia, as they sing their praises of the Messenger of God. However, going back to Arab pre-Islamic history, divination had a place in Islam, which peoples of the *dar al-Islam* in Africa pursued. Islam did not condemn the belief in and consultation of the "spirits of the wild" in the form of the jinn, but only the worship of them (Kirby 1986).

Divination was not unknown to the people of West Africa. But Muslims, from pre-Islamic Arabia, were familiar with sand-divining, *khatt al-raml*. Based on a form of numerology or geomancy, the diviner is able to predict the future. There are signs that deal with health, wealth, and high social position. There are also signs that touch upon poverty, ill-health, and worries of the moment. Finally, there are signs related to sex, the male's control over female reproduction, and lovers (Kirby 1986). Just as the arrangement of letters and numbers that stand for verses of the Qur'an (along with literacy) was considered magical, the *malam* was master of amulets and of astrology. Many non-Muslim Asante warriors wore coats the *malams* made, hung with verses and squares from the Qur'an (Hiskett 1984).

6. Just as the evil force is a major concern in Traditional Religions, so too is life after death. If the ancestors are replaced by Islam with the major prophets of old, and perhaps with the dead marabouts and their shrines, the question remains concerning the uncertainty of life after death. Islam provides a solution in a theology of eschatology, or a future hope of an afterlife in a paradise of pleasure. There shall be a bodily resurrection of the dead and a reward or punishment, the latter meted out to infidels.

7. Finally, the intersection of Islam with religious traditions in West Africa becomes very clear with the use of amulets. Muslims believe that the holy words of the Qur'an possess their own power against the evil force in their own world. West African Muslims quickly appropriated the words of the Qur'an as a powerful talisman against every evil, whether in battle or at home. Bits of parchment or paper that contained verses of the Qur'an were folded in pouches worn on the breast. The charm was even regarded by non-Muslims to be just as powerful as any of their own concoctions of medicine. There are words in the Qur'an (Surah 113) and commentaries that discuss the treatment of the threat of the "evil eye" and wicked "blowers on knots," probably referring to witches. Allah's words were somehow incarnate on paper or even in the chalk script left on children's slates. Once washed off the boards, the chalk in the water wrung out of cloths was retained as "holy water" for protection against the machinations of any evil

spirit, even Iblis, the devil. Muslims taken into captivity in the Americas brought with them this powerful talisman, just as they did other artifacts of root work to be utilized for conjuration. Since many Muslims were transported to Brazil from the Senegal River region, the name of the Mandinka became synonymous with the Muslim charm among other African slaves (Clarke 1982).

The West African Muslim consciousness is what the purist calls an *al-Mukhlit* one, a "mixer" of traditions (Johnson 1991). At once cabalistic and orthodox in their liturgy and moral viewpoint, West African *malams* have rituals that are not too far from the hieratic symbols created by the local priests in their shrines and, as we shall observe in the next chapter, not too distant either from the healing arts of the Christian indigenous churches.

One has only to read D. T. Niane's version of *Sundiata: An Epic of Old Mali* to grasp the extent of the marriage between the Crescent and Malinke religious practices. The griot right from the start claims legitimization from the Prophet, while going on later to describe sacrifices by the hero to hundreds of jinns in a pool of magic water (Niane 1992). That was a long time ago. Islam today, wherever it thrives in West Africa, has been Africanized. It is not as Arab either in custom or in language as any upright Sunni would desire. Ibn Battuta, were he to return today to modern Mali, or Ghana, or Nigeria, would probably agree. Nevertheless, Islam has its attractions for this very reason. It has been transformed from Arabian or Arabic into an indigenous reality, perhaps purloined and then owned by West African traditions. The only exception perhaps would be in Hausaland, where everything in the culture has been Islamized and Arabized. Islam remains—for example in Nigeria—a political force to be reckoned with, but politics are not the only indicator of peoples' affairs, in spite of what the leaders may claim. As Traditional Religions start to wane and Christianity itself is on the roll, a drum beating out a new rhythm and calling for a new song and dance, and as the latter associates itself more closely with economic progress, leaders in Nigeria and elsewhere have to recognize that Islam is not the only way to salvation. Islam, however, has some lessons to teach Christians in West Africa. We now turn to this formidable arena, where West African Religious Traditions are being played out in a new tune.

BIBLIOGRAPHY

Abercrombie, Thomas J. "Ibn Battuta: Prince of Travelers." *National Geographic*, December 1991, 2-49.

Clarke, Peter B. *West Africa and Islam: A Study of Religious Development from the 8th to the 20th Century*. London: Edward Arnold (Publishers) Ltd, 1982.

Conde, Maryse. *Segu*. New York: Ballantine Books, 1987.

Geertz, Clifford. *Islam Observed*. Chicago: University of Chicago Press, 1968.

Hiskett, Marvyn. *The Development of Islam in West Africa*. New York: Longman Group Ltd, 1984.

Johnson, Lemuel A. "Crescent and Consciousness: Islamic Orthodoxies and the West African Novel." In *Faces of Islam in African Literature*, ed. Kenneth W. Harrow, 239-60. Portsmouth, N.H.: Heinemann Educational Books, 1991.

Kirby, Jon P. *God, Shrines, and Problem-solving among the Anufo of Northern Ghana*. Collectanea Instituti Anthropos, vol. 34. Berlin: Dietrich Reimer Verlag, 1986.

Niane, D. T. *Sundiata: An Epic of Old Mali*. Harlow, Essex, England: Longman Group, 1992.

Ousmane, Sembene. "The False Prophet." In *African Short Stories: Twenty Short Stories from across the Continent*, ed. Chinua Achebe and C. L. Innes, 2-7. Portsmouth, N.H.: Heinemann African Writers Series, 1985.

Robinson, David. "An Approach to Islam in West African History." In *Faces of Islam in African Literature*, ed. Kenneth W. Harrow, 107-29. Portsmouth, N.H.: Heinemann Educational Books, 1991.

Sanneh, Lamin. *Translating the Message: The Missionary Impact on Culture*. American Society of Missiology Series, no. 13. Maryknoll, N.Y.: Orbis Books, 1990.

STUDY GUIDE

1. Why should not West African Islam be studied from the viewpoint of Arab or Oriental Islam?

2. Which are the three distortions of African Islam that some commentators commit?

3. Locate on maps the great centers of West African Islam. Where was Segu, Djenne, Sokoto?

4. Discuss each of the "complexes" defined by Geertz. Indicate how Traditional Religions were perhaps influencing a view concerning the dead among the Muslims. Note the different approaches taken by the marabouts and the warrior leaders such as dan Fodio.

5. Discuss the three-level paradigms proposed by Humphrey Fisher and show how they are borne out in the history of West African Islam.

6. Discuss Ibn Battuta and his contribution to the knowledge of Old Mali.

7. What is the meaning of *dar al-Islam* and *dar al-Harb?* Show how Islam is territorial. What influence did this distinction have on the slave trade by Africans?

8. What is a *malam?* What was his influence on the African practice of Islam?

9. Discuss the reason for the lack of complete penetration of Islam in the forest regions, such as among the Asante.

10. List and comment on the areas of intersection of Islam with Traditional Religions. Note especially where Islam dealt with evil and how it discerned the solution to problems through divination. How have Muslims used amulets?

9

"The Green Mamba Dies at the Sight of Jesus"

Christianity in West Africa

HOW IT STARTED

There is a place on the Gulf of Guinea, where the forest meets the sea. The mouth of the Pra River empties into the Gulf at a location near Shama (Ghana), a natural harbor. There, in January 1471, two Portuguese sea captains dropped anchor from their caravels and waded ashore in search of fresh water. While bartering with the Africans, the Europeans found that gold was plentiful there. Immediately they staked out a claim on Shama and reported the news to Prince Henry back in Lisbon (Sanneh 1983).

Prince Henry the Navigator dispatched more explorers south to reconnoiter the coast and to stake out locations for more permanent settlements. His motives were both for trade and for the advancement of Portugal, a country virtually untrammeled by strife, contrary to the experience of many other European countries at the time. Henry was known for his zeal for the spread of the gospel of Jesus Christ in foreign lands touched by his naval expeditions. However, other Portuguese and eventually Spaniards, traders mostly, who were not so highly motivated, penetrated the West African coastal area searching for easy wealth.

Further east of Shama, at a place the Efutu, a Twi-speaking people, call Edina, there is a sandy shore where fishermen are contentedly mending their nets. Nearby, a rocky hillock overlooks the Gulf. A spring of fresh water gushes from the rocks and tumbles quickly down to join the sea waters crashing against the rusty rocks. A few naked men splash in a pool of the fresh water, bathing themselves, their wet black skin glistening in the sunlight. The day is January 19, 1482. A fleet of Portuguese caravels drops anchor and a large number of bearded men gather on the shore, breaking the tranquility of the scene. They kiss the ground. One of them, Diogo da Azambuja, the leader of the expedition, plants a cross firmly in the sand. Behind him stand five hundred soldiers. They are fully armed, but their weapons are concealed beneath their tunics. With them are over a hundred artisans and a few priests, their black robes flapping in the breeze. Immediately they turn and head as a group toward the highest point overlooking the water and set up a table. The priests celebrate the Mass, the first one ever recorded in West Africa. Weeping with devotion, many of the men vow that the church will soon be planted here and last until the end of the world. (Sanneh 1983). Soon they built a fortress on the hilltop, a place sacred to the Efutu, surrounded it with high walls and a moat, isolating themselves in their castle and chapel, dedicated to São Jorge (St. George), except to go out and trade for the plentiful supply of gold. They called the town *la mina*. It was like a gold mine! The coastal area they named the Gold Coast. But soon Edina and *la mina* combined to become Elmina, a name that in future decades would be associated with the slave trade at that same castle.

Thus Christianity made its dubious entry into West Africa and Akan territory. And, right from the start, except for a few brave efforts elsewhere in West Africa, Christianity would exist in quarantine for a long time.

THE EARLY CHRISTIAN STORY IN AFRICA

The Christian story in Africa goes back to the New Testament, where, in Matthew's gospel, Joseph fled King Herod's wrath and took his little family to hide in Egypt (Mt 2:14). Some thirty years later, on the way to his execution, when Jesus lost control while trying to carry the cross, the soldiers forced a passerby to help him by shouldering the cross. Mark's gospel mentions the man's name as Simon from Cyrenia in Libya, a Roman province. Simon was said to be the father of Christians known to Mark's community, Alexander and Rufus ("Red") (Mk 15:21). On the day of Pentecost, North Africans, most likely Jews or Jewish converts from Egypt and Libya, were among those who heard Peter's sermon in their own language (Acts 2:9). Most clearly a black African, an Ethiopian, or perhaps more precisely, an official from the kingdom of Meroe in the Upper Nile valley, met the deacon Philip, who baptized him (Acts 8:26-39). We do not know whether this official converted any Africans. We do know that Nubians became Christians and remained so for many centuries.

The Church of Alexandria in Egypt had apostolic connections, beginning with Mark and perhaps Thomas on his way to India. Christianity spread the gospel across North Africa throughout the Roman provinces. Most important, Alexandria had been a Jewish center of learning, and now Christian scholars emerged from its citizens, including Clement, Origen, Cyril, and Athanasius. The Coptic Church in the Nile Valley and, further south, the

Ethiopian Church were truly ethnic in spirit and in culture. The Coptic Church, more than the Church of Alexandria, preserved many ancient Egyptian customs and ritual (Meyer and Smith 1994). The Ethiopian Church, founded in the fourth century, was the most African in culture and language. North Africa along the Mediterranean Sea was dominated by the Roman and Phoenician cultures. Eventually Latin became the adopted language of even the Berbers, who spoke an Afro-Asian language at home. This area produced great theologians and saints of the church, especially Cyprian, Augustine and his mother, Monica, Tertullian at Carthage, and the martyrs Perpetua and Felicity. The Egyptian desert produced the great monks Antony and Pachomius and the monastic rule and liturgical style of praying the psalms. But Christianity failed in North Africa, mainly because it was the religion of a minority closely aligned with Rome and the Latin Church. Culturally, the church was Greco-Roman. The Christian Berbers, sometimes called Donatists, rejected the Catholic Church because of this background, although there were doctrinal problems. When Islam swept through North Africa, only after a brief resistance the Berber population accepted Islam and drove out the descendants of the Phoenicians and Romans. The Coptic Church survived in the Upper Nile basin mainly because it became the religion of the Egyptians who resisted Arabization and who retained a form of Egyptian language and art in their monophysite liturgy. The Ethiopian Church survived because it became the religion of the nation and culture of the people, in language, symbol, and in liturgical style. It was truly African to the core (Oduyoye 1986; Sindima 1994).

The lesson to be learned from this experience of the early African Christian Church is that Christianity will survive only if it answers the needs of the local church and its people. Does it do that in West Africa?

CHRISTIANITY AND EUROPEAN EXPANSIONISM

When the Portuguese first set foot on African soil at Elmina, the representatives of religion just tagged along. They were not leaders. Later on they were practically confined to their castle chapels to say Mass for their dead rulers and to receive royal stipends for their religious work in the castle. A few Augustinian missionaries ventured forth to the Komenda fields a few miles west of Elmina, only to be slaughtered for their efforts (Sanneh 1983).

Further south the Portuguese worked more vigorously to spread the gospel. In fact, the missionaries met with some degree of success in the Kongo region from the mouth of the Congo River further south to Luanda. The sub-kingdom of Soyo in the sixteenth century, from royalty to lowest commoner, converted to Catholicism, not just for political reasons but because they probably did believe with all their hearts that salvation was theirs (Gray 1990). Alfonso I ascended the royal office in the early years of the sixteenth century and sought through the help of the Portuguese to consolidate his power against the larger Kongo kingdom. He sought diplomatic relations with the papacy and sent a certain citizen by the name of Antonio with a legation to Rome. Antonio's bust still stands in the church of Santa Maria Maggiore in Rome (Sindima 1994). Alfonso packed off one of his sons, Henrique, to Lisbon to study in the seminary. He eventually became the first African south of the Sahara to be ordained bishop. Because of poor health, he never accomplished much (Sindima 1994). Alfonso was like his Muslim counterparts to the north, who used the new religion for the consolidation of power. He was succeeded by other kings who in the seventeenth century expelled the Portuguese with the help of the Dutch. The latter wanted Soyo's business in ivory, copper, and slaves in exchange for firearms and ammunition. Nonetheless, the Soyo citizenry never did accept Calvinism in exchange for their Catholicism (Gray 1990).

Against this historical background Capuchins arrived from Naples in the late seventeenth century. They were somewhat neutral as far as politics were concerned, and they continued the spread of the gospel among the peoples of the Kongo region. Their neutrality extended not only to their dealings with the Europeans but also to relations between the peoples of Soyo and others beyond in the region. In Soyo, the Capuchins were the sole evangelists, although they were challenged in Kongo by diocesan priests of mixed ethnicity.

While the Christian liturgical calendar became central to many annual events in Soyo life, with even the king decked in royal splendor in attendance, many times actively inserting his own cultural dances into the celebrations, the Capuchins met with minimal success in changing the people's attitudes about their shrines and charms. The Capuchins made their first mistake by not learning the language and the culture of the people sufficiently. Second, they identified traditional religious practices as the work of the devil. On the part of the populace, the ruling elite slowly accepted the teachings of the Capuchins, including their insistence on canonical marriage according to the Council of Trent, a thing that not many in Europe were even willing to comply with. The rest of the population accepted a mixed form of religion, Catholicism and its feasts, and Catholicism mixed with traditional religious practices, where medals were the new charms, again a thing that many European Catholics believed, as well as the continuance of the use of ancestral rituals and shrines (Gray 1990). Soon many regarded their own ancestors to be comparable to the foreign Catholic saints. The worst policy was that the missionaries never permitted the local Christians to rise higher than interpreter. No one was ordained to the priesthood. Hence, no one was available to deepen the faith of the people in a truly African fashion in the context of language and culture.

The Christian experience of Soyo in the late seventeenth and early eighteenth centuries was more an exception than the rule. The Portuguese method of *padreado,* which required that the Africans in their territories accept both Catholicism and the rule of the king of Portugal, met with strong opposition from Africans almost everywhere. Moreover, the policy of *requerimento* meant that Christianity in its totality required obedience to church authorities. Nothing of traditional practices was to remain. Nothing of traditional value was permitted to continue. Either rulers accepted this in order to obtain the technology of the Europeans or they were rejected altogether.

It was not until the nineteenth century that a surge of evangelization occurred in West Africa. While European missionaries often colluded with the colonial powers and continued to cooperate with them or were used by them for their purposes of exploiting the vast wealth of Africa, they also managed to counter many colonial policies. Nonetheless, many African novelists have tried to illustrate that there was hardly any difference between the colonial administrator and the missionary. As Achebe notes in *Things Fall Apart:*

> From the very beginning religion and education went hand in hand. Mr. Brown's mission grew from strength to strength, and because of its link with the new administration it earned a new social prestige. (Achebe 1989, 166-67)

Certainly the missionary's objectives were closely aligned with those of the administrator. Christianity and civilization seemed to go hand in hand, but according to the version of the missionary's country of origin. He may have softened the demands of the administrator, but many times he dealt with him in order to exploit the treasure-house mentality promoted by the likes of a Cecil Rhodes in East Africa.

PROTESTANT ENDEAVORS AND TRANSLATION

Yet Christianity in West Africa was not to be identified with the Western missionary. The Protestant initiative originated with Africans themselves or with their descendants from the African diaspora. And there were Western missionaries who initiated a first and a very significant step toward the Africanization of Christianity—the translation of the Bible.

As Lamin Sanneh remarks,

> However much mission may have been conceived as the arm of European political expansion, missionaries still had to rely on indigenous languages to preach their message, and this created a distinction between European culture and the indigenous traditions. Consequently, however much mission tried to suppress local populations, the issue of the vernacular helped to undermine its foreign character. By the same token, the new interest in creating vernacular Scriptures for societies

that had no Scriptures of their own ushered in a fundamental religious revolution, with new religious structures coming into being to preside over the changes. One of the most dramatic changes was undoubtedly the popular, mass participation of Africans in this process. It began to dawn on African populations that the missionary adoption of vernacular categories for Scriptures was in effect a written sanction for the indigenous religious vocation. (Sanneh 1990, 159)

One of the first to advocate the use of the local language was a secretary of the Church Missionary Society of the Church of England, Henry Venn, sometimes called the father of the indigenous church. He was one of the first to advocate the appointment of local pastors with the effect of what he termed the "euthanasia of mission" (Sanneh 1983). In other words, foreign missionaries should hand over the church to the local people as soon as possible. Venn in fact encouraged the pastorate and episcopal ordination of a Yoruba *aku,* a recaptive, who found Christianity in the place where the British dumped him after he was rescued by them from a Portuguese slave ship, in Sierra Leone. His name was Adjai. After his baptism he was known as Samuel Ajayi Crowther (Walls 1992).

One of the many accomplishments of this able clergyman was that he helped gather orthographic material to aid a committee of experts in the translation of the Bible into Yoruba by collecting over the years many proverbs, vocabularies, and idiomatic expressions from elders. Being a Yoruba speaker himself, Ajayi was better able than many missionaries to construct a tonal alphabet and the best idiomatic translation of the Bible possible. He even enlisted the advice of Muslims, inquiring how they translated the ancient words of the Qur'an when they quoted from it in sermons delivered in the local language (Walls 1992). Crowther saw the connection between the Qur'an and the Bible as a bridge over which he could pass to reach the mind-set of the many Muslims in his Niger Mission. He later encouraged the limited distribution of the Bible in Arabic, but only insofar as the verses were not used like the Qur'anic charms (Walls 1992). Ajayi Crowther was truly a pioneer in the Africanization of Christianity, although his fellow church members failed to recognize his accomplishments. For a long while no other Yoruba was chosen to succeed him in the episcopate, and many Yoruba left the Anglican Church to found their own African Churches (see below), sometimes called "African Independent Churches." Crowther's treatment provided fuel for Edward W. Blyden's call for the nationalist movement (Walls 1992).

German-speaking Presbyterians from Basel founded a missionary enterprise known as the Basel Mission. Some of their men had worked in Liberia and with Crowther on the Niger Mission. Eventually they entered the Gold Coast (Ghana) to establish their mission in the interior; their favorite areas were the higher altitudes, with less humidity and heat and fewer mosquitoes. In the mid-nineteenth century they established firm church settlements

in the Akwapim traditional region at Akropong and on the Kwahu escarpment at Abetifi. One of the mission's outstanding scholars was a German,
Johannes Christaller, who undertook the huge task of learning everything
he could about the Akwapim dialect of Twi. He translated the Bible in
Akwapim by 1871. He published a Twi dictionary and grammar. Finally, by
1879, he had collected thirty-six hundred Asante and Fante proverbs and
idioms (Sanneh 1990; Bediako 1995). Back in Switzerland, at Basel, he
founded a newspaper, which in the early years of the twentieth century was
transferred to the Gold Coast, where articles were written in Twi, Ga, and
English about current world events (Sanneh 1990; Bediako 1995). Christaller's
affirmation of the Akan culture and language was itself a work of the great-
est achievement, one which was recognized as a foundation of the nationalist movement in the emerging Ghana. Not to be forgotten are the works
done by Dr. Clement A. Akrofi, who built upon the works of Christaller. His
collection of proverbs with their English interpretations was itself an achievement, aside from his revision of the Twi Bible (Bediako 1995).

As Sanneh and other Africans have noted, the translation of the Christian
scriptures into the languages of Africans resulted in an affirmation of their
ancient languages and cultures in a revolutionary form, the written medium
of grammar and alphabet. It provided not only a continuity between the
ancestral religions and Christianity but a new lever in the brave new world
which required the peoples of clan, ethnic group, and nation to stand proudly
in the face of foreign cultures. No longer needing to express themselves in
a foreign language, Africans have through Christian efforts been able to
write about themselves, keeping in mind their own ancestral origins. Thus
the Christian translation project resulted in the emergence of African literature and in the African independence movement. Many decades before the
proposals of the notion of "negritude" in the Pan-African Movement suggested by Aimé Cesaire in 1939 (Masolo 1994), and long before the claims
of Afrocentrism to reaffirm African cultures and languages so grossly dero-
gated by Western slavery and colonialism, and in the face of Muslim denial
of the very existence of spirituality in local traditions, Christian efforts affirmed them and provided an avenue for their presentation to all who cared
to understand that sub-Saharan Africa was a reserve of high culture and
religion from ancient times. At first with the European mainline churches,
such as the Methodists and Presbyterians, then later under the leadership of
African prophets and ministers with the foundation of independent movements, Africans ceased to regard Christianity as a foreign intrusion. Beginning with translation of the Bible, then with further adaptations and innova-
tions, Christianity became truly African. Nova Scotian settlers of African
descent developed an evangelical culture in Freetown. From there, the neo-
Sierra Leoneans branched out into the Niger River basin as far as Yoruba
country. Methodists were invited to Cape Coast, in the Gold Coast, by Fante
Christians. Still today the Methodist Church buildings in Cape Coast and
Elmina are imposing. And the "Presby" Church arrived in West Africa both

from Basel and from the Caribbean (Gray 1990). Their foundations still endure to this day in Akropong, in Abetifi, and in Kibi in modern Ghana.

Several outstanding individuals of African descent, who were probably very influential in the promotion of African nationalism, and who thought of their Christianity as providential, a gift from God, returned to Africa with their faith and their English language. The first was Alexander Crummell, an Episcopalian clergyman born in New York in 1819, educated at Queen's College, Cambridge, England, and Liberian by adoption. He spent twenty years in Liberia and Sierra Leone, largely in the field of education. Crummell's ideology centered around the notion that the Africans "exiled" in the New World had received from divine providence "at least one item of compensation, namely the possession of the Anglo-Saxon tongue" (Appiah 1992, 3). According to him, English was without the slightest doubt superior to the "various tongues and dialects" of the native African populations (Appiah 1992, 3; see 20). English "was superior in its euphony, its conceptual resources, and its capacity to express the 'supernal truths' of Christianity" (Appiah 1992, 3).

Ironically, Crummell claimed that his authority for thus lecturing Africans and those of African descent at Cape Palmas in Maryland County, Liberia, in 1860, was that he too was a Negro. He was one of the earliest nineteenth-century blacks to express ideologically a common destiny for the people of Africa because of the notion of race (Appiah 1992). Yet, he said, they were inferior to him and those like him, because he was a Christian and he spoke a European language. His low opinion of Africans, while at the same time initiating an early stage of pan-Africanism and nationalism, simply reflected notions on race he learned from Anglo-Americans in his country of origin. Crummell introduced to Africans the ideology that all Africans are alike solely due to their skin color. He ignored where they differed due to cultures, religious traditions, and languages. His view of Africans was lumped together into one category of culture as "anarchic, unprincipled, ignorant," and "heathen and savage" (Appiah 1992, 21).

Similar to Crummell in many ways, but more prolific in his theology of race, was Edward W. Blyden. Born on St. Thomas in the Danish Caribbean in 1832, educated in New York, a Presbyterian minister, and Liberian by adoption, he returned to the United States between 1872 and 1888 eleven times to speak to many audiences in behalf of Africa on the solidarity of black people. Together with Carter G. Woodson and W. E. B. Du Bois, Blyden helped to establish the black history movement in the United States (Wilmore 1987). He was a professor and president at Liberia College, and eventually, as ambassador of Liberia to Queen Victoria, he corresponded with William Gladstone, Charles Dickens, and Charles Sumner (Appiah 1992). Like Crummell, Blyden believed that Africans needed to learn the English language to better themselves and to rise out of their "savagery" (Mudimbe 1988). However, Blyden went further. Sympathizing with the goals of the American Colonization Society, Blyden advocated the return of black Americans to Africa. He stated that *black* for him meant pure black and not any-one of "mixed blood" or mulattoes (Mudimbe 1988). Later he would ex-pound on what he meant by the "black personality," anticipating later ideas espoused by the notion of negritude promoted by Leopold Senghor. Afri-cans had to be educated by pure blacks from the Americas to become Chris-tian and civilized. Yet Blyden was more subtle than Crummell by distin-guishing "Negroes from Negroes," clearly critical of those who wish to lump all Africans into one race (Appiah 1992; Mudimbe 1988). The great com-mon trait of Africans was that they lacked Christianity. And the only ones capable of bringing Christianity to all peoples of Africa were those of Afri-can descent who had been converted in exile.

Interesting enough is the fact that as time progressed Blyden came to accept the "independence" of Islam. He remained quite critical of Protes-tant efforts, which remained close to European settlements along the West African coast in the nineteenth century. He saw Islam as a religion that had integrated better into African cultures. His "nationalist" outlook is reflected in his wish to introduce Arabic and African languages into the curriculum at Liberia College, so that Christians could communicate better with the many peoples of the interior (Mudimbe 1988). Arabic was a good prepara-tion for Christianity, Blyden thought. In his old age Blyden was at least spiritually Muslim, while at the same time he promoted black nationalism and the unity of Africa by black Christians. All in all, Blyden's ideas were partially represented in the African independence movement advocated by Kwame Nkrumah, with his political philosophy of "conscencism." A three-fold framework embraced this approach: African tradition, Islamic contri-bution, and Western legacy (Mudimbe 1988). The only difference was that Nkrumah held to a materialistic and Marxist philosophy.

Others would follow in Blyden's footsteps, and his theology and philoso-phy would later be accepted one way or another by them. One such person-ality from the United States was Bishop Henry McNeal Turner of the AME Church. Products of AME and AME Zion Churches and other Methodist affiliations were educated at Wesleyan High School, which changed to Mfantsipim in 1905 at Cape Coast. These included J. Mensah Sarbah and J. E. Casely Hayford from Mfantsipim, and J. E. K. Aggrey, born at Anomabu in Fante country—all leaders in the future independence of Ghana. They demonstrated how the connection between their Christianity and their poli-tics arose out of the culture of their own people. And the legacy they re-ceived from the written form of their languages from Christian scholars was not forgotten.

INDIGENOUS AFRICAN CHRISTIAN CHURCHES

The great achievements of Christianity—due to translation of the Bible and other Christian texts—include the phenomenon known as African Independent Churches. Kofi Appiah-Kubi prefers "Indigenous African Christian Churches" (hereafter IACC) to distinguish them from the elder (or missionary) churches derived from outside of Africa (Appiah-Kubi 1979). Sometimes local Akan people call them "spiritual churches."

Aside from the skirmishes about who could or should evangelize West Africa or other places on the continent, and about the methods to be used, such as translation of the Bible and other texts, there were the Africans themselves, perhaps like Okonkwo, who reacted in different ways to the foreigners who presumed to tell them about religion. Yet some of them, again like Okonkwo, did not respect Igbo or Akan religion, or continue to follow the ritual path to peace with their communities. Is Okonkwo really Achebe in disguise? At the end of *Things Fall Apart* the gods and the ancestors are weeping because there are new and more powerful forces at work on the land that have made them impotent and useless (Onwubiko 1991). Achebe has, in the last analysis, yearned not for a return of the Igbo ancestral religion or for the permanent establishment of the religion of the queen of (Victorian) England, but for a religionless secular society in Nigeria. His writing was to make a deep impression on the youth of Nigeria (Onwubiko 1991).

Other African writers and novelists have criticized Christianity for being divisive of the sense of community and for being totally unappreciative of the role of the ancestors in the clan and kinship systems. Christian missionaries were unable to understand and therefore to tolerate traditional religions and cultures. However, as Mercy Amba Oduyoye explains, once the foreigners got a foothold in their country, the Asante took a wait-and-see attitude. Would the invaders eventually understand them? The Asante claimed the Fante were already corrupted. A benign tolerance of these other new religions set in (Oduyoye 1986). *Ehia oburoni a oka Twi,* "When the white man gets into hot water, he will learn to speak Twi!" Meanwhile, *Ohoho te se abrofra,* "The stranger is like a child." As Dr. Akrofi himself explains the maxim: *[Ohoho] onnim oman hwee,* "The foreigner is ignorant of the internal affairs of the country" (Akrofi n/d). People known to be Christian also consulted the shrines deities. The missionaries had not shown the Africans how completely to conquer the *honhom fi,* the evil force, still rampant over the land and manifest in discord and disease. Oduyoye and other African scholars have now demonstrated that a huge gap surfaced between the gospel that was proclaimed by the missionaries and the gospel that was heard and thus finally accepted. She refers to the Yoruba for "I have heard" *(gbo),* which almost sounds like the Yoruba for "I accept" *(gba),* which are nonetheless not the same (Oduyoye 1986).

Secessions from European-based missionary churches began principally in South Africa around the 1890s as a protest against the rising racism in the white churches. The movement was known as "Ethiopianism," already perceived as a form of pan-African conspiracy of nationalism. In fact, the name *Ethiopia* was derived from the biblical references to Africa. The tag

Ethiopian or *Abyssinian* before a church title meant that its members were blacks in Africa or from Africa. Even the Ras Tafari Movement in Jamaica was derived from Marcus Garvey's campaign to have all blacks in the diaspora return to "Ethiopia." At any rate, the first IACCs were not only protests against the European churches and their cultural baggage but protests against a social problem, chiefly racism. While not termed such, the movements were incipient models for later liberation concepts culturally, politically, and theologically (Onwubiko 1991). Certainly in South Africa, the IACCs were truly independent in the sense of their rebelliousness against early outbreaks of apartheid and European expressions of the faith. The new church leaders, like Simon Kimbangu in the Belgian Congo, were prophets who desired intensely to reform the church to fit African sensibilities (Cox 1995).

According to Harvey Cox, the IACCs at the early part of the twentieth century were influenced by pentecostal missionaries who arrived at first in South Africa soon after "fire fell" in Los Angeles at the Azusa Street revival in 1906. From there it spread throughout sub-Saharan Africa with glad tidings of the outpouring of the Holy Spirit (Cox 1995). There are now over five thousand independent Christian denominations, all born in the twentieth century, all bearing the marks of pentecostal spirituality, but also with truly African qualities of their own. They are expanding faster than Islam, twice as fast as the Catholic Church, and three times as fast as the other non-Catholic groups (Cox 1995). In Zaire, the Church of the Lord Jesus Christ on Earth of the Prophet Simon Kimbangu, founded by Kimbangu in 1921 before he was jailed by Belgian and Catholic authorities, now has more than eight million members, making it the largest of such denominations in Africa. It is the first of the IACCs to be affiliated with the World Council of Churches. Besides the five thousand known churches, there are other innumerable ones founded by local prophets, with various titles bearing the name *prophet, apostolic, spiritual,* or *Zion.* According to Cox, by the year 2000 (he writes in 1995) there will be more members in these churches in Africa than in the Catholic Church or in all the Protestant denominations put together (Cox 1995).

In West Africa the twentieth century witnessed a progression of Africans accepting Christianity from the European mainline churches, with their efforts in translation of the Bible, a large step toward affirmation of African cultures, to the IACC total immersion in them. Contemporary scholars, for example Robert J. Schreiter, distinguish among three models of evangelization that account for the Christian encounter with cultures (Schreiter 1985; Fisher 1990). The first is the *translation* model, such as the work done by Crowther and Christaller. In a sense this model is a form of indigenization, which at least affirms the local languages and idioms as templates of cultural value.

The second model is sometimes called adaptation or, more scientifically, according to anthropology, *acculturation*. This is the process we find in the early twentieth-century break-away Christian churches, especially in Nigeria, such as the United Native African Church in Lagos. Adaptation was evident in the promotion of drumming, choir singing, and African versions of western hymns during services. The question of polygamy was addressed, though not entirely solved to the African way of thinking. Many of the churches were lay-oriented and tended to give more prominent roles to women. Even some of the mainline churches soon followed suit, such as the Basel Mission in the Gold Coast, which always had a local person as moderator or president of the Presbyterian Church. One of the more important endeavors of these churches was dealing with the ownership of property and development of agricultural projects. For example, the Basel Mission established a large palm-oil farm at Akropong. The Basel Trading Company, in time known as the Union Trading Company (U.T.C.), built up a huge palm-oil industry, which expanded into the production and the sale of cocoa (Sanneh 1983; Miller 1993).

The third model of evangelization, *contextualization*, is exemplified early on in the IACCs. In Catholic theology the term *inculturation* has been coined and widely accepted (Dulles 1995; Fisher 1990). This model proposes that Christians do not live their faith in a style and language alien to their own culture; in other words, they discover their own forms of worship and their own methods of evangelization. Stated yet another way, the local people themselves are engaged in the evangelization of their own culture. The IACCs retained many elements of African Traditional Religions. But some have complained that the IACCs have practiced syncretism rather than inculturation. Syncretism may involve all or any of content, process, or simply deep respect between two religious symbol systems (Luzbetak 1988). Theologically speaking, with regard to content, if a particular IACC retains or adapts any element untenable to Christianity in its teaching or morals, syncretism pure and simple is nothing other than a form of reverse cultural domination. For example, resorting to direct worship of the river deities among the Akan and dressing it with Christian elements would constitute such a form of syncretism. In that sense it is bad. Most of the IACCs do not practice syncretism along these lines to my knowledge (see below). As regards process, the IACCs have adapted the Bible translations already prepared for them by the mainline churches and incorporated them within their styles of worship. Most often use of the Bible is rather literal. But where syncretism evolves further, we should regard their actions as similar to the translation and acculturation models of evangelization. The third level of syncretism is simply contextualization or inculturation. This is the level where perhaps we may say the IACCs have surpassed the historic churches. They certainly have maintained a deep respect for West African sensibilities.

We have learned that for West Africans, culture and religion go hand in hand. No wonder, then, that the historic churches were perceived as culturally and in every other respect European or American. Very central to all West African beliefs is that the living and the ancestors are of prime importance in God's creation. But there pervades within this cosmic order the evil force, the *honhom fi,* which can be thwarted if certain rituals and practices are followed. Traditional religions and cultures maintained order in society with taboos and with rituals. Religious leaders were thus able to exercise systemic control—to judge whether the kings and chiefs, as well as the subjects, were or were not in step with the cosmic order. Ritual is not the mere sustainer of the status quo, but the thorn in the side and the promoter of social change. When the Christian churches arrived in West Africa, they eventually took over this task. We have noted how the Basel Mission encouraged intensive farming and business. Many of its young students were the future leaders in the independence movement of Ghana, guided by Christian visions mixing culture with a view to freedom in what today we would call liberation theology. The proverb declares: "Slowly, slowly, the chicken drinks her water." Slowly, yet resolutely, the Akan and other Africans were Africanizing the foreign religion and making it their own.

The IACCs have certainly manifest how truly close to the culture they are. With their pentecostal viewpoint they have moreover married the two questions of ethnic identity and of liberation theology. They quote the psalms to justify the use of drums and other African instruments in their worship. They refer to King David, who danced before the Ark of the Covenant, to explain why they dance in their services (Cox 1995). They have found spiritual and political liberation in the power and the guidance of the Holy Spirit. In seeking what is lacking to them as Africans, members of the IACCs struggle for selfhood as Akan, Yoruba, Ewe, and so on. According to Appiah-Kubi, for these churches Jesus Christ is the supreme object of devotion, as Savior, Baptizer in the Spirit, the Soon-Coming-King, and the Healer (Appiah-Kubi 1979). He says they are free, emotional, and to some extent fanatical in their Christian worship. Preserving traditional values, they emphasize healing, reverence of the ancestors, and helping members to cope with the stresses of modern urban life (Appiah-Kubi 1979). The intentions of their intercessory prayers are much like those of libation pouring: healing and health, fertility for the women and potency for the men, employment, success in examinations, help in overcoming addictions, safety on the road against car accidents, power against possible witchcraft or sorcery, protection from another person's ill-will, and so on (Bediako 1995; Appiah-Kubi 1981). While very much this-worldly, like Traditional Religions, the IACCs also look to a future messianic fulfillment.

While it is not our purpose to provide a history of the Christian churches in West Africa, we should note the more famous of the IACCs. In Nigeria, between 1920 and 1930, pentecostal revivalist movements enhanced the fire of the Holy Spirit in the hearts of many Christians who had belonged to the mainstream churches, such as the Anglican Church. The emphasis was on healing through prayer. One prophet was Josiah Olunowo Oshirelu, who became the founder of the Church of the Lord, known simply as Aladura, from the Yoruba for prayer. At first it was a gathering of Yoruba people, who drew from Africanized Islam and the Bible, to emphasize healing and prayer along with a millennialist condemnation of the colonial system. His following split several times. Among the splinter groups were the Precious Stone Church, and the Cherubim and Seraphim Church, founded by Moses Orimulade Tunolashe, who became known as Baba Aladura, the "Praying Father," along with a young lady, Christiana Abiodun Akinsowon, both of whom led a "Praying Band," the Egbe Aladura. This latter movement retained many elements of Yoruba Traditional Religion, including belief in the *orisha* and the use of Ifa divination to determine the will of Olodumare (Sanneh 1983). Belief in the deities is a clear example of our discussion above about the use of syncretism in regard to content. However, divination is probably on the level of contextualization in the sense that it is a vehicle for giving religious advice and for communal reconciliation (Kirby 1992). The Christ Apostolic Church centered more on the person of Jesus Christ, who outflanked the deities (Sanneh 1983). The Aladura movement in its several modifications spread eventually to other West African countries, including Ghana. Ghana had its own share of pentecostal revivalist movements, including the Musama Disco Christo Church, established in 1922, and the F'Eden Revival Movement, begun in Ghana in 1963 (Assimeng 1989).

While Christianity has challenged many of the beliefs of Traditional Religions, it has itself been criticized by African religious systems for the need to view the human experience in this world as spirit-filled. Even with the advent of Western technology, Africa has resisted and challenged materialism, and it has persisted in the belief that culture and religion must work hand in hand. Those modern states that experimented with various brands of atheistic communism had to come to terms with this realization. Even now, Benin, which formerly had assumed a socialist posture, has accepted a festival of Traditional Religions as a national holiday.

THE ROMAN CATHOLIC CHURCH

Elmina was the site of the "second coming" of the Catholic Mission to the Gold Coast in 1880. Priests of the Society of African Missions (SMA), Fathers Auguste Moreau and Eugene Murat, arrived to set up a renewed attempt to evangelize the peoples of the Gold Coast to the Catholic faith. Though ravaged by malaria, yellow fever, and other problems, sometimes resulting in death, Catholics sent more missionaries to establish a frontier along the coastal areas. Slowly, the number of baptized Catholics increased, and the work spread further to the north. An ecclesiastical territory was entrusted to the Society of African Missions with its own bishop, Maximillian Albert, in 1901. Meanwhile, further north, at Navrongo, the White Fathers (now known as Missionaries of Africa), so called because they wore white robes similar in design to those worn by Muslim men, founded a mission that would prove at first very difficult. They endeavored from the start to learn the Kassena language, and soon they had written a grammar and a dictionary in that language. Two Canadians, Oscar Morin and Leonide Barsalou, were outstanding in their work of evangelization in the language of the people. The first Catholics were baptized in 1913 after a rather strenuous catechumenate.

The Catholic Mission excelled in the work of extending the faith into rural areas. The missionaries soon brought education in church-sponsored primary and middle schools and, with time, in quite a few secondary schools. With funds arriving from overseas, the Catholic Mission constructed strong school buildings and eventually added churches and rectories. They insisted on well-trained teachers. When Catholic religious sisters arrived, clinics and hospitals became popular centers, especially for the rural people. While the priests lived in central stations, maintaining a certain clear element of a ghetto mentality, they extended their work to outstations, sometimes in great numbers. They succeeded because of the work of those who learned the language of the foreigners and, knowing their own people, served as catechists, instructing the people of their villages and surrounding areas. Without them, the missionaries could not have survived. The catechists in many ways were linguists in the traditional sense of an *okyeame*, as well as interpreters, if the missionary could not speak the language of the people. The church instructed the catechists in ways of handing on the faith and in faith community leadership. Among the Ewe in eastern Ghana, catechists are called "head Christians." In fact, the catechists, together with the school teachers, men and women, as well as leading elders of small villages, have been the backbone of the Catholic Church even in the face of lack of cultural conversion on the part of the missionary. As in the historic Protestant churches, the laity excelled in leadership, which overflowed into the political effort to make the Gold Coast an independent country. Although Kwame Nkrumah had been educated in Catholic schools, he declared himself later to be a radical nationalist, a Marxian socialist, and a nondenominational Christian, in that order (Miller 1993).

The Catholic Mission impressed the local Africans with its concern for health and education as means to cope with life as it changed in the new colonial world. In its worship, its use of sacraments and sacramental signs, such as holy water, oil, incense, and so on, it appealed to African sensibilities. In fact, many Protestant church members soon adopted similar signs. Just as Catholics availed themselves of the Bible translations and dictionaries, such as those created by Christaller, and adopted the mission station system and some of the Protestant fund-raising methods, so the Protestants adopted Catholic symbols, such as the Palm Sunday procession. On the other hand, before the Second Vatican Council the church's Latin liturgy did not encourage much contextualization of worship into the full culture of the people. European customs were coupled with liturgical signs, such as gift-giving on Boxing Day, the day after Christmas. Since the Catholic Church was stringent in its insistence on married life "until death," many Catholics have married according to traditional rites but remained literally excommunicated and do not take communion. Just in case a divorce might be necessary, many Catholics delay sacramental marriage for many years. An interesting development in this regard is the church's insistence that Catholics should first marry according to traditional rites, have at least one child, and only then come forward to request a church marriage. The liturgical celebration still seems to require all the trappings of a Western-style wedding with bridal gown and suit, rings, and even a wedding Bible.

Some Protestant usages the Catholics adopted almost completely. For example, choirs in Ghana almost always dress in academic graduation gowns. When asked why they do this, they say, "It's Ghanaian custom." Similarly, every month a collection is taken up for the church in the form of a "Kofi and Ama" collection. Each day of the week is called out from Kwasi and Akosua on Sunday to Kofi on Friday and Ama on Saturday. Each day group comes forward, accompanied by drumming and singing of hymns, and each competes with the others for which one will contribute the most. It's a fun thing, and everyone hopes his or her "soul name" will win with the most contributions. Then there are the annual harvest festivals, where dignitaries are invited to chair the function and to contribute from their wealth for the good of the church, while the members compete in auction for ordinary African yams and cassava, or chickens, or sometimes a kitschy picture of Jesus or Mary. Everyone has fun, and the church gains its best financial contribution for the year; in fact, this one event normally helps to make each parish community self-supporting. While Protestant churches have been successful at tithing and with pastor appreciation days, the Catholic communities have never taken the collection that seriously, due largely perhaps to the large foreign allocations made to the missionaries, who use the funds to promote their personal projects, such as the expansion of the schools and clinics. The result of this has been a certain amount of clerical paternalism. Even when local clergy have assumed the leadership role in the church and the number of missionaries has receded, clerical paternalism remains an issue that needs to be addressed.

Since the Second Vatican Council reforms in the liturgy in 1963, the Catholic Church has launched a concerted effort everywhere in Africa to advance further than adaptation to a truly incarnational African celebration of the mass and sacraments. This required that Catholics look more seriously into learning the language of the people. This is not to say that language learning on the part of Catholic missionaries had not been tried, sometimes even to perfection. The Divine Word Missionaries in Ghana have been outstanding in this regard; one need only look at two Americans, Fathers Clement Hotze and Curtis Washington, and listen to them joking with the Krobo in their own language. In the north of Ghana, Bishop Peter Dery, brought up as the son of a shrine priest, later a Christian and a diocesan priest, a product of the work of the White Fathers, moved quickly in the Wa diocese to translate the texts of the mass into Dagare and to have the music sung in local melodies. His successor in Wa, Bishop Gregory Kpiebaya, went further and promoted dance during the liturgy. Both bishops would later succeed each other as archbishop in Tamale. In Kumasi, Bishop Peter Sarpong provided the necessary leadership in composing new forms of prayers and music with proper lyrics in Asante Twi. He has experimented with rituals that remind one of traditional rites; for example, during ordination the candidates swear allegiance to their bishop with a cross in their hand in much the same manner and language as sub-chiefs swear their fealty to their *omanhene* (see Obeng 1996).

The Divine Word Missionaries, great builders of schools and churches, also pioneered a Catholic center for the acculturation of missionaries in the Akan culture and language. Father Kofi Ron Lange, who translated Christaller's book of proverbs, founded a language school that has moved from Nsawam to Kwahu Nkwatia to Kwahu Tafo to Abetifi. He was aided in this work by several persevering schoolteachers, some still there today. Products of his work include pastors who have promoted cultural inculturation, such as the Dutchman Father Henry Noordemeer, the German Father Norbert Mushof, and, most of all, the American anthropologist Father Jon Kirby, himself a speaker fluent in three Ghanaian languages, who founded and is still director of the Tamale Institute of Cross-Cultural Studies. This school trains incoming missionaries as well as Africans in applied cross-cultural ministry.

After Vatican II African bishops were appointed. More than anyone, they realized the need for a change in approach to evangelization, and translation was only one step in the right direction. In 1974 at Rome, during a bishops' synod, the African bishops present there issued a call for change:

> The bishops of Africa and Madagascar consider as completely out of date the so-called theology of adaptation. In its stead, they adopt the theology of incarnation. . . . Theology must be open to the aspirations of the People of Africa if it is to help Christianity become incarnate in the life of the African continent. (Fisher 1990, 75)

Perhaps one could say that this mission statement has been fulfilled more in East Africa than in West Africa. Only in more recent times has this change in theology progressed in the West, but more in the interior than along the coastal dioceses of the church. In Ghana most of the active African theologians are Protestants, such as Kwame Bediako, Kofi Appiah-Kubi, Kwesi A. Dickson, John Pobee, and Mercy Amba Oduyoye. Bishop Peter Akwasi Sarpong is perhaps the only Catholic persistent in writing and creating along this field. Those who have written their doctoral dissertations on culture and theology have since disappeared, perhaps into the obscurity of their stations.

In 1994, from April 10 to May 8, representatives of all of the some 102 million Catholics, bishops from everywhere on the continent, held an African Synod of Bishops in Rome under the leadership of Pope John Paul II. They celebrated African liturgies every day, rich in song, dance, and ritual acclamations. Most of the discussions centered on Africa's contemporary problems, mainly along the lines of justice and peace. Even in post-apartheid days, African countries are ruled by dictators and war-lords. Bishop Sarpong was present. While his emphasis has been on the culture of the Asante, he has not ignored social issues. For him there is no conflict between the culturalists and the liberation theologians. Culture for him goes hand in hand with the liberation questions in Ghana as well as on the whole continent. In comments written at the end of a publication dealing with the 1994 synod, its documents, and reflections by theologians (Browne 1996), Sarpong rather sadly remarks:

> Inculturation is not something different, apart from, or opposed to the other topics—justice and peace, proclamation, dialogue, and social communications. . . . One African bishop who remarked that we were wasting time discussing dancing instead of talking about justice and peace demonstrated a lamentable misunderstanding of the meaning of inculturation. If inculturation means no more than dancing, clapping hands, or drumming, then I feel I am experiencing a totally different Church. . . . Dancing, joy, and excitement are important to Christianity and to Catholicism if they are well understood; otherwise they are useless. (Sarpong 1996, 222-23)

The bishop goes on to tell how he gave a lecture to many of the African bishops only to discover they had a negative view of their own culture and religious history. In their discussions they used such pejorative words as *polygamy, paganism, heathenism, fetishism, animism, idolatry,* and *primitive* to describe their African Traditional Religions. Almost with tears in his eyes, he says: "I realized the gigantic task ahead of us" (Sarpong 1996, 223).

I bring this up at the end of this book only to let the reader know that not everyone will agree with the approach I have assumed. Not even all Africans will agree! But what I point out here is what Bediako also declares: Christianity in Africa is Africa's religion; Christianity is a non-Western religion (Bediako 1995). To say that, one must accept all that is good in African Religious Traditions.

SOME THEOLOGICAL POINTS

It is not within the scope of this chapter to develop in detail matters about which one could write a book. African theologians, however, have done so; one such book is the work quoted above by Kwame Bediako, *Christianity in Africa: The Renewal of a Non-Western Religion.* We shall, however, address a few major points. Since "in the beginning was the dance, which reflected on itself and so gave birth to the word," tradition was born out of the ancestors' experience of the mystery of the Divine. In chapter 7 we noted that God may be called "the Great Ancestor." By whatever name God was called upon by the ancient Africans, it must have been something like Onyame or Olorun. God was connected with the earth; God was the source of life; God was the First. And they danced their joy on the earth. Then, when their parents died, they went to the abode in the earth where God was the Lord. God, Nyame, and the *nananom,* the ancestors, were all that counted. If they recognized other spirits, which the Akan called *abosom,* they are not God, not on the same level as Nyame. God and the ancestors "count." When the Christian missionaries arrived, they looked askance at libation pouring and other activities and festivals, such as the Akwasidae, as worship of the ancestors. The ancestors, it turned out, are not worshiped as God, or even invoked as the deities, but they are extremely important to the circle of life. There is a need, as Bediako recommends, along with Fasholé-Luke, to develop a Christian theology of the ancestors (Bediako 1995). To my mind, such a theology of ancestors not only connects well with an ancestor-Christology, but with what we can term an ancestor-Theology, with a capital "T." Coupled with that, there is a need for an earth theology in the African sense. Starting with the ancient ones, even those who certainly were not Christians, God must have been at work. The story of the making of Christian Africa has indeed to start from the beginning. God the Great Ancestor was the founder of the traditions that were handed down from one generation to the next. Even though Jesus, the Son of God, Nyame Ba, was born a Jew, he, as a human being with God's *'kra,* is the brother of all human beings. His death also has universal significance. He is now the firstborn of those who have died. His work brings God back to earth to bring to it his peace. His blood spilled on the earth has cleared for itself a new sacral space. While the title *king,* in the African sense, like *chief,* suffers from ambiguity, nevertheless, its priestly function still perhaps holds true today, even though the office of chief has been desacralized by the modern state. The form of worship with dance and drumming, however, can signify a form of reverence for Christ that is due to the *omanhene.* In the sense that the risen Christ is the Great Ancestor, sharing with God his Father in the same title, like a king he stands in as the first of the ancestors. Truly Christ is Nana. And the ancestors' land is his.

Bediako points to the Letter to the Hebrews to develop an African Christology based on sacrifice. Christ now is the Head Ancestor. By his one sacrifice, once and for all, he has replaced all others, which have meaning only in his. Bediako then goes on to quote from the RSV:

When he had made purification for sins, he sat down at the right hand of the Majesty on high. (Heb 1:3)

Then he quotes the Akwapim version of the same text:

Ode n'ankasa ne ho dwiraa yen bone no, okotraa anuonyam kese no nifa so osorosoro.

Bediako says that if Akan readers study their lesson carefully, they will note the word for purifying, *dwiraa*. The annual Odwira Festival (see chapter 1) with its purification rituals has now been transcended by the sacrifice of the cross once and for all, for all people. Christ's work replaces the old ritual with a new and perfect Odwira (Bediako 1990, 45; see 70-71). Catholic theology would pinpoint that festival with the Easter Triduum in the first place, and with the Sunday eucharist otherwise.

There is certainly much more to be said about the development of an African theology, and African theologians have been busy producing such a theology in recent years (see the bibliography below for examples). Recent African theologians are developing these and other themes, which are contextual. As important as the themes of Ancestor and Elder Brother are the themes dealing with the problem of evil and salvation and healing. Certainly Jesus as healer of all illness is one dear to the African heart. The IACCs have been adamant on this matter. The Catholic Church, with its sacraments of reconciliation and anointing, needs to take note of the centrality of healing not only in the clinics but in ritual as well. A pastoral theology of healing is sorely needed.

"In the beginning was the dance." Dr. Jon Kirby, an anthropologist, has recorded the psalm-like poetry of Madam Afua Kuma, a pentecostal from the Kwahu village of Asempaneye in Ghana. Her song is a testimony of how a new African faith can come to light when Jesus is encountered within a non-Western culture:

Jesus: you are a solid rock!
The green mamba dies at the sight of Jesus.
Iron rod that cannot be coiled into a head-pad;
The cobra turns on his back, prostrate before you!
Jesus, you are the Elephant Hunter, Fearless one!
You have killed the evil spirit, and cut off its head!
The drums of the king have announced it in the morning.

All of your attendants lead the way, dancing with joy!
Chief of young women:
They have strung a necklace of gold nuggets and beads,
and hung it around your neck.
So we go before you,
shouting out praises, *"Ose. Ose!"*
Chief of young men:
they are covered with precious beads
and gold pendants worn by princes.
They follow you playing musical instruments.

Jesus! You are *okyerema Nyanno:*
the God of all drummers
who are seen in the moon beating your drum
as your young maidens dance around you.
Soldiers, police, and crowds of young men
leap in jubilation.
Priests and pastors in procession,
thousands of them!
lift state swords high in salute.
You have adorned your young maidens
with gold finery,
and strewn precious beads before them.
Let us beat gong-gong
and announce it to the nations:
Let us bring your Beauty and show him to them.
        (Kuma 1981, 32-33)

If in the beginning was the dance, then surely the Word has become African flesh and dwelt among us in Jesus of the Deep Forest.
Momma yenka se: Amen! "Let us all say: Amen!"

BIBLIOGRAPHY

Achebe, Chinua. *Things Fall Apart.* New York: Fawcett Crest, 1989.

Akrofi, C. A. *Twi Mmebusem: Twi Proverbs.* Dictionary. Accra, Ghana: Presbyterian Book Depot, n/d.

Appiah, Kwame Anthony. *In My Father's House: Africa in the Philosophy of Culture.* New York: Oxford University Press, 1992.

Appiah-Kubi, Kofi. "Indigenous African Christian Churches: Signs of Authenticity." In *African Theology en Route,* ed. Kofi Appiah-Kubi and Sergio Torres, 117-25. Maryknoll, N.Y.: Orbis Books, 1979.

———. *Man Cures, God Heals: Religion and Medical Practice among the Akans of Ghana.* Totowa, N.J.: Allanheld, Osmun & Co., Publishers, 1981.

Assimeng, Max. *Religion and Social Change in West Africa: An Introduction to the Sociology of Religion.* Accra, Ghana: Ghana Universities Press, 1989.

Bediako, Kwame. *Christainty in Africa: The Renewal of a Non-Western Religion.* Maryknoll, N.Y.: Orbis Books, 1995.

————.*Jesus in African Culture: A Ghanaian Perspective.* Pamphlet. Accra, Ghana: Asempa Publishers, 1990.

Browne, Maura. *The African Synod: Documents, Reflections, Perspectives.* Africa Faith and Justice Network, ed. Maura Browne. Maryknoll, N.Y.: Orbis Books, 1996.

Cox, Harvey. *Fire from Heaven: The Rise of Pentecostal Spirituality and the Reshaping of Religion in the Twenty-first Century.* Reading, Pa.: Addison-Wesley Publishing Company, 1995.

Dulles, Avery. "Seven Essentials of Evangelization." Speech. *Origins* 25, no. 23 (November 23, 1995): 397-400.

Fisher, Robert B. "Cross-cultural Implications of Liturgical Translation in Ghana and Efforts toward Inculturation." *Verbum SVD* 31, no. 1 (1990): 75-94.

Gray, Richard. *Black Christians and White Missionaries.* New Haven: Yale University Press, 1990.

Kirby, Jon P. "Anthropology of Knowledge and the Christian Dialogue with African Traditional Religions: Lessons from Anufo Divination." *Missiology: An International Review* 20, no. 3 (July 1992): 323-41.

Kuma, Afua. *Jesus of the Deep Forest: Prayers and Praises of Afua Kuma.* Translated by Jon P. Kirby from the Twi. Accra, Ghana: Asempa Publishers, 1981.

Luzbetak, Louis J. *The Church and Cultures: New Perspectives in Missiological Anthropology.* American Society of Missiology Series, vol. 12. Maryknoll, N.Y.: Orbis Books, 1988.

Masolo, D. A. *African Philosophy in Search of Identity.* African Systems of Thought. Bloomington: Indiana University Press, 1994.

Meyer, Marvin, and Richard Smith. "Introduction." In *Ancient Christian Magic: Coptic Texts of Ritual Power,* ed. Marvin Meyer and Richard Smith, 1-9. San Francisco: HarperSanFrancisco, 1994.

Miller, Jon. "Missions, Social Change, and Resistance to Authority: Notes toward an Understanding of the Relative Autonomy of Religion." *Journal of the Scientific Study of Religion* 32, no. 1 (March 1993): 29-50.

Mudimbe, V. Y. *The Invention of Africa: Gnosis, Philosophy, and the Order of Knowledge.* Bloomington: Indiana University Press, 1988.

Obeng, J. Pashington. *Asante Catholicism: Religious and Cultural Reproduction among the Akan of Ghana.* New York: E. J. Brill, 1996.

Oduyoye, Mercy Amba. *Hearing and Knowing: Theological Reflections on Christianity in Africa.* Maryknoll, N.Y.: Orbis Books, 1986.

Onwubiko, Oliver A. *African Thought, Religion, and Culture.* The Christian Mission and Culture in Africa Series, vol. 1. Enugu, Nigeria: SNAAP Press, 1991.

Sanneh, Lamin. *Translating the Message: The Missionary Impact on Culture*. American Society of Missiology Series, vol. 13. Maryknoll, N.Y.: Orbis Books, 1990.

———. *West African Christianity: The Religious Impact*. Maryknoll, N.Y.: Orbis Books, 1983.

Sarpong, Peter K. "Conclusion." In *The African Synod: Documents, Reflections, Perspectives*, ed. Maura Browne, 220-26. Maryknoll, N.Y.: Orbis Books, 1996.

Schreiter, Robert J. *Constructing Local Theologies*. Maryknoll, N.Y.: Orbis Books, 1985.

Sindima, Harvey J. *Drums of Redemption: An Introduction to African Christianity*. Westport, Conn.: Greenwood Press, 1994.

Walls, Andrew F. "The Legacy of Samuel Ajayi Crowther." *International Bulletin of Missionary Research* 16, no. 1 (January 1992): 15-21.

Wilmore, Gayraud S. *Black Religion and Black Radicalism: An Interpretation of the Religious History of Afro-American People*. 2d ed., revised. Maryknoll, N.Y.: Orbis Books, 1987.

Additional Sources Not Cited in Text

Bediako, Kwame. *Theology and Identity: The Impact of Culture upon Christian Thought in the Second Century and in Modern Africa*. Oxford, U.K.: Oxford Regnum Books, 1992.

Berends, William. "African Traditional Healing Practices and the Christian Community." *Missiology: An International Review* 21, no. 3 (July 1993): 275-88.

Bujo, Benezet. *African Theology in Context*. Maryknoll, N.Y.: Orbis Books, 1992.

Kirby, Jon P. "Language and Culture Learning IS Conversion . . . IS Ministry." *Missiology: An International Review* 23, no. 2 (April 1995): 131-43.

Pastoral Care and Counselling in Africa Today. Vol. 1 of *African Pastoral Studies,* ed. Jean Msamba ma Mpolo and Daisy Nwachuku. New York: Peter Lang, 1991.

Sanneh, Lamin. *Encountering the West: Christianity and the Global Cultural Process*. Maryknoll, N.Y.: Orbis Books, 1993.

———. "The Yogi and the Commissar: Christian Missions and the African Response." *International Bulletin of Missionary Research* 15, no. 1 (January 1991): 2-12.

Schreiter, Robert J., ed. *Faces of Jesus in Africa*. Faith and Culture Series. Maryknoll, N.Y.: Orbis Books, 1991.

Thomas, Norman E. "Images of Church and Mission in African Independent Churches." *Missiology: An International Review* 23, no. 1 (January 1995): 17-29.

Also Recommended

Kane, Thomas A. *The Dancing Church: Video Impressions of the Church in Africa.* Video Tape. Mahwah, N.J.: Paulist Press, 1991.

STUDY GUIDE

1. Discuss the motives the Portuguese had for exploring the West Coast of Africa. Was their attempt at Christian evangelization serious? Explain your answer.

2. Elaborate on the early history of Christianity in North Africa. Who were some of the famous church leaders and theologians at the time? Why did Christianity fail in North Africa but succeed among the Copts, the Nubians, and the Ethiopians? Elaborate on the history of the church in those areas.

3. Compare the efforts of consolidation of King Alfonso I in the Kongo with the similar efforts of Muslim rulers of West Africa recounted in chapter 8.

4. Explain the role of the Italian Capuchins in the Soyo Kingdom. Why did they succeed to a certain extent? What method of conversion did the Capuchins employ? See Mudimbe 1988, chap. 3, "The Power of Speech," for that author's idea that the missionary's language was a form of oppression. Note what he says about one of the leaders of the Capuchins, Father Giovanni F. Romano, and about Crowther and Tempels (48-50; recall Tempels from chapter 7 in this book).

5. Against this background, comment on the statement Sanneh makes about the work of translation done by missionaries, including Crowther, as well as Christaller.

6. Research the role of Africans and African-Americans in the conversion of Africans to Christianity.

7. Research further on Crummell and Blyden. Also look into the African interests of such men as Martin R. Delaney, Paul Cuffee, Daniel Coker, Lott Carey, and Henry M. Turner. How did these men influence the "back to Africa movement" that later inspired Marcus Garvey and the Rastafarians? What is the connection of these men with liberationists in sub-Saharan Africa?

8. Why should more attention be paid to the Indigenous African Christian Churches? How do these churches respond to the sensibilities of Africans with regard to the problem of evil, disease, and personal and social problems? What can the historic Christian churches learn from the IACCs?

9. Research the story of Simon Kimbangu. Compare his church to the Murid Movement in Islam in Senegal.

10. Discuss the three models of evangelization. How do the IACCs make use of the second and third models?

11. What is syncretism? How do the models of evangelization and syncretism sometimes coincide?

12. Since religion and culture are so indistinguishable in sub-Saharan Africa, why did the Africans look with suspicion upon the new religions from Europe and America?

13. Find out more on the Aladura Church in Nigeria. Discuss its concern for healing.

14. Discuss the contemporary missionary work of the Roman Catholic Church. Show how it intends to make use of a theology of incarnation, explain what this means, and illustrate it by examples.

15. Discuss some of the ways Africans have Africanized Christianity in ritual as well as in theology.

16. In what ways can a theology of liberation combine with a theology of culture in West Africa?

17. What is meant by a theology of the ancestors and an earth theology in an Akan sense? How is God regarded as the Great Ancestor? How is this applied to Jesus Christ? How is Jesus regarded as healer in an African sense? Does the title king or chief seem appropriate? Why or why not?

18. As you come to the end of this book, what is the most significant thought with which it leaves you about West African/Akan Traditional Religions? What can you learn from dealing with cultures different from your own? How can Christians or Muslims learn to deal with Traditional Religious Systems in a positive and non-ethnocentric manner? Is there still a cultural apartheid?

19. Comment on the following statement: "An African Church must necessarily be the product of an organic growth on the African soil, an institution in which Christianity is incarnate within the African milieu" (Wilbert R. Shenk, "Toward a Global Church History," in *International Bulletin of Missionary Research* 20, no. 2 [April 1996]: 53; Shenk is quoting from J. F. Ade Ajayi and E. A. Ayandele, "Writing African Church History," in *The Church Crossing Frontiers: Essays on the Nature of the Church*, ed. Peter Beyerhaus and Carl F. Hallencreutz [Uppsala: Gleerup, 1969], 90-91).

Glossary

Twi and other African languages sometimes have their own orthography and phonetics. Please note the following:

ky is like ch in chin
gy is like g in gem
hy is like a whispered h
tw, as in twi, is like trying to say chew and a w at the same time
dw is like a j in jump and a w
hw is like am s together with a w
In this book I have not made use of the symbols for a short e, as in bet, and
  a nasalized o
Vowels are generally pronounced as in European languages. Spellings vary
  in the dialects, for example, *agya* in most Akan dialects, but *egya* in Fante.

abadinto	the naming of an infant
abe, ebe	proverb, maxim, saying
abayifo	witches
abenkwan	palm-nut soup
Aboakyer Festival	deer-hunting festival at Winneba taking place in May to renew a deity
abosom (s. *obosom)*	deities, gods (in the text called "no-gods" since they are created by Nyame, God)
aberewa	old woman, the mythical foundress of an ethnic group
abusua	lineage
abusuaban	clan
abusuapanyin	lineage or clan head (blood relatives head)
abadan	first steps of the *akom* (possession) dance
Adae	monthly festival in honor of the royal ancestors (see Akwasidae, Wukudae), literally the sleeping place where the ancestors lie in the stool rooms where their memorials in the form of the black stools are kept
adaebutuw	ritual of retirement of ancestors, elders, and drums at the end of the eighth month in preparation for the *Odwira* Festival and the new year

adaekese	the ninth or great *Adae,* the beginning of the *Odwira* Festival
adinkra	type of funeral cloth with stamped symbols; referring to the symbols
adowa	Akan court dance performed by women
aduanekese	sumptuous meal prepared by the bride at the wedding
aduru	medicine, herbs
adwira	plant grown in home gardens, the leaves of which are used for purification (from the verb *dwira,* to cleanse, to purify, hence Odwira Festival), ritual cleansing
afo	stick, symbol of authority (Igbo)
afona	state swords
ahenfo, ahemfo	chiefs, royalty
ahooden	strength
ajo l'aye	life's journey (Yoruba)
aklama	guardian spirit (Ewe)
akomfo	priests
akonnwa	stool, chair (*akonnwa tuntum* blackened stool)
akpeteshi	sugar-cane gin
akraguare	washing of souls ritual
aku	recaptive from slavery (Yoruba)
Akwasidae	monthly major festival in honor of the royal ancestors in a given traditional area, the beginning of the traditional month of 42 days
akyeneboa	mortal embodiment or incarnation
akyiwadie	taboos
alaafin	kings (Yoruba)
amanhene	kings of traditional states or lands, senior chiefs
amantoo	states, kingdoms
anansesem	the Spider stories of Kwaku Ananse
Ani, Ala, Ana, Ale	the Earth, earth goddess (Igbo)
anopa	morning
anyansafo	wise men
aponakyibo	"knocking at the door" or betrothal ceremony
Apoo Festival	Akan festival at Wenchi in the Brong Ahafo Region of Ghana
asafo	military association, especially among the Fante men, *ntoro* group
asafohen	company captains (in the *asafo)*
Asante Nkramo	Asante converts to Islam

asantehene	king of Kumasi, first among equals in the Asante alliance
Asase (Asaase) Yaa	the Earth Goddess, her day being Thursday
Asase Efua	the Earth Goddess (Fante), her day being Friday
asenhyerenee	good luck sign
Asikadwa Kofi	Friday's Golden Stool; symbol of the Asante Nation
asokwahene	head drummer
asusuebre	rainy, planting season (April-June)
ata	twin
atumpan	medium-sized single-headed drum, coming in twos as the talking drum
atweneboa	totem, sacred animal or plant
awadee	customary marriage ceremony
aware gyae	divorce ritual (also called *awadee gyae)*
ayehyia	the "wife-meeting" day
ayie	funeral
bamporobere	small rainy season (September-November)
barima	male (*obarima, obabarema,* young man, boy)
bayie	witchcraft
benkum	left
bomaa	large open-headed drum
chi	vital force, soul (Igbo), similar to Akan *'kra*
dame	game, similar to checkers, played in Ghana
donno	double-headed "armpit" drum, may be played by women
durbar	a royal reception, term imported by British from colonial India
duyefoo	a medicine-man
dwamu kasa	public speaking
dwiraa	purifying
dzemawei	deities (Krobo)
dzo	fire spirits (Ewe)
ebo	the exterior body
efulefu	worthless empty men, useless persons, some of whom became Christian converts in Achebe's novels (Igbo).
egwugwu	founding ancestors (Igbo)
egyabosom	river deity (Fante)
egyasunsum	father's soul (Fante), like the *ntoro*
emi	spirit given by God (Yoruba), similar to the Akan *'kra*

ennye kwa	out of the ordinary
esen	crier, herald
esono gwa	elephant stool
eye bone; enfata	"it is morally wrong; unfitting"
fo	people, group, class (suffix added to words to signify the group, e.g., *ahenfo,* the royalty or the chiefs as a group)
fontomfrom	variety of large drum; a dance of the Akan
gba	I accept (Yoruba)
gbo	I have heard (Yoruba)
griot	poet, oral historian, sometimes regarded as a bearer of divine revelation
gyasehene	palace administrator
gye Nyame	"Except God," an adinkra symbol
haadzii	twins (Ga)
harmattan	dry wind blowing south from the Sahara bringing dust, coincidental with the Twi *opebere,* the dry season, from December to March
high life	modern form of music in which traditional rhythms and local language in Ghana are mixed with Western instruments and sometimes Western forms of music, such as jazz and reggae
honam	exterior body
honhom fi	evil force, filth, dirt
hyirew	white clay, sign of joy or victory
idi	buttocks (Yoruba), euphemism for sexual organs
Ifa Odu	oral tradition related to divination (Yoruba)
ife	wide (Yoruba), as in Ile Ife
ikenga	personal ancestor (Igbo)
ilo	park, place for games (Igbo)
indichie	ancestors (Igbo)
iyi-uwa	evil stone (Igbo)
kenkey	a cornmeal dough ball (Fante), like the Accra *dokunu* (Ga)
kente	silk and cotton hand-woven colored strips, the entire cloth made up of the strips, worn as a wrapper cloth by Ghanaians
koda	the evil force that negates a bountiful harvest (Krobo)
kokokyinaka	dark-blue bird, the drummer's totem or patron animal
kotokodwa	porcupine stool
'kra (okra)	vital force, soul, "spark from God"

krada	soul day
kradin	soul name (sometimes called the day name)
krontihene	commander-in-chief of the national army in a traditional territory
kukuba	"pot-child," infant who dies within the first week after birth (Fante)
kuntunkuni	usually a red or other dark wrapper cloth worn by chief in the stool house
kwadwumfo	court poet among the Akan
kwamu kwabrafo	executioner
kyidom	rear guard
mamponghene	chief of Mampong in Ashanti, vice-regent of the Asante Alliance in the absence of the *asantehene*
marabout	Muslim spiritual leader, bearer of supernatural powers and revelation
Mawa or Mawuga	God of the Ewe
mbari	shrine-like huts (Igbo)
mmoatia	dwarf spirits, spirits of the wild, genies
mogya	blood; female principle; the bond of the *abusua;* the matrilinear system
mpae	libation prayers
musuo	an offense, abomination
nana	grandmother or grandfather; title given to elders, royalty, hence to the ancestors; title for persons considered reincarnation of ancestors
nananom nsamanfo	the ancestors
nananom	ancestors
ndichie	titled elders and initiates into the *ozo* society (Igbo)
nifa	right
nipadua	the body
nsa	schnapps, whiskey (for outdooring rites it must be clear like water)
nsaguda	libation-pouring day for funeral rites
nsu	water
ntafo	identical twins
ntetia	naming ceremony of an infant
ntoma	toga-like wrapper cloth, such as kente or adinkra
ntoro	semen; the male principle; the bond with the father and the river deities
Nyame (or Onyame)	God
Nyankopon	God the Great One

Nyamedua	"God's tree," both the forked branch in the yard and the adinkra symbol
oba	child
obaa	girl, female
obaapanyin	senior woman of a clan or lineage
obaso	"He hanged himself" (Yoruba)
obayi	witch
obo	stone
obosom	divinity, deity, divine spirit (not Nyame)
obra or *abrabo*	earthly life, destiny
oburoni (pl. *aborofo*)	European , American, Asian, non-African (from *aburo,* corn, maize) (the African is *obibini*)
oburoni koko	literally, "a pink-skinned person from behind the corn field," like the author
odehye	those of free-born ancestry
Odomankoma	the Almighty
odoso	skirt made of raffia
Odwira Festival	purification ritual for the new year, the major festival in honor of the stool ancestors usually in August or September
ofupebere	small dry season (July-August)
ogbanje	evil spirit (Igbo)
ohemaa	queen mother
okomfo	shrine priest
okomfopanin	chief priest
okpensi	ritual stick (Igbo)
okposi	ancestral stool (Igbo)
okyeame	spokesperson, "linguist"
okyerema	drummer
oman	state, traditional territory
omanhemaa	queen mother of a state
omanhene	king or chief of a state, paramount chief
omenani	customs, "ways of the land" (Igbo)
omusu kyerefo	diviners, interpreters of mischief or misfortune
opebere	dry season
orisha	deity (Yoruba); person possessed by a deity
osebo gwa	leopard stool
osom obosom	worship of a divinity
osu	outcast, slave of a deity (Igbo)
otumfoo	great chief
saman	spirit of the deceased, ghost
samando	world of the ancestors, abode of the dead

sankofa	adinkra symbol, like a bird with its head turned backwards, meaning for one to return to the past to seek one's heritage
sasa	a spiritual power, usually one seeking revenge
sasabonsam	the evil spirit, the forest monster, associate with witches
som	to serve, worship
suban	character
suman	amulet, talisman, charm
sunsum	soul, personality, the spiritual element underlying the *suban*
tawia	child born after twins
tete bosom	tutelar spirits, principal or ancestral deities
tete kasa	speech from ancient times, like the proverbs
tiri aseda	bridewealth; literally, "the appreciation for the head"
tiri nsa	bridewealth; literally, "the head rum"
togbuitrowo	similar to tutelar deities (Ewe)
tro-tros	locally made buses, lorries
trowo	earth deities; lesser deities (Ewe)
tufohen	general of the *asafo*
tutuw-bo	process of public exposure of a criminal
ukwu	great (Igbo)
vo	"set apart" (Fon)
vodu	deity (Fon), probable source of the word *voodoo*
waly	bearer of revelation, holy man (among the Malinke)
wofa	uncle
Wukudae	minor celebration in honor of the stool ancestors, halfway through the traditional month
yi	to take
zongo	Muslim quarter of town

Index

Other Titles in the Faith Meets Faith Series